Accession no.
36137032

KU-695-569

Political Bodies/Body Politic

Political Bodies/Body Politic
The Semiotics of Gender

Darlene M. Juschka

LIS - LIBRARY	
Date 8·5·14	Fund ┌ -che
Order No. 2501533	
University of Chester	

LONDON   OAKVILLE

Published by Equinox Publishing Ltd.

UK: Unit 6, The Village, 101 Amies St., London SW11 2JW
USA: DBBC, 28 Main Street, Oakville, CT 06779

www.equinoxpub.com

First published 2009

© Darlene M. Juschka 2009

All rights reserved. No part of this publication may be reproduced or transmitted in any form or by any means, electronic or mechanical, including photocopying, recording or any information storage or retrieval system, without prior permission in writing from the publishers.

British Library Cataloguing-in-Publication Data

ISBN 978 1 84553 206 2 (hardback)
ISBN 978 1 84553 207 9 (paperback)

A catalogue record for this book is available from the British Library.

Library of Congress Cataloging-in-Publication Data

Juschka, Darlene M., 1957-
    Political bodies/body politic : the semiotics of gender / Darlene M. Juschka.
        p. cm.
    Includes bibliographical references and index.
    ISBN 978-1-84553-206-2 (hb)—ISBN 978-1-84553-207-9 (pb) 1.
Feminist theory. 2. Gender identity. 3. Signs and symbols. 4.
Feminism—Religious aspects. 5. Feminism and literature. I. Title.
    HQ1190.J87 2009
    305.4201—dc22
                                2008017429

Typeset by S.J.I. Services, New Delhi
Printed and bound in Great Britain by Lightning Source UK Ltd, Milton Keynes

Contents

Conclusion

Tables and Figures

Acknowledgements

As with any project, there are multiple people who influence, support, and provide feedback. In the development of *The Semiotics of Gender* there were numerous people whose influence, feedback, and support assisted in the shaping of the text. Of influences there are many, but Christine Delphy, Angela Carter, and Judith Butler shape my theory of gender/sex; Claude Lévi-Strauss, Bruce Lincoln, and Jonathan Z. Smith my theory of systems of belief and practice, along with myth and ritual; Ferdinand de Saussure, Roland Barthes, and Robert Innis my development of semiotics (and symbols therein); Antonio Gramsci and Louis Althusser my understanding of ideology; Michel Foucault and Chris Weedon my poststructural orientation towards discursive analyses; and Arnold van Gennep, Stanley Tambiah, and Ronald Grimes with regard to my understanding of ritual. Lest one think that I am rhyming off a roster of who is who in the above, my intention is to make apparent my awareness that I do not work in isolation when I theoretically engage the various subjects of this text. So my intention is to acknowledge those theorists whose work has been very influential on my own.

The project took several years to complete, but the majority of the work took place during my sabbatical year spanning 2006–2007. Sabbaticals are wonderful things and I think every working person should be given one as it refreshes the mind and body. I wish to thank the University of Regina for providing me with the sabbatical that allowed me to complete the book.

Equally supportive were friends and family who had to listen endlessly and with great patience to my constant referencing of the project and the struggles I faced therein. They provided support by the way of confidence when indeed I often did not have it. So thanks go to my partner William Arnal for his patience and suggestions, as well as his reading of a number of the chapters in the book, to my children Justin and Amy for their unconditional support with regard to my abilities, and to my dear friends Helen Ramirez, Stephanie Kirkwood Walker, Leona Anderson, Wendee Kubik, Jackie Kuikman, Willi Braun, Kenneth MacKendrick, and Russell McCutcheon for their insights, suggestions, support and general well-wishes on the project. I also wish to thank Janet Joyce founder and editor of Equinox Press who agreed to publish this book, and Val Hall who worked with me in its preparation.

Finally, I want to acknowledge Dr. Gary Lease who died in January of 2008. Gary was a wonderful man and colleague. Indeed his letter supporting my bid for tenure in 2002 provided me with some necessary confidence to negotiate the academic scene. Gary respected the kind of work I do and for that I am eternally grateful. He was a wonderful man, one who I will remember with respectful fondness until my own death greets me. Here's to you Gary, a man among men; a human among humans!

Introduction
Topographical Excursions on
Theoretical Paths

Language, then, is not a medium; it is a constitutive element of material social practice ... Language is in fact a special kind of material practice: that of human sociality.

Raymond Williams, *Marxism and Literature* (1977, 165)

Gender/sex[1] as a category of analysis

The semiotics of gender/sex is a venture I initiated in the early part of the new millennium. I began this (ad)venture because I was interested in developing some sort of theoretical apparatus that could further my understanding of the logic and mechanisms of gender/sex ideology. Why and how is gender/sex engraved on the hearts and minds of so many different peoples separated by time and space? How is it that gender/sex, as a primary source of identity and social formation, is often ignored, overlooked, or considered unworthy of investigation in the field of religious studies? Why is it that I can get my students to understand that gender/sex is a constructed socio-political category in the classroom, but not outside the classroom? In many ways gender/sex remains a theoretical enigma even though it has been extremely well-researched in the last twenty years. We know it operates throughout the majority of societies as a significant category that determines social organisation, we know it acts as a core aspect of identity, and yet how and why it functions this way remains somewhat of a mystery.

There have been efforts to theorise gender and to explain its social, economic and political power,[2] but some of these efforts have ended up bogged down by individualism or do not pay enough attention to social and historical change. For example, efforts have been made in the field of sociology toward understanding the operations of gender in social

formations.[3] However, in these kinds of analyses either description of
gender's processes or the outcomes in terms of its application have often
acted as theories of gender. Often times the category of gender is taken
as whole, fixed, and/or singular at the outset while little effort is ex-
pended to think about it as a linguistic and fluid category, although certainly there are exceptions to this such as the work of R. W. Connell or
Stevi Jackson. Anthropology as well has sought to theorise gender by
examining it in relation to kinship systems or distinct and limited social
groups.[4] These studies are most edifying, but gender is engaged at times
as if it is a discrete object with particular properties while in other studies
it remains locked in its originating context with little to no application
beyond the borders of the particular social body.[5] Finally, but not definitively, cultural studies, and those influenced by cultural studies, have also
sought to analyse gender/sex and gender/sex ideology.[6] In this kind of
engagement gender/sex is taken from the outset to be a linguistic sign
used to organise the social body. Equally, the dialectical play between
culture, social body, person, and language is a developed aspect of such
efforts. However, often times gender/sex ideology, as ideology or the
mystification of social categories, lacks a developed assessment of on-
the-ground implications. This means there is little attention paid to oppression, and in the theorising, under the sway of Michel Foucault, power
is so infused throughout the social body and in the psyche of the individual that real social outcomes such as death, violence, poverty, and/or
power and privilege tend not to be strong aspects of the analysis.

My work, which tends to be interdisciplinary in nature, requires that I
pay attention to multiple theories and methods for understanding the
category of gender/sex and gender/sex ideology. Working in feminist studies, the study of myth, ritual and symbol, semiotics, religious studies, and
the ancient world, along with my interest in epistemology, and theoretical formulations in a variety of disciplines, for example, literature, film,
and feminism, allows me to bring a variety of tools to the analysis. This is,
then, the academic context from which this text emerges. Although the
kind of interdisciplinarity that comes with my work can have its weak-
nesses, it also has its strengths; and it is with these strengths that I hope
to critically contribute to the discursive analysis of gender/sex.

So to better understand the kind of work that makes up this text, this
introductory chapter begins by discussing some of the theorists who have
influenced the writing of this book. The multiple theories that I draw
upon are engaged in such a way that best suits the examination of, and
thinking about, gender/sex and gender/sex ideology. Ultimately, I am interested in developing a semiotics of gender/sex because I think that the
complexity of gender/sex and gender/sex ideology, and their multi-

layered and multi-levelled deployment, their interrelationship with other significant categories such as race, class, sexuality, age, status, power and so forth, are missed when only a single lens is employed. It is my hope, then, that this text will promote further thought concerning gender/sex and gender/sex ideology.

Theoretical considerations: Ideology and gender/sex ideology

Defining ideology is a difficult task. The term is used equivocally and its meaning tends to shift from text to text, article to article, surfacing in a number of different ways. Slavoj Žižek remarks that "'[i]deology' can designate anything from a contemplative attitude that misrecognizes its dependence on social reality to an action-oriented set of beliefs, from the indispensable medium, in which individuals live out their relations to a social structure, to false ideas which legitimate a dominant political power" (1994, 3–4). The elusiveness of ideology lies in the fact that it is not a thing in and of itself, although it can become a thing inasmuch as ideas are things and therefore have material existence and in this, then, ideology is material, but its materiality is located in an "apparatus, and its practice or practices" (Althusser 1995, 125–126). Louis Althusser, when engaging the history of the term ideology, notes that "the expression 'ideology' was developed by [Pierre J. G.] Cabanis, [Antoine Louis Claude] Desutt de Tracy and their friends in 1796, who assigned to it, as an object, the (generic) theory of ideas" (1995, 120). In their reading ideology was not a means of social control, and instead meant the theory of ideas. Fifty years later Karl Marx picked up the term but moved it in a new direction and for him ideology became "the system of the ideas and representations which dominate the mind of a man [sic] or a social group" (Althusser 1995, 120). In Marx's development, the concept of ideology is seen an oppressive system, one developed and maintained in order to secure the dominance of the ruling class, even if the ruling class should find themselves captured by the same ideology meant to control the ruled.

Some of the difficulty of defining ideology is that it is a theory about human social relations, but "theory of" and "concrete social relations" are frequently conflated so that ideology is often perceived as a thing in and of itself. In its initial usage by Dessut de Tracy, Althusser tells us, it was assigned the status of an object, but ideology is never a concrete thing in and of itself. Rather, it is a theory of social relations and not the relations in and of themselves. Furthermore, in the instance of the control by, and the manufacturing of, ideology the subject (ruler)/object (ruled) dichotomy is blurred so that the subject is also an object of ideology. In other words, all are objects in any given ideology, but some will be interpellated as subjects, and therefore have normative access to power, scarce resources, and so forth (for example, adult men in patriarchal relations), while others will have less access (for example, all women in patriarchal relations regardless of, or in conjunction with, other social markers such as class, sexual desire, race, etc.). However, even if there are those who secure greater benefits and those "others" who secure less, all are shaped by the operative ideology.[7] This does not mean, however, that ideology is self-generating. It does not have existence unto itself although it may seem as if does. Rather, ideology is produced, propagated, extended, altered, and enforced by human beings.

Following Louis Althusser, to understand ideology one must recognise two steps: the first is the realisation that there are two aspects to ideology, and the second that these two aspects are called general ideology (language) and particular ideologies (social institutions) (1995). In the instance of particular ideologies Althusser names two modes of generation and dissemination, the Institutional State Apparatus (ISA) and the Repressive State Apparatus (RSA), both of which are linked to hegemony. Its second and more implicit form of manifestation he calls general ideology, and, although it appears eternal and trans-historical, it achieves materiality in the ISAs and RSAs.

According to Althusser then, "a theory of ideolog*ies* depends in the last resort on the history of social formations, and thus of the modes of production combined in social formations, and of the class struggle which develops in them" (Althusser 1995, 121, emphasis original). This leads first to Institutional State Apparatuses (ISAs) which are named by Althusser as religious, educational, trade-union, family, legal, political, communicational, and cultural. These are not to be confused with Repressive State Apparatuses (RSAs), he argues, which function in large measure in the public domain. RSAs are state controlled and function by coercion, violence and repression. RSAs are supported by, and support, ideology: they use ideology, but repression is their primary means of operation.

ISAs, on the other hand, tend to function in the private domain. Although some of what is indicated as private such as law, education, communication, and culture appear to be in the public domain, Althusser explains that they *function* as if they belong to the private domain (1995, 111). ISAs ensure that the individual is both self-regulated (system of belief and practice supported by social apparatuses such as education) and governmentally regulated (system of belief and practice, and managing systems that support the operations of the social body such as health care). ISAs function first and foremost by ideology and secondarily and often symbolically by repression (1995, 112).[8]

Having defined particular ideologies, Althusser continued his investigation of ideology, and in a second step he proposes a contingent general ideology. In Althusser's theory of general ideology, ideology is not bound by history and instead "it is endowed with a structure and a functioning such as to make it a non-historical reality…in its Freudian conception this time—our proposition *ideology has no history* can and must…be related directly to Freud's proposition that the *unconscious is eternal*, that is, that it has no history" (1995, 122, emphasis original). Ideology as omnihistorical does not mean that ideology transcends history; rather it refers to ideology as "omnipresent and trans-historical" and therefore present throughout history. Drawing upon Freud's theory of the eternal unconscious, Althusser argued that ideology in general, that is, non-historically specific ideology, is, like the unconscious, eternal and, while it has no history *per se*, it remains "the history of social formations containing social classes" (1995, 122). How this operates is in relation to language. Language is the most significant mechanism through which individuals are governed by the ideological state apparatuses in the interest of the elite, however that elite is determined. It is in ISAs and RSAs that general ideology through language (or discourse as Bruce Lincoln names it) is made material and given a history of its own (Althusser 1995, 122). Language is always already there: it holds us, shapes us, contains us and gives rise to the world we are born into, move through, and depart from. General ideology, as linguistic, is like the air we breathe and we are, more often than not, unaware of it. General ideology is shaped and deployed through language and reinforced and given concrete form in the ISAs and RSAs.

Further to ideology is subjectivity, the process of which is achieved through, argued Althusser, interpellation. According to Althusser (1995, 130–136), the process of interpellation refers to recognition and misrecognition of an individual as Subject and/or Object. By hailing an individual, group, nation, and so forth, one names the Subject or Object, and in the process of hailing one recognises the Subject or Object location and attempts to locate oneself in it, subsequently taking on the identity, for example, woman, man, white, black, and so forth. Acquiring this identity one then has experiences related to this identity—or rather the experiences one has are shaped in accordance with this identity. Therefore, not only is a politics of identity generated that treats identity as fixed and outside of history, this identity is further buttressed by the category of

experience, which is understood to give epistemological certitude to this
identity (Scott 1992).

Connected and important to the recognition of the hail, is misrecognition.
Misrecognition refers to the belief that one is the author of one's subjectivity. Instead of understanding that concepts like human, woman, black,
or Canadian, among others, are social constructs that, like language, are
always already there and subsequently imposed-absorbed; the hail and
one's response to it are partially repressed and operate unconsciously so
that one is never fully cognizant of the process of subjectivity. Chris Weedon
comments that: "In the position of the Subject [as an object of ideology]
the individual assumes that she is the author of the ideology or discourse
which she is speaking. She imagines that she is indeed the type or subject
which humanism proposes—rational, unified, the source rather than the
effect of language." (2001, 31)

In another kind of ideological play, one that draws upon the metaphysical, divine legitimation can be conferred on identity when deity is
understood to *recognise* it. Myth, ritual, and symbol are consummate
examples of Althusser's concept of interpellation, and ritual in particular
functions to confer metaphysical legitimation on identity, for example the
identity of "woman" (adult and marriageable) with the rite of female
genital cutting found among a number of peoples of western and northern Africa. Althusser comments that "...ideology 'acts' or 'functions' in
such a way that it 'recruits' subjects among the individuals (it recruits
them all), or 'transforms' the individuals into subjects (it transforms them
all) by that very precise operation which I have called *interpellation* or
hailing..." (1995, 130 emphasis original).

Gender/sex is equally ideological in that the category functions to
determine and then recruit a certain kind of subjectivity (male, female,
homo-heterosexual, transsexual, transvestite) from a more general subjectivity, human, transforming the general into a particular, and
recognisable, subject of ideology, for example, women who have fe-
male/feminine experiences—"when Suzie and the girls get together to
share some food and stories, Whistler's rum is part of the fun" or men
who have male/masculine experiences—"when Tom and the boys get
together to blow off some steam and play some pool, Labatt Blue is there
too". These commercials propose gender/sex ideology through the activities of Suzie and the girls, who are represented as oriented toward
relationality (sharing stories) and nurturance (sharing food), and Tom and
the boys, who are represented as oriented toward aggression (blowing off
steam) and competition (playing pool). The commercial fixes the category of gender/sex via recourse to a gender/sex ideology and what it

erases is how gender/sex is "…a shifting and contextual phenomenon" one that "does not denote a substantive being, but a relative point of convergence among culturally and historically specific sets of relations" (Butler 1999, 15). Bombarded by such gender/sex ideology in popular culture and the media, those who wish to recognise themselves as *real* women and *real* men ought to evince these same kinds of activities and in doing so will properly perform their gender.

Antonio Gramsci, imprisoned in Fascist Italy from 1926 until 1934, developed the term hegemony in relation to ideology (Gramsci 1971). Traditionally hegemony referred to political rule or domination especially with regard to relations between countries or states. However, the meaning of this term was extended by Karl Marx who incorporated the idea of rule or domination with regard to relations between social classes and especially toward the idea of a ruling class. Drawing upon Marx, then, Gramsci furthered the concept of hegemony by making a distinction between rule and hegemony arguing that rule is expressed directly in political forms and in times of crisis by direct or effective coercion, while hegemony is called upon to enforce ideology in the day-to-day. Hegemony, he contended, is a web of interlocking political, social, and cultural forces. Raymond Williams explains that in Gramsci's theory hegemony is

> a whole body of practices and expectations, over the whole of living: our senses and assignment of energy, our shaping perceptions of ourselves and our world. It is a lived system of meanings and values—constitutive and constituting—which as they are experienced as practices appear as reciprocally confirming. (1977, 110)

In other words, hegemony is both the rulers and their ideology, the latter being understood to be the way things are, and those ruled within the system understand themselves as part of the system. Hegemony constitutes a sense of reality so that experiencing reality outside of that frame is almost impossible. Hegemony is culture and all its operations, hierarchies, classes, and formation and is that which roots culture in a reality of its own construction.

Althusser and Gramsci's theories of ideology (general and particular ideology, interpellation, and hegemony) are foundational for my theorising of gender/sex and gender/sex ideology. Gender/sex and gender/sex ideology and their deployment within masculine hegemonies are central to the work of this text. Although many feminist orientations employed and continue to employ the concept of patriarchy, or "rule of the father", I prefer to use the phrase patriarchal relations, and to use it with some specificity, often in relation to gender/sex ideology deployed within systems defined by kinship. When examining social bodies where kinship operates in a muted form I instead use the phrase masculine hegemony as rule and social organisation are established and shaped with reference to maleness, men, and masculinity however these categories have been constructed. In a masculine hegemony a primary method of social organisation is gender/sex ideology and that ideology determines the rulers from the ruled, the former who have full access to, and control of, scarce resources and determine in detail the operations of the social body, while the latter, operations of the social body, ensure and legitimate such privileging.

Drawing on the theories of Althusser and Gramsci, in a masculine hegemony language models and communicates categories of gender/sex and gender/sex ideology. In such an ideological system the value of male/man/masculine over and above female/woman/feminine is primary, although it certainly links with other social identity markers such as class, race, ethnicity, age, religion, and so on. Such markers are important and often work in tandem with the category of gender/sex, or on their own, but in a masculine hegemony the pre-eminent ideological category is gender/sex, which is then used to shape the ideology related to other categories such as class, race, ethnicity, sexuality, and so forth. A good example of this kind of interplay is the notion of hypersexuality that was, and continues to be, ascribed to black men and women in a white-supremacist ideology: gender/sex ideology becomes a means by which to shape and deploy racism. However, gender/sex is not always the pre-eminent category of social organisation. As Sherry Ortner has argued, other categories such as age can act as a primary category by which to organise a social body (1996). Gender/sex can take a second, third or even fourth position in terms of importance for social organisation (see the concluding chapter of this book), but rarely if ever is it absent from social organisation while its performance is mandatory to belong to most social bodies.

The performance of gender/sex is a theoretical engagement mostly closely associated with Judith Butler. Gender/sex is performed and often much of the performance operates with little critical awareness. The performance of gender/sex is simply that; we ascribe to and perform female and feminine, and male and masculine, however they are defined within one's group and the larger social body that one occupies, to become *real* women or men (or in cases of transgression both or neither). As Butler comments:

> If gender is a kind of a doing, an incessant activity performed, in part, without one's knowing and without one's willing, it is not for that reason automatic or mechanical. On the contrary, it is a practice of improvisation within a scene of

constraint. Moreover, one does not "do" one's gender alone. One is always "doing" with or for another, even if the other is imaginary. (2004, 1)

To say that most of the performance of gender/sex operates under the radar of our consciousness does not mean it is instinctual and biologically grounded in oestrogen, progesterone, and testosterone or in the chromosomes XX or XY. Although certainly I do not reject that hormones and genes play a role in the development of any animal body, along with a plethora of other factors such as insulin or the growth hormone (GH or hGH), what I do reject is that hormones and genes are essential truths of gender/sex that present themselves to the theorists rather than having been interpreted by theorists. Following Anne Fausto-Sterling (2000), then, among others such as Christine Delphy (1996), Michel Foucault (1980), Eve Kosofsky Sedgwick (1990), and Thomas Laqueur (1992), I take sex, like gender, to be a socially constructed category even if it is also a physical category. I say this because categories, for example ear size or eyebrows, are also physical categories that have not been developed and deployed to designate groups or people, while other physical categories, for example skin pore size or whiteness of teeth, have be developed and deployed to designate class in primarily the United States and Canada: upper and middle classes, particularly females, are bodily signified by small pores and whiter than white teeth, while lower classes have larger pores and stained or yellowed teeth.[9]

Positioning this text, and myself therein, as supporting the view that gender and sex are interrelated and socially constructed, hence gender/sex, makes apparent my adherence to feminist poststructuralism. Assuming this epistemological position means that I employ a semiotic and systematic analysis to examine gender/sex, while working within this frame is indicative of my understanding of meaning as constituted within language; but more than this, that language itself is not removed from social and historical specificity. Following Chris Weedon, then:

> Poststructuralism, while building on Saussure's theory, radically modifies and transforms some of its important aspects. It takes from Saussure the principle that meaning is produced within language rather than reflected by language, and that individual signs do not have intrinsic meaning but acquire meaning through the language chain and their difference within it from other signs....To gain the full benefit of Saussure's theory of meaning, we need to view language as a system always existing in historically specific discourses. Once language is understood in terms of competing discourses, competing ways of giving meaning to the world, which imply differences in the organisation of social power, then language becomes an important site of political struggle. (2001, 23)

Further theoretical considerations: Myth, ritual and symbol

The next chapter, 'A Semiotics of Gender', provides greater detail concerning my understanding of myth, ritual and symbol, but in this introduction I will provide some preliminary remarks. Over the last two and one half millennia there have been a plethora of treatises that seek to define myth (mythology or mythography) by asking what it is, what it does, and how it does it. This search for the definitive word on myth often, but not always, begins with Plato. Going back to these classical Greek thinkers is not surprising since, aside from the fact that Plato talks about myth, he is a synecdoche that evokes the foundation myth that secures the Eurowest's[10] white masculine, "secular" and "reason-orientated" origins. The writings of Plato, then, act as the springboard for modernist orientations toward myth.[11] However, my intention in this discussion on myth is not to chronologically chart the vast corpus of texts that have sought to explicate, define and/or delimit myth. Instead, my purpose is to make apparent how it is I understand myth and to discuss briefly those theories that have come to influence my work as evidenced in this text.[12] There are many theorists of myth, but the theoretical formation that most shapes my understanding of myth is poststructuralism; but a poststructuralism with a clear focus on issues related to power.

Ritual, unlike myth and symbol, has a more limited history in academic work, although like symbol it began to garner attention at the end of the nineteenth century and beginning of the twentieth century. In the early twentieth century Arnold van Gennep (1960; Fr. 1909) laid the ground for a processual theory of ritual, noting that ritual, particularly rites of passage, could be divided into three separate phases; separation, transition (liminality), and incorporation.[13] This schema became foundational for ritual studies and was carried forward particularly in the work of Victor and Edith Turner. Drawing on van Gennep, Turner very much universalised the concept of liminality or the second phase of van Gennep's tripartite structure. The liminal phase was considered to be betwixt and between wherein one is neither inside nor outside but on the threshold—the Latin *līmen*. But Turner was also interested in the performative aspect of ritual, although his interest continued to be shaped by the concept of liminality.[14]

However, ritual, like myth and symbol, has ideological implications and my engagement with ritual is a process of focussing on the very socio-political nature of ritual disseminated through its structural *and* performative aspects. The structure of ritual is important to understand insofar as it is the mechanism that acts as the engine to uphold and deploy ideological imperatives embedded in the ritual, while performance speaks to the dissemination of ritual as both convincing and authoritative. Ritual is a powerful medium of modelling and communication and its performance is both cognitive and physical being as it is both thought in motion and motion in thought. Ritual is ever changing, but also "never" changing, as it, like myth, draws on tradition for its authority: "it has always been thus, and will always be thus".

According to Raymond Williams:

> Tradition has been commonly understood as a relatively inert, historicised segment of a social structure: tradition as the surviving past....For tradition is in practice the most evident expression of the dominant and hegemonic pressures and limits. It is always more than an inert historicised segment; indeed it is the most powerful practical means of incorporation....Most versions of "tradition" can be quickly shown to be radically selective. From a whole possible area of past and present, in a particular culture, certain meanings and practices are selected for emphasis and certain other meanings and practices are neglected or excluded. (1977, 115)

From this vantage point it is quite obvious that tradition is neither neutral nor benign: it is ideological from the outset and a means by which to obscure operative social power. In both myth and ritual tradition functions implicitly and/or explicitly and serves to cloak myth and ritual with an aura of authority, while, at the same time, it presents a sense of order through reference to fixed time. The very messiness of life and the swift and continual change in every given moment of existence are smoothed out by the careful choice of objects, events, or referents that are lifted up from a plethora of others and given signification. Each is then locked in time, a time of the past, as either an originary moment or a repetition of that originary moment. This labour is the labour of the *bricoleur*, and the outcome is *bricolage*, as Claude Lévi-Strauss made apparent in his work.[15]

The category of symbol in the last century has also been a subject of academic inquiry and there have been a goodly number of significant thinkers who have engaged it. The list is fairly extensive, more of which I speak about within the text, but from the outset I engage the category of symbol through a poststructuralist lens. This means that I engage symbol as a sign, hence my use of the term sign-symbol, working in line with semiotic theory, following in particular the work of Ferdinand de Saussure, Claude Lévi-Strauss, Michel de Certeau, and Roland Barthes.

Among many contributions made by Lévi-Strauss, *bricolage* is significant to my understanding of myth. At the outset I understand myth to be a narrative (oral or written) full of significance (negative or positive) for those who share it. The myth, however it is couched, holds meaning and is often understood to represent a truth for the group or social body from which it emerges. For example, in the majority of Christianities, a central foundational myth is this: two thousand and some years ago a deity of human and divine descent was born into the world and subsequently died in the world, and this event is seen to provide guidance in life and death for those who adhere to the myth. This foundational myth, then, is understood by Christian actors as an historical event that took place in the distant past. Interestingly, when a scriptural canon was compiled and trans-lated by Jerome in the late fourth century CE, the foundation of the myth of the deity who was born and died was further grounded by being linked to an earlier myth that related the origin of existence and humanity, Gen-esis 1 and 2.[16] For Christian actors, then, the foundational myth is a truth that their lives as Christians are built upon.

Myth, then, in my usage is a meaningful narrative, and as a narrative it is both social and ideological, even if, in the instance of the latter, it purports to hold a utopian impulse. Consequently, as ideology, myth is structured and disseminated in such a way as to obscure its social origins, even in the moment that the myth supports these social origins. But as narrative, the roots of myth, ideological as they may be, are grounded in the social realm, the place of human activity. The referent and/or origina-tor of the myth may be understood to stand outside of this social realm, but production of the myth clearly is not. So while myth is perceived by actors to refer to, or have a referent from, an otherworldly dimension, it is equally perceived to be a product of social activity: the telling or speak-ing of the tale. The discursive power of myth, then, relates to this dialec-tical play between recognising the social construction of myth and obscuring it. This may sound paradoxical but it is not. Through what Lévi-Strauss termed *bricolage*, the social construction of myth is evidenced, but this *bricolage* is mystified, or separated from its sociality, in order that it may take on an aura of truth.

Further linked to my understanding of myth, ritual, and sign-symbol is the work of Bruce Lincoln. In his intellectual labours, myth, ritual, and sign-symbol are a powerful means by which to shape and deploy ideol-ogy, but equally, as Lincoln argues, to challenge ideology; a point he admirably demonstrates in his text *Discourse and the Construction of So-ciety*. Lincoln comments that "[c]hange comes not when groups or indi-viduals use 'knowledge' to challenge ideological mystification, but rather when they employ thought and discourse, including even such modes as myth and ritual, as effective instruments of struggle" (1989, 7). Lincoln does not reject the idea that myth, ritual, and sign-symbol are ideological; rather he argues that they are ideological tools that can be employed by both those who seek to disseminate their ideology and those who might contest it. Unlike Roland Barthes, or (less so) Maurice Bloch, the latter in the instance of ritual, Lincoln does not suppose that there are non-ideological discourses such as, in the case of Barthes "the language of man [sic] the producer...or revolutionary language" (1972, 146) or, in the instance of Bloch, the grounding of ideological ritual in economic and political history so that the latter demystifies the former (Bloch 1986, 7–11, 187–195). Lincoln's introduction of the concept of discourse to his work allows him to bring together myth, ritual, and sign-symbol, and to examine them in relation to "the tensions, contradictions, superficial stability, and potential fluidity of any given society *as a whole*" (1989, 7, emphasis original).

A performative theory of ritual is one that was developed by Stanley Tambiah and delivered as the Radcliffe-Brown lecture in Social Anthropology in 1979. Here Tambiah argued for a performative approach to ritual:

> Ritual is a culturally constructed system of symbolic communication. It is constituted of patterned and ordered sequences of words and acts, often expressed in multiple media, whose content and arrangement are characterised in varying degree by formality (conventionality), stereotypy (rigidity), condensation (fusion), and redundancy (repetition). Ritual action in its constitutive features is *performative* in these three senses: in the Austinian sense of performative wherein saying something is also doing something as a conventional act; in the quite different sense of a staged performance that uses multiple media by which the participants experience the event intensively; and in the sense of indexical values—I derive this concept from Peirce—being attached to and inferred by actors during the performance. (1985, 128)

Victor Turner was also interested in the performativity of ritual, although his interests lead him instead to the Theatre (see for example 1982; 1988). A central ritual concept of interest for Turner was liminality (liminoid), the place of "betwixt and between", which he developed fully in his work in line with the notion of communitas. Although certainly there are problems with Turner's development of liminality and communitas,[17] he, along with Edith Turner, extended further thinking and theorising on ritual.

The interplay of ideology with gender/sex, myth, ritual, and sign-symbol is central to the semiotics of gender/sex that this text elaborates. In an effort to better understand the complexity of social organisation and how gender/sex is more often than not the primary category by which it is organised, this text focuses on the confluent categories of myth, ritual, and sign-symbol. These categories are of primary importance for the dissemination of gender/sex, as rites of passage such as initiation make apparent. For example, central to the Jewish initiation rite of male penile circumcision or Igbo female genital cutting is gender/sex. In the former, a

necessary link (was) is made between a masculine deity and the masculinity of his followers. In the bris maleness and masculinity are central to
defining a relationship between deity and the potential adherent. In the
instance of female genital cutting, excising the clitoris was central to ensuring the femaleness and proper femininity of the adherent. In both
instances, the rite uses gender/sex as a primary means to speak about
what it means to be part of the social body in question. Certainly other
identity categories are equally deployed or challenged via myth, ritual,
and sign-symbol, categories such as age, kinship, citizenship, nationality,
race, and so forth, but in this text my primary focus is gender/sex and its
deployment through myth, ritual, and sign-symbol. It is not that I think
race, class, kinship, and so forth are of less importance, I do not and
indeed they also come into the analysis in some measure. However, as
the sites of analysis for this text vary in time and space, and paying attention to social and historical location is central to my engagement, it seemed
to me that the analysis of the categories of gender/sex provided a constant theme for a rather variegated text.

The logic of the text

The Semiotics of Gender is divided into six chapters. The first chapter lays
out the semiotics of gender/sex as I have developed it. This chapter is
largely theoretical and it provides the reader with an understanding of
how I understand gender/sex and how I understand its interplay with
myth, ritual, and sign-symbol. Using grids as visual cues, this chapter provides the theory for what follows in the subsequent chapters.

    The second chapter is a developed look at a feminist mythographer
who thought to demystify gender/sex through fictional (and non-fictional)
engagement. The literary work of Angela Carter has intrigued many feminists and she is known for her deconstructive fairy tales such as "The
Bloody Chamber" in her text of the same name (1993). This fairy tale is
a variation of the Bluebeard story, but in Carter's version the heroine and
her masculine rescuer are in the end saved by the heroine's mother.
Carter wondered how it could be that women might escape the brutal
clutches of a gender/sex ideology produced by and in a masculine hegemony, and toward this end she wrote the two novels of which I engage in
chapter two. Her imaginative efforts were unsuccessful as there is no
"outside" of patriarchal relations since there is no "outside" of the social
body. Still, such efforts are not futile insofar as they make visible
the interplay between gender/sex and myth along with their social

construction. Carter was very much influenced by Karl Marx and Louis Althusser, and thought deeply about ideology; in particular gender/sex ideology. Her efforts, which took place largely in the nineteen seventies and eighties (Carter died in 1992), blazed a path for other feminists to follow. For Carter gender and sex are not inherent to humans; rather they are imbued and imbibed.

Chapter three also focuses on myth, although ritual is linked to myth in the event of male sacrifice. This chapter examines the mytheme of man the hunter and woman the gatherer in a modern American context to ask what it is that brings young men to offer their lives for the state. Certainly not all young men, and particularly not young men of the elite class, offer up their lives, but all are touched by this mytheme which in the end requires that they submit to the rule of the father.

Chapter four shifts from a focus on myth to a focus on ritual and the latter's intersection with gender. In this chapter the rites of possession and exorcism in early modern France provide a useful analysis of gender/ sex. Here public ritual with gender/sex at the centre expressed and mollified anxiety related to political change, a pandemic plague, social upheaval in the form of religious wars, and the colonisation of unfamiliar worlds.

Chapter five delves into the ancient Roman world and gender/sex ideology as is it deployed in the figure of the gladiator and its subsequent use in modern American film. This chapter discusses how the gladiator figured in Roman masculinities and how this figuring becomes a sign-symbol by which to speak about true heroic masculinity, a masculinity that is proposed to reside at the core of U.S. culture as it did in ancient Rome.

Finally, chapter six deviates from an analysis of gender/sex to theorise sign-symbol and icon, and from here to examine the concept of the icon in relation with the Indian deity Gaṇeśa. Although Gaṇeśa is gender/ sexed and this is central to his myth, this chapter sets gender/sex aside to think about theorising sign-symbols and icons. In the past I have come across the icon in the work of a number of anthropologists and the concept has intrigued me. Is the icon simply a sign-symbol and its treatment as different from a sign-symbol something simply to be avoided? Or is there something intrinsic to the concept of the icon that calls for furthering theorisation? The chapter argues the latter rather than the former.

The intention of this book is to examine myth, ritual and sign-symbol, and their deployment of gender/sex. To my mind, gender/sex is discursive although this is very often not evident. Ritual and symbolic representational narratives, located in the biological and metaphysical domains respectively, are linked with myth in the social domain (see chapter one)

and together that which is produced in and through the social is made to
appear as if rooted in the deep, deep earth and a natural inhabitant of
some unearthly realm far removed from human action. By examining
myth, ritual, and sign-symbol and their deployment of gender/sex the
interplay of the material and the abstract is made visible. It is this visibility
that this text focuses upon to make apparent the ideological mystification
of gender/sex.

Notes

1. To emphasise the interrelation the social categories of gender and sex and to
prioritise gender as the initial category, I use a forward slash between the terms and
place gender before sex—gender/sex—throughout this book treating them as a linked
categories. My rationale will become apparent as the reader moves further into the
text.

2. See for example, Jessica Benjamin 1988; 1995; 1998, Nancy Chodorow 1978;
1994; 1999, Page DuBois 1988, Jane Gallop 1982, and Carol Gilligan 1982; 1992.

3. See for example, Seyla Benhabib and Drucilla Cornell 1987, R.W. Connell 1987;
2002, Stevi Jackson and Sue Scott 2001, Laura Kramer 2005, Judith Lorber 1991; 1994;
1999; 2005, Barbara Smith 1998 and Dorothy Smith 1987.

4. See for example, Ifi Amadiume 1987, Evelyn Blackwood 2000, Micaela di Leonardo
and Roger Lancaster (eds.) 1997, Miriam Goheen 1996, Gilbert Herdt 1987, Aiwa Ong
1998, Sherry Ortner 1996, Peggy Reeve Sanday and Ruth Gallagher Goodenough
1990, Susan Starr Sered 1994, and Marilyn Strathern 1988; 1980.

5. Sherry Ortner (1996) is an exception to this along with di Leonardo and Lancaster
(eds.) (1997).

6. See for example, Barbara Adam and Stuart Allen (eds.) 1995, Helen Baehr and
Ann Gray (eds.) 1996, Anne Balsamo 1996, Sarah Banet-Weiser 1999, Gail Bederman
1995, Elizabeth Bell, Lynda Haas and Laura Sells (eds.) 1995, Gargi Bhattacharyya 1998;
Josiah Blackmore and Gregory Hutcheson (eds.) 1999, Lisa Bloom 1999, Jacqueline
Bobo 1995, Bram Dijkstra 1996, Ann Douglas 1988, Sherrie A. Innes 2004, E. Ann
Kaplan 2005; 1997, Peter Lehman (ed.) 2001; Paula Treichler 1998, Jeffery Weeks
1991 and Todd Penner and Caroline Vander Stichele (eds.) 2006.

7. Following Althusser, in the process of mystification we all appear as objects of this
naturalised law, but some are able to occupy the position of subject as they most
approximate this category. Those who are subjects benefit most by the ideology proffered
because they are recognised as the subject since they fit the model of the ideal subject.
Those who benefit the least are interpellated within the ideological framework as
object because they resemble least the ideal subject. For example, women in a hegemony
oriented toward a masculinist ideology or people marked by colour in a white-supremacist
ideology cannot approximate the subject.

8. In Bruce Lincoln's work a similar formulation is laid out. However, he uses the
terms force, which is similar to RSAs and discourse, which is similar to ISAs, as a primary

means by which to ensure (or challenge) and protect (or supplant) the interests of the ruling elite (1989, 3–4).

9. As lower classes have insufficient resources to direct at culturally determined forms of beauty, beauty is a means by which class is marked.

10. I use the term Eurowest to represent an epistemological, social and political orientation that is generally shared by Europe and its colonial off-shoots.

11. For further discussion on this subject see Buxton 1999 and Most 1999.

12. For developed discussions on theories of myth in the nineteenth and twentieth centuries see the work of William Doty 1986, Bruce Lincoln 1999, and Robert A. Segal 2004; 1999; 1998; 1996.

13. van Gennep also argued that rites could be grouped into six classes: sympathetic and contagious, direct and indirect, positive and negative. Once having determined the class of the ritual, one can then relate the classes to each other in order to have a better understanding of the ritual under study. This aspect of his work, however, is often not developed by those who use his tripartite structure of ritual.

14. See for example Turner 1967; 1969.

15. Although I use Lévi-Strauss' concept of *bricolage*, I am not setting up a dichotomy between the engineer and *bricoleur* as he did. This dichotomy was useful to support his notion of hot and cold societies but, since I do not support this view of societies, I have separated bricoleur from engineer. Instead, my use of *bricolage* is somewhat similar to Niklas Luhmann's theory of autopoiesis wherein "elements of system are (re)produced by the elements of the system" (Seidl and Becker 2006, 15). He argues that "[e]lements are elements only for the system that employs them as units and they are such [elements] only through this system" (Luhmann 1995, 22). Furthermore, it is only by making use of an element (relating it to other elements) that it becomes an element in the system (Seidl, *et al.* 2006, 16). So too *bricolage* in that forms, e.g. Christ, that are part of a system (Christianity) can be reformed within the system in a substantially new way, e.g. liberation theology. As to the notion of system that I am using throughout this text, I suspect my use is not completely reflective of Luhmann's intentions. In his theoretical frame something called Christianity would be classified as a sub-system. But in my usage I am likening it to his notion of system, arguing that myth, ritual, and symbol are elements within a system of belief and practice and make sense only in relation to each other and operating as elements within the system to reproduce the system. I suspect that in some measure I am stretching Luhmann's theory of social system, but hopefully not to the breaking point. I would like to thank Willi Braun for bringing Luhmann's theory of system to my attention.

16. For purposes of simplicity I will use the Vulgate Bible as the first instance of a fully authorised bible. It was compiled by Jerome of Dalmatia (c. 347–420 CE), who drew on the work of Eusebius (275–339 CE) and Athanasius (298–373 CE).

17. See Juschka 2003a.

1 A Semiotics of Gender
Prolegomena

The mythico-ritual system here plays a role equivalent to that performed by the legal system in differentiated societies; in so far as the principles of vision and division that it proposes are objectively adjusted to the pre-existing division, it consecrates the established order, by bringing it to known and recognized, official existence.

The division between the sexes appears to be 'in the order of things', as people sometimes say to refer to what is normal, natural, to the point of being inevitable...

Pierre Bourdieu, *Masculine Domination* (2001, 8)

Introduction

Gender/sex signing systems have been of interest to anthropologists as early as Margaret Mead and to feminists since the inception of what is called the second wave (1960–1990). Typically the gender/sex signing system has been articulated as two different systems: sex is a system locked in immutable biology while gender is a social system that was/is open to critique and rearticulation. However, following Angela Carter, Christine Delphy, Judith Butler, and other eminent feminist thinkers[1] who have engaged the gender/sex signing system, I reject the idea that sex is a natural category and gender a social category, and instead treat both as social categories that are interrelated so that both work in tandem to produce a gender/sex signing system otherwise called gender/sex ideology (see also Herdt 1994). With this in mind, this text is an effort toward developing a theoretical apparatus to better understand gender/sex signing systems. This theoretical apparatus I call a semiotics of gender and it includes relating gender/sex to the categories of myth, ritual, and sign-symbol. I examine gender/sex in relation to myth, ritual, and sign-symbol because they are powerful ideological mechanisms that entrench, uphold, and signify gender/sex. Although gender/sex signing systems have often been treated in the study of religion as only somewhat interesting, it is my belief that gender/sex, more times than not, is a central category of systems of belief and practice. Because of the problematic nature of the concept "religion"[2] I resist using the term "religion" throughout this text and instead opt to use the phrase "system(s) of belief and practice" as I feel this latter allows me more latitude. Also myth, ritual, and sign-symbol do not always make their appearances within so-called "religions" and in order to take them up, particularly in relation to gender/sex signing systems, I have opted for wider conceptualisation in the phrase "system(s) of belief and practice."

Myth, ritual, and sign-symbol: What else but *semeia*?

Table 1.1 Representational narratives: Myth, ritual, and sign-symbol

Representational narrative	Domain	Linguistic tool
Sign-symbol	Metaphysical	Synecdoche
Myth	Social	Metaphor
Ritual	Biological	Metonymy

It is not new, of course, that myth, ritual, and sign-symbol are understood as signifying mechanisms that provide and elaborate meaning within social bodies. Often, however, the power of these signifying mechanisms is dismissed or thought to belong solely to the realm of "religion". Rejecting this position, then, in this text I argue that myth, ritual, and sign-symbol are integral to the construction of systems of belief and practice in the majority of social formations. They are representational processes that not only signify meaning, but are also employed to "speak excessively about reality". As Roland Barthes argued nearly half a century ago:

> The fact that we cannot manage to achieve more than an unstable grasp of reality doubtless gives measure of our present alienation: we constantly drift between the object and its demystification, powerless to render its wholeness. For if we penetrate the object, we liberate it but we destroy it; and if we acknowledge its full weight, we respect it, but we restore it to a state which is still mystified. It would seem that we are condemned for some time yet always to speak *excessively* about reality. (1972, 159, emphasis original)

Myth

Myth, like any literary genre, is a particular kind of story with a set of particular outcomes. Said simply, like the mystery novel, which has as its centripetal force uncovering an unknown, myth has truth as its centripetal force, be it about the nature of existence, gender/sex, human beings, animals, rocks, stars, or deities. But myth does not need to be explicitly aimed at the truth, as it can also operate inferentially so that "truth" is arrived at implicitly. Equally, whatever truth seen to be operative in the myth does not have to be profound; it can simply corroborate the "order of things". For example, the cosmogonic myth found in Genesis of the Hebrew Bible is an explicit statement about the truth of creation, whereas the myth of the lamp central to the festival of Hanukkah speaks implicitly about the truth of creation. In the latter myth, the truth of creation is inferred through the miracle of the light burning for eight days since such an event refers the reader to the "truth" of a creator deity. Although the cosmogonic myth is considered by some to be quite profound, the second is less so and yet by its inferring of the cosmogonic myth the Hanukkah myth also gains in authority.

Explicit myths, or narratives classified as myth, can be broken down into a variety of kinds. There are cosmogonic myths that define the parameters of the existential world and its creation and anthropogonic myths that speak to the creation of existential human(s) and their order. There are demogonic myths[3] that speak of the formation and makeup of the social body and its affiliations with other groups, the world, deity or existence, while another kind of myth is the eschatological myth that announces the culmination and completion of the world, group, or whatever category is underscored. Finally there are historical myths, often working in tandem with demogonic myths, which recall the path, the origin, development, events, or particular and meaningful circumstances for the person, group, gender/sex, and so forth. The kinds of myths indicated above are clearly and explicitly myths and serve to relate the context, tradition, history, and reality of the group, people, country, or nation. These myths are often explicitly integral to systems of belief and practice.

However there is another category of myth called mythemes. Mythemes, as I use the term, deviating somewhat from Claude Lévi-Strauss,[4] are elemental themes or singular strands that act as aphoristic presentments relating cultural truths. In my usage I have generalised Lévi-Strauss' definition of mythemes and although I also understand mythemes to be gross constituent units, they are units that interweave with the socio-cultural body of knowledge rather than just myths as Lévi-Strauss understood them to function. These constituent units or mythemes are often considered to be profound and/or relevant truths that are accepted, rejected or contested within the social body. A gender/sex example of this is the mytheme "man the hunter and woman the gatherer" (see chapter three) that many in the Eurowest under the influence of paleoanthropology and evolutionary biology take to speak the truth of gender/sex. Mythemes tend to operate on the level of folk culture, but certainly they can and do operate in any part of the social body where knowledge is produced, whatever kind of knowledge, for example the figure of "the communist" in the political realm during the period of McCarthyism in the United States. Or the mytheme that men and women are *opposite* sexes, a belief central to modern Eurowestern gender/sex ideologies that acts as a truth that demarcates the group called women from the group called men. This notion of "opposite sexes" came under criticism in the work of Thomas Laqueur who has argued that the notion of opposite sexes was a product of the nineteenth century while prior to this, he convincingly contends, women and men belonged to the same sex, but were different genders (1992). Mythemes are generated and operative in social bodies and tend to impart what are understood to be normative truths.

Explicit myths and mythemes are often interrelated and therefore supportive of each other. In the instance of the category of sex delineated along the lines of the "same" prior to 1800 and the "opposite" after 1800, the anthropogonic myth of Adam and Eve was employed as metaphysical rationalisation and legitimation for both mythemes. In the Genesis myth the woman (Eve) is derived from Adam and this was seen as confirmation of the truth of women and men sharing the same sex but having different genders. In this interpretation the idea that woman was derived from man meant that they shared essences, but not genders. However, the same Genesis myth works equally well with women and men as opposite sexes when the emphasis is placed on the link between the woman (named Eve by Adam) and the Satan-serpent (in the myth they are made to speak together), and the deity and Adam (in the myth they are made to speak together). Linking the deity with Adam and the Satan-serpent with Eve allows for the opposition functional in the relationship between deity and Satan-serpent (one is good and one is evil) to transfer to Adam and Eve. Adam, who is all men, is the opposite of Eve, who is all women. The anthropogonic myth of Adam and Eve is able to work with both mythemes of gender/sex, same and opposite, because emphasis is placed on different aspects of the myth. In this example we see how the explicit myth of Adam and Eve works with the mythemes of gender/sex, but what is of further significance is that by bringing together a myth and mytheme the "truth" of gender/sex is given metaphysical credence.

Myths generally work in tandem with sign-symbols and indeed at times the two are difficult to differentiate. For example, in the colonies of the nineteenth century United States Horatio Alger's rags to riches dime-store novels acted a masculine myth of perseverance, hard work, dedication, loyalty, and justice that, if enacted, would not only produce success but ensure that the downtrodden who overcame adversity would take on heroic proportions.[5] The myth of perseverance and success in the stories of Horatio Alger, when linked as it was with American democracy, the latter symbolised by the Statue of Liberty, acted as a significant truth. Together, this myth of perseverance and the historical emergence of American democracy signified by the Statue of Liberty combined to speak *"America"* as the home of the free, the brave, the equal; a brave new world that was a refuge for the oppressed of Europe. In Emma Lazarus' now famous words,

> 'Keep, ancient lands, your storied pomp!' cries she
> With silent lips. 'Give me your tired, your poor,
> Your huddled masses yearning to breathe free,
> The wretched refuse of your teeming shore.'

Together the myth of Horatio Alger and the Statue of Liberty functioned as a twentieth century mytheme of the United States of America as the land of equal opportunity where the playing field was level and all could secure their dreams with simple hard work and perseverance. The reality of course was very different so that those marked by race met slavery, those by gender/sex subordination, those by indigeneity slaughter, and those by class poverty.

Myths and mythemes are useful to shape and police social bodies. Bruce Lincoln suggests that myths function to manufacture "estrangement" and "affinity" (1989). Myth, Roland Barthes argued,

> has the task of giving historical intention a natural justification, and making contingency appear eternal. ... If our society is objectively the privileged field of mythical significations [seen in media, narrative, sacred text, proper social relations, censorship, science, medicine, and so forth], it is because formally myth is the most appropriate instrument for the ideological inversion which defines this society. (1972, 142)

That is, myth locates the historical and social operations of society in nature—this is not about what we humans have developed; rather it is merely a reflection of what has been determined by nature or god or whatever is perceived as a directive force.

Ritual

Similar to an analysis of the ideological underpinnings of myth, is a theory of ritual articulated by Bruce Lincoln following, but emending, Maurice Bloch. In Lincoln's engagement with ritual, ritual, much like myth, has both ideological and utopian horizons. In other words, ritual is both constructive and deconstructive in terms of ideology and social organisation. Ritual is a heuristic term or a taxonomic category that includes a multitude of intentional actions and effects—what we might call rites. Ronald Grimes comments that

> "Ritual" (from the Latin adjective *ritualis*) refers here to the general idea of which a rite is a specific instance. As such, ritual does not "exist" even though it is what we must try to define; ritual is an idea scholars formulate. Strictly speaking then, one would not refer to "a" ritual or to "rituals" but to "ritual' and to "a rite" or "rites". Ritual is what one defines in formal definitions and characterisations; rites are what people enact. (Grimes 1990, 10)

Bloch suggests that "…what characterises ritual is that it lies somewhere between an action and a statement" (1986, 10), which of course makes it rather difficult to get a hold of. In light of this difficultly he suggests that ritual be analysed both symbolically and historically (1986, 11) so that both content and form are engaged in the analysis. Bruce Lincoln, influenced by Bloch's orientation to ritual, also pays attention to the symbolic propositions and the historical contexts of ritual in order to capture both its ideological and utopian horizons.

The category of ritual includes such actions and affects as "greetings, and fixed polite formula, formal behaviour and above all rituals, whether social, religious or state" (Bloch 1977, 284–285 quoted in Lincoln 1989, 5). Here the category of ritual is broadly constructed, but following Grimes (among others) only actions and effects, precipitated and accompanied by thought of course,[6] that are intended to be ritual or, following Catherine Bell, intentionally ritualised, are engaged as ritual in this text. Therefore brushing one's teeth would not be taken to be a rite, but the securing of a driver's licence for sixteen-year-olds in Canada and the United States, particularly sixteen year old *boys*, could be construed as a rite of passage.

The idea that ritual is the thing of the past, unchanging and traditional, is part of its ideological core and has often meant that rites are not something that should be subjected to social critique (see also Bloch 1977). Ritual (as well as myth) is seen to be traditional and constructed along the lines of what is believed to be normatively true; hence, as Lincoln and Bloch among others argue, ritual is ideologically oriented. For example, the "Hindu" rite of sati assumes a normative maleness and femaleness; a normativity that when enacted in the ritual and linked to myth eschews any kind of critique. In sati female and male are understood to be natural categories rather than socially constructed categories. Such a perspective of gender/sex is in itself a gender/sex ideology and already a mystification of social identities and roles. This mystification of gender/sex is a propositional element of the ritual of sati. The rite is understood "to tease out" the players' true female and male natures allowing either to surface. In the rite of sati femaleness acts as the core or central proposition of the rite and it is this femaleness, or the essence of female, of the wife that must be released in order to ensure the full and proper realisation of the maleness of the husband whose death has preceded hers. Ritual is often understood and used to realise some aspect of human potential, the effect of which is to ensure proper sociality. Meanwhile, those who have the temerity to challenge the legitimacy of the sati rite (or rites in general), particularly Indian feminists, as evinced in the 1987 case of the sati of Roop Kanwar in Delore, Rajasthan, are delegitimised by suggesting that such critiques are modern and Eurowestern while the practice of sati itself is legitimated by encapsulating it in tradition and referencing said tradition to authentic "Hinduism". However, the ideological play found in the ritual and responses to it can be exposed by paying attention to the social and historical context as suggested by Bloch and Lincoln.[7]

Categories delineated within the frame of ritual are typically proposed as authentic and unchanging. For example, in many rites of passage the necessity is to bring the non-gender/sexed human, typically a child, into a state of being gender/sexed. This process, of course, assumes from the outset that there is a substantial and necessary difference between maleness and femaleness and such assumptions are typically grounded in myth, enacted in ritual and given form in sign-symbol.

Sign-symbol

A sign-symbol is a figure, a shape, an object, a word, a phrase, a gesture that has been given cultural meaning while its realisation is in and through language. In order to make apparent the linguisticality of what are called symbols throughout this text I use the term sign-symbol. The sign-symbol is a feature of all human societies throughout time and space, but unlike Mircea Eliade (see chapter six), and those who follow him, the sign-symbol is not a mystical entity, although certainly this is how it has been understood under the sway of a crypto-Christianity. As Roland Barthes, among others, has argued, the sign-symbol is a linguistic device created by and shaped within human social bodies. For example, in twentieth century Cameroon among the Nso' the hoe is a tool that women use to till the fields and their gardens. It is a useful and everyday device. However, the hoe used in the marriage rite is still a hoe, but now it is more than a hoe and it is made to "speak excessively" within the rite itself. Linked with conceptualisations of humanity, particularly a gender/ sexed humanity, the hoe is used in the marriage rite to speak about kinship relations, femininity, heterosexuality, women and men's gender/sexed roles, ancestors, and the nature of the land and earth (Goheen 1996). How can such a simple object be made to carry so much meaning?

The hoe explicitly carries such weight when embedded in the rite of marriage, but equally the hoe implicitly continues to carry such weight even when leaning against a wall, in the hands of a woman or quite problematically in the hands of a man.[8] This is because the hoe is more than a hoe; it is also a sign-symbol that relates the Nso' gender/sex ideology as it is shaped within the Nso' kinship system and women's usufructuary relations to the land mapped through a patriarchal kinship structure. As seen in this example, sign-symbols represent something beyond their literal signing, and could be said "to speak" inferentially. Inferences are made by logical links, moving from one proposition or idea to the next to arrive at a logical theory, conclusion, supposition and so forth: so too the sign-symbol. Why the hoe can signify gender/sex, kinship systems, land use, and ancestors is through associative linguistic links all of which are shaped and made sense by their relation to myth and ritual. The sign-symbol is a condensation of ideas that through the synecdochical function allows the object, for example a hoe, to signify beyond its literal meaning. This is how the hoe can signify gender/sex, kinship, ancestors, and land among the Nso'.

Domains

Significant aspects of systems of belief and practice are, as indicated above, the representational narratives myth, ritual, and sign-symbol. These representational narratives are not free floating; rather they emerge from and are grounded in contexts that for the purposes of the semiotics of gender I term "domains". The term "domain" is intended to evoke a sense of constructedness while avoiding the notion of extra-sociality. Two of these domains, the biological and the metaphysical, risk reinforcing the mystification of ritual and sign-symbol respectively, but both domains have tended to be associated with their linked representational narratives in the past, that is, body and ritual, abstraction and sign-symbol, and in Table 1.1, column 2 I have adhered to this association. However, by linking the biological and metaphysical with the social, and establishing the social as the primary ground of production, I hope to mitigate potential mystification.

The social domain mediates between the biological and the metaphysical, while it acts as the ground for both these domains. The social domain, the domain wherein language is generated, is the ground and context for the production and interpretation of myth. Language is the "always already there" that defines, organises, shapes and mediates meaning so that order is created. And, as the social mediates between the metaphysical and biological, so too myth mediates between ritual and sign-symbol in that authorship of the myth, regardless of its perceived source (for example, the deity) is clearly located in the realm of humans. Both ritual and sign-symbol are equally produced in a social context, but the domains they are deployed within, the biological and the metaphysical respectively, make this less apparent.

In this text, the domains are treated as the epistemological ground that allows the representational narratives to make sense. For example, the rite of circumcision makes sense in relation to the body which is a concept understood to exist in time and space, hence the domain of the biological. The myth of the founding of Rome located in the figures of Romulus and Remus makes sense in relation to narrative that is situated in the domain of the social. And a sign-symbol such as the host, understood to represent the body of the deity Jesus Christ, functions linguistically as a category of thought which of course operates in the domain of the metaphysical.

The three domains are, as indicated in Table 1.1, the metaphysical, social and biological and each acts as the ground of the representational narrative that is most appropriate to it. Again, these domains are sociolinguistic constructions and are not real in the sense that they exist in physical space, although it may appear otherwise, particularly with the domain of the biological. Rather, the domains emerge in affiliation with systems of belief and practice largely because they allow for the categorisation of existence (see Lakoff 1987). The domain most strongly engaged by each of myth, ritual, and sign-symbol is the one that each most comfortably occupies: the social with regard to myth; and the biological with regard to ritual; and the metaphysical with regard to sign-symbol.

The domanial framework in this text is conceptually similar to Bruce Lincoln's schema of macrocosm (the world or universe), mesocosm (the social body), and microcosm (the individual) developed in his text *Myth, Cosmos, and Society* (1986, 4). However I have amended his domanial categories in order to resist the existential implications that I believe are inherent to his schema. Rather than attempt to construct a bridge between representational narratives and the existential world, I have instead used a domanial schema that I believe emphasises the epistemological rather than the existential. By engaging the epistemological rather than the existential my intention is to adhere to the social construction of systems of belief and practice and their indebtedness to language as a primary means to construct "worlds", to use William Paden's concept (2000). Therefore the epistemological domain of the metaphysical produces abstract, universal, atemporal (outside of time), and transcendent kinds of constructs, the epistemological domain of the social generates material, demarcated, temporal (in time), and medial kinds of constructs, while the epistemological domain of the biological gives rise to concrete, local, subtemporal (beneath time), and immanent kinds of constructs. One could say, then, that operative in the domain of the biological the representational narrative of ritual shapes the physical world much as circumcision is understood to shape the male or female genitals; operative in the domain of the social the representational narrative of myth shapes the social world producing such constructs as gender/sex, deity, demons, or fate; and operative in the domain of the metaphysical the representational narrative of sign-symbol shapes the conceptual world so that a hoe is more than a hoe in the hills of Cameroon.

Linguistic tools

The linguistic mechanisms that demonstrate the interplay between the domains of the social, biological and metaphysical, and myth, ritual and sign-symbol are, respectively, metaphor, metonymy and synecdoche (Table 1.1, column 3).[9] In each instance, the trope operates as a linguistic link between the representational narrative and its operative domain permitting, as Hayden White suggests, "the characterisation of objects in different kinds of indirect, or figurative, discourse" (1973, 31 and 34). Furthermore, the linguistic linkage makes apparent the discursive and epistemological character inherent to the domains of the social, biological, and metaphysical along with the linguisticality of the representational narratives of myth, ritual, and sign-symbol. Although each trope is not limited to its associated representational narrative and domain, the linguistic logic operative in each suggests a certain affinity with it.

Metaphor (linking myth with the social)

In my development of a semiotics of gender metaphor is the linguistic trope operating with myth in the domain of the social. The trope of metaphor mirrors the double intentionality that functions in relation to myth (literality and figurativeness) while its interplay is one of drawing upon the mundane with a twist in order to signify. To explain, myth is a symbolic narrative (as symbolic it participates in double intentionality) that mediates between the sign-symbol and ritual, while, as earlier indicated, the social mediates between the biological and the metaphysical. Working in line with Barthes' exegesis of myth, myth draws upon language, but signs language anew in order to make meaning. In other words, myth takes already formed signs, or language, which then act as the signifiers to new signifieds (concepts) in order to produce new signs. Therefore, a narrative that relates the first sacrifice such as the Song of Purusa in the *Rg. Veda* tells a story of that first sacrifice which acts metaphorically to speak about the formation of the social body and the creation of the universe:

> When they divided Purusa ("Man"), how many pieces did they prepare? What was his mouth? What are his arms, thighs, and feet called? The priest was his mouth, the warrior was made from his arms; His thighs were the commoners, and the servant was made from his feet....The Moon was born of his mind; of his eyes, the sun was born; From his mouth Indra and fire; from his breath, wind was born. (Rg. Veda 10.90 in Lincoln 1986, 3)

The myth uses metaphor in order to reflect its "truth" so that the priest is his mouth, the warrior his arms, the commoners his thighs, and servants his feet: as the body of Purusa is divided up in the first sacrifice, so too the social body. The metaphor is central to making sense of the myth as it invokes the double intentionality "speaking" both literality, referring us to the body and social body, and figuratively referring us to the relationship between the first sacrifice and the structure of the social body.

Metaphor is a complex trope and its complexity is related to its double intentionality. To begin with metaphor uses similarity to make its meaning and is, as White comments, "essentially *representational*" (1973, 34 emphasis original). For example, the phrase "eyes are the windows of the soul" is read literally only in the first intention, but must be read figuratively in order to grasp the intention of the metaphor. Eyes are not windows to be seen into and nor is the soul something visible to, or in, the eyes. However, read metaphorically, the body is likened to a building or structure and in association with this eyes are equated with windows, the latter of which allows for the interiority of the building to be glimpsed. In the metaphor bodies and buildings, and windows and eyes, act as homologies. In other words, there is a perceived structural relationship between bodies and buildings: the body is the building that houses the soul of which is glimpsed through the windows (eyes).[10] As Bruce Lincoln has argued, homology moves one beyond likeness (analogy) to propose a structural relationship: as a building houses people and windows are the means to see into (and out of) the building, so too the body houses a soul and eyes are the means to see into (and out of) the body. A structural relationship is proposed and this relationship allows for a second intentionality to surface. Although a building and a body are different, they are also similar insofar as each is understood to hold or contain something other than itself.

Metonymy (linking ritual with the biological)

Metonymy operates according to association in which a single aspect of something is able to represent a more complex whole. Hayden White suggests that metonymy is reductionist in that there is a part-part relationship so that a part of the object is made to represent the whole object (White 1973, 35). Therefore a part, for example the press, can represent the whole, news media. According to White, in metonymy it is the "extrinsic" relationship that is underscored, for example sail for ship, and it is this that brings about extra signification (White 1973, 35).

The aspect of metonymy that I find helpful for engaging ritual is its concrete and material orientation, in that implied in metonymy is a sense of contiguity or a touching (see Jakobson 2002), while ritual also appears to touch or be contiguous with the domain of the biological: the actions, gestures, movements, speech, and so forth carried out in the ritual allow ritual to be perceived as "speaking" with flesh and therefore operative in the domain of the biological. There is, then, a perceptual materiality inherent to metonymy that allows for a logical connection between the domain of the biological and ritual. For example in Classical Greece exiting from a house within which a deceased person was laid out (the *prothesis*) required that one sprinkle oneself with water as a rite of purification. Outside, at the entrance of the house, was a pitcher-like vessel *(lekythos)* containing the water that allowed one to perform the simple rite: to not perform it was to imperil the social body at large, the temples of the deities, and so forth since one's contamination was contagious (see Garland 2001; Johnston 1999; Vermeule 1979; Kurtz and Boardman 1971). In this rite, as with most ritual, what is central to its logic is the materiality, the body and water, while the linguistic tool of metonymy, here represented by the gesture/act of ablution, links and grounds the rite in the domain of the biological. The linking and grounding of the rite in the domain of the biological is achieved through the physicality of the water and the act of ablution both of which signify as a metonym referring one to "world" and its perceived operations wherein a presupposed order is assumed. In this instance water is understood to have purifying properties and the act of ablution transfers those properties to the ritual actor. As White comments

> By metonymy, then, one can simultaneously distinguish between two phenom-
> ena and reduce one to the status of a manifestation of the other. This reduction
> may take the form of an agent-act relationship ("the thunder *roars*") or a cause-
> effect ("the roar *of* thunder"). And, by such reductions, as Vico, Hegel and
> Nietzsche all pointed out, the phenomenal world can be populated with a host
> of agents and agencies that are presumed to exist *behind* it. (1973, 35, emphasis
> original)

Synecdoche (linking sign-symbol with the metaphysical)

Although it has been argued that synecdoche is a subcategory of metonymy and therefore distinguishing them is unnecessary, I do distinguish
them. Certainly synecdoche and metonymy, along with metaphor, are
linguistically related in that each is a trope that resists literality and embraces symbolism. However, in synecdoche the logic or function is one
of condensation and abstraction wherein a quality is suggested, while in
metonymy the logic or function is one of reduction and association through
approximation or contiguity. White comments:

> Unlike the Metonymical expression "fifty sail" used as a figure for "fifty ships," it
> [synecdoche] is meant to signal not simply a "name change" [metonymy literally
> means name change] but a name change designating a totality...which possesses
> some quality...that suffuses and constitutes the essential nature of all the parts
> that make it up. (1973, 36)

Synecdoche is the linguistic mechanism that links the domain of the metaphysical and the sign-symbol. As a linguistic trope synecdoche, when
played out with relation to the sign-symbol, is a part that represents a
quality of the whole understood to be intrinsic to it. Hayden White argues that "[w]ith Synecdoche... a phenomenon can be characterized by
using the part to symbolise some *quality* presumed to inhere in the totality, as in the expression 'He is all heart'" (1973, 34, emphasis original).
For example, as sign-symbols a crown signifies kingship while a sceptre
signifies rule. Both crown and sceptre, operating as sign-symbols, use the
synecdochical function of condensation in order to signify beyond their
literality. Condensation, as I am using it here, refers to the process of
concentration that produces increased density and complexity pointing
one toward the quality of the whole that is intrinsic to the thing. Therefore, synecdoche links complex abstractions or ideals with a singularity so
that a part is able to represent the quality inherent to the whole.

A sign-symbol, because of condensation and abstraction, can mean
beyond the literal, moving one from the concrete to the abstract, hence
its domanial location of the metaphysical. The sign-symbol also operates
via double intentionality in that it is the thing, for example, crown, but
equally it points beyond this initial signing to the qualities of kingship

(historically and socially delimited) perceived therein. It is the dual function of condensation and abstraction found in synecdoche that allows for interplay between the domain of the metaphysical and the sign-symbol.

The tropes of metaphor, metonymy and synecdoche function in terms of double intentionality as they allow for something to mean beyond its literal reference. Following George Lakoff I believe these tropes are a creative means by which to extend knowledge and understanding. As he comments, "human categorisation is essentially a matter of both human experience and imagination—of perception, motor activity, and culture on the one hand, and of metaphor, metonymy, and mental imagery on the other" (1987, 8). Equally, I would argue that through the linguistic tools of metaphor, metonymy, and synecdoche myth, ritual, and sign-symbol, respectively, are linked to the domains of the social, biological, and metaphysical. What is evident in these linguistic relationships are the social origins of myth, ritual, and sign-symbol.

Cultural artefacts and *bricolage*

In order that belief occur, that the individual, the group, and/or the society's belief be engaged, that which is encoded, sign-symbol, myth or ritual (often through recourse to deity, nature or abstract mathematical laws of the universe), must have social meaning from the outset. Therefore, a hoe, to use the example of the Nso' people of Cameroon, is a hoe and recognised as such. It is a sign in the Sausurrean linguistic frame and therefore carries social meaning. But the hoe becomes more than just a hoe when it takes on the synecdoche function and becomes a part that represents some quality of the whole: the hoe is a sign-symbol that "speaks" from within and about the system of the belief and practice among the Nso'. Beginning as an everyday item or cultural artefact the hoe used in ritual signifies a contract between the man and woman: he will provide land which she will till. At the outset, then, cultural artefacts do not hold any inherent meaning beyond their initial function within the social/cultural frame. A hoe is simply a tool for a particular type of farming. Significant meaning, or meaning *more* than the mundane of the quotidian, is invested in the item when it is called upon to play a ritual and/or mythic role—the hoe, then, becomes more that a simple tool of cultivation (its literality) and further signifies the totality of human relations through kinship and marriage, and the qualities of heteronormativity, femininity, and masculinity. The hoe is the *bricolage* the *bricoleur* uses to construct sign-symbols.

Another example of *bricolage* is Dominique Blain's 1993 artistic instal-lation entitled *The World*. This installation consisted of a book entitled *The World* lodged between a pair of army boots. Exterior to the installation the boots are simply boots, but within the installation they are more than boots as they now act as bookends that fix and enclose the book, *The World*. In this installation the cultural artefacts of army boots and a book entitled *The World* are doubly intended and now signify war as an enclos-ing and containing force for the world, a force that shapes the human condition. Or Blain's installation entitled *Village*, which is comprised of newspapers recording the events of the Bosnian War (1992–1995), is another example of *bricolage*. The newspapers used in the installation are products of human culture and often are the refuse that blow around the streets or are found in the houses of human habitats. In this installation Blain took this remnant of human sociality and used it to construct husks of houses (with windows blown out) in a vast Tower of Babel. Alluding to the Tower of Babel, and the many words and stories that represent hu-man lives found in print news, the installation signifies human inability to understand each other even when millions of words are employed; com-munication is truncated and such truncation leads to violent conflict. In this piece the remnants of cultural debris such as newsprint is the *bricolage* used to construct a new object that, when signifying as the Tower of Babel, critically engages the past and the future of the Eurowest.[11]

Bricolage is made up of already formed cultural objects or the constant accumulative signifiers that take on meaning and act as myth, ritual, and sign-symbols all of which are doubly signified (engage in symbolic dis-course). The basis of belief is a process of assembling *bricolage* or cultural artefacts from the social domain and using these in order to make mean-ing, but meaning that is significant and of course understood to be true. With *bricolage* one is employing previously formed signs from the past to construct new signs. *Bricolage* comprises the stories, signs, actions and the like when reshaped and signified anew to become myth, ritual, and sign-symbol and used to establish, or disestablish, ways to understand existence. In this way *bricolage*, through myth, ritual, and sign-symbol, is deemed important to the group holding up or establishing as it does a system of belief and practice[12] wherein the self, humanity, the social body, the world, existence, and so forth are extrapolated.[13]

The gender/sex signing system

Table 1.2 The gender/sex signing system

Domain	Representational narrative	Linguistic tool	Linguistic designator
Metaphysical	Sign-symbol	Synecdoche	Feminine/masculine
Social	Myth	Metaphor	Woman/man
Biological	Ritual	Metonymy	Female/male

In the semiotics of gender, or the gender/sex signing system, my first move is not to separate gender and sex as if they are separate categories that merely influence each other, as I indicated in the first part of this chapter. Initially feminist theorists of second wave feminism set out to separate gender from sex in order to underscore the social constructiveness of gender. In this kind of theorizing sex is understood to be immutable and fixed, while gender is understood to be flexible and mutable depending on socio-cultural and historical parameters.

The dimorphism between sex and gender has been challenged by a number of theorists. Gilbert Herdt (1996) calls into question this opposition and suggests that it is a legitimating aspect of Eurowestern heterosexism. Christine Delphy (1996) calls into question the gender/sex dimorphism indicating that this process may have been useful at one juncture toward theorising masculine hegemony, but it now has become prohibitive to clear thinking about gender/sex. In her formulation of gender/sex she argues that the category sex does not precede the category of gender; rather gender precedes sex. Here two ideas are underscored: the first is that sex is as much a social construct and category of social organisation as is gender; and the second is that gender defines sex and not the other way around:

> We continue to think of gender in terms of sex: to see it as a social dichotomy determined by a natural dichotomy We now see gender as the content with sex as the *container*. The content may vary, and some consider it *must* vary, but the container is considered to be invariable because it is part of nature, and nature 'does not change'. (1996, 33, emphasis original)

To some it may appear that we are dealing with the chicken and the egg problem, but we are not. A chicken and an egg are things in the world (this is of course aside from their linguistic designation), while gender and sex are categories and therefore not things in the world. There are those who of course argue that sex difference, that is, female/male, is a thing and point to genitalia as proof. But sex difference or distinction is not the same thing a penis or a vagina. A penis and vagina are aspects of the body, like an arm, fin, head or tail, and do not mean beyond their being what they are, although certainly linguistic designators do carry cultural meaning, for example, vagina derived from the Latin meaning sheath or scabbard. However, by using them in such a way as to mark, for example, female and male as different or further as "opposite" is to have vagina and penis act as sign-symbols to signify *difference* particularly sex difference. We do not, for example, signify *difference* through eye colour. We do not perceive brown eyes as the opposite of blue eyes, or that violet eyes signify those people as different from brown-eyed people. We know that eye colour varies, but in the Eurowest eye colour is not used to signify *difference* as it does not carry that kind of cultural value.

Delphy's argument, then, is to say that sex itself is a sign that emerges from the domain of the social while *"gender* precedes sex...sex itself simply marks a social division; it serves to allow social recognition and identification of those who are dominants and those who are dominated" (1996, 35, emphasis original). In the gender/sex signing system, my first move, then, is to link the concepts of gender and sex, and prioritise gender as the determinative category, hence my use of "gender/sex" throughout this book. This formulation of gender/sex works in tandem with my location of the social as the primary and pivotal site of the production of all symbolism: gender, myth, and metaphor working in the social domain are the origins for the biological (and therefore sex, ritual, and metonymy) and the metaphysical (and therefore sign-symbol and synecdoche).

The semiotics of gender is a theoretical frame by which to understand the processes of the signing of gender/sex. It is a theory that operates on the level of language and therefore is useful in the analysis of gender/sex, regardless of social and historical location. The theory is one wherein the signing of gender/sex is analysed in relation to the three domains of the social, biological, and metaphysical (Table 1.2, column 1), the categories of myth, ritual, and sign-symbol, (Table 1.2, column 2), and the tropes of metaphor, metonymy, and synecdoche (Table 1.2, column 3). With regard to gender/sex as signing system, then, in the domain of the social related to the category of myth and the trope of metaphor the linguistic designators of woman and man (and girl and boy) operate (Table 1.2, column 4); in the domain of the biological, in relation to ritual and metonymy, the linguistic designators of female and male operate (Table 1.2, column 4); and in the domain of the metaphysical, in relation to sign-symbol and synecdoche, the linguistic designators of feminine and masculine function (Table 1.2 column 4). Each pair of linguistic designators registers different levels and conceptualisations of the gender/sex signing system. Therefore woman and man register social roles and relationships, for example mother and father, female and male register embodied (tactile) characteristics and qualities, for example smooth and hard, and feminine and masculine register abstract characteristics and qualities, for example emotional and logical. Each set is linked and supportive of the other and together the three sets represent a gender/sex signing system.

The social as the primary site of production: myth, metaphor, and woman/man

In my theory of gender/sex signing systems, I privilege the category of myth without taking up the long-standing discussion concerning the link between, or the priority of, myth and ritual.[14] I do this because I understand the domain of the social, following Marxist materialism, as the site for all human production. Although Barthes, among others, has argued that myth is a reified and ideological discourse raising the problem of engaging it in a materialist fashion, I would argue that myth, although certainly ideological in that it "transforms history into nature" (Barthes 1972, 129), is first and foremost a narrative produced in, by and through social relations. Myth in either written or oral form is necessarily, because of its form, linked to a human authorship, regardless that human authorship is denied, absent, or indicated as secondary, as in the divine revelation of a text, for example Muhammad or Joseph Smith. As myth operates in the domain of the social it mediates between ritual (in the domain of the biological and employing metonymy) and sign-symbol (in the domain of the metaphysical and employing synecdoche). As the mediation point it links sign-symbol and ritual while lending them, as it is itself lent through association with both, an air of authority, and a sense of veracity, and, most importantly, it provides the weight of tradition. It is tradition, produced from the intertwining of myth and history that allows authority and veracity to be associated with the representational narratives (see Williams 1977, 115).

In the semiotics of gender, then, woman/man is the primary site for the production of the gender/sex signing systems. Female/male, associated with ritual, operates within the domain of the biological and is signed through the linguistic mechanism of metonymy. As myth is the ground of origin, when linked to ritual, myth is naturalised (made to appear as if in nature) while ritual of course takes on authority, veracity, and traditionality. To make this statement clearer through example below I draw upon the mid-twentieth century ethnographic work of Marcel Griaule in relation to the Dogon people of Southern Mali and Northern Burkina Faso.

Among the Dogon people, the rite of passage that marks the transition from childhood to adult status is circumcision, while adult status is understood as gendered status. In this socio-cultural location, the anthropogonic myth asserts that humans are born with a female and male soul. As children, then, humans are bisexual containing both maleness and femaleness.

The Dogon anthropogonic myth relates that the masculine creator deity was unable to have sex with the earth because of a termite hill. We read "[a]t God's approach the termite hill rose up, barring the passage and displaying its masculinity" (Griaule 1958, 17). In order to deal with the masculine obstruction, the creator deity cut down the termite hill and subsequently was able to have sexual relations with the earth. The product of this first sexual union was the jackal, but as a single being rather than a twinned being the jackal was considered to be the defective product of a defective union. The deity, however, again sought to have sexual concourse with the earth and as nothing prohibitive occurred, such as the raising of the termite hill, the twins were born. This sexual union was considered to be efficacious and from it came the male and female twins called the Nummo. The Nummo themselves take on a creative role and assist in the creation of the ancestors. It is they who ensured the ancestors are born with two souls: the male is given a female soul located in the foreskin, while the female is given a male soul located in the clitoris. However, the Nummo understood that human life would be challenging and femaleness and maleness contained in one being would be too difficult for humans. With this in mind, then, they determined that each person must of necessity take up the gender most suited them, and, toward this end, they circumcised the male ancestor, removing from him the femininity of his foreskin, and the female ancestor removing from her the masculinity of her clitoris[15] (Griaule 1958, 22–23).

The act of circumcision among the Dogon is given legitimation and authority by reference to the myth. In the myth it is deity that initiates the creation of the male and female twins who then assist with the creation of the ancestors. As the first act of creation was problematic, so too the first act of creation carried out by the twins. In order to correct the problem, the twins enact the first circumcision removing the foreskin from male/female ancestor and the clitoris from the female/male ancestor. In order that people and existence be as they ought to be, the rite of circumcision must be performed since, as stated in the myth, life was too difficult to support bisexual humans. The rite, then, is understood to end the bisexuality of children; a bisexuality that ultimately is understood to obstruct proper heterosexual relations and reproduction.

If a child should happen not to be circumcised, its identity will be confused and this confusion would bring dis-ease into the group. As it is explained by the Dogon, a female/male with clitoris intact would be too aggressive and not take to her role as subordinate to her husband and unselfish to her children. "S/he" would act like a man. Or the male/female with foreskin intact would be disinclined to find a mate and set up a household. Neither would fit well into the society because neither fits well into themselves. Furthermore, in terms of fit, it is believed that two souls in one person would mean that neither soul was firmly lodged and this would of course create even more difficulties for the person, the family and the social body at large. The rite of circumcision, then, is a necessary act toward ensuring proper human and social relations.

The combining of myth and ritual in the above example makes apparent how the two are intertwined and supportive of each other. The anthropogonic myth legitimates and gives authority to the ritual, while the ritual concretises, or gives flesh to, the myth. The speaking of the myth takes up the metaphorical function that allows the earth to be female, and a termite hill to be a clitoris, while the metonymical function allows the act of circumcision, the removal of "excess", the foreskin or clitoris, to approximate the first circumcision and every other circumcision thereafter. Dialectically related, the myth and the ritual together speak the Dogon system of belief and practice and in the process define and uphold the gender/sex signing system.

The domain of the metaphysical is equally interrelated with the domain of the social, but it is also connected to the biological through the social domain. The social is the ground of intentional social action wherein objects, gestures, words, and actions are given a telling and it is this telling that allows sign-symbols to carry meaning. An object, gesture, etc. without a context cannot be a sign-symbol, for context is everything when it comes to sign-symbols (Turner 1967). Clifford Geertz (1971), among others, has made this argument, but Victor Turner (1969) extended it further arguing that the meaning of the sign-symbol is not only socially bound, but ritually bound as well.

A sign-symbol given meaning via the social and myth is concretised in ritual and the domain of the biological. The sign-symbol in its double intentionality is an abstraction, but when captured by ritual it is enfleshed and given concrete existence. Emergent from the social and tethered to the world by ritual, or reference to ritual, the sign-symbol ascends to a place of pre-eminence as it is given metaphysical status. It is this status of pre-eminence that sign-symbol then bestows on myth and ritual ensuring that they too are perceived as operating in line with universal law and truth.

Concluding comments: signing systems and gender/sex ideology

The biological and metaphysical domains operate in order to uphold and legitimate human operations and relations in the domain of the social. By locating truth in the domains of both the biological and the metaphysical, the social and its human relationships are of course mystified. How humans relate in all cultural locations is determined in part by their gender/sex signing system. Gender/sex signing systems are manifested in a variety of methods: hierarchically, complimentarily, or even neutrally. Gender/sex signing systems can and do change and when the understanding of domains change, as a result of epistemology, representational narratives are also invested with new meaning. But in all instances change is generated within the domain of the social while myths are assigned new meaning to reflect this change.[16]

The semiotics of gender is a theory that seeks to understand the complexity of human signing systems and how they operate to define the parameters and mechanisms of social bodies. In terms of this, and in light of my pedagogic inclinations, myth, ritual, and sign-symbol seem to me to be lucrative avenues by which to understand the operations of the gender/sex signing system since gender/sex ideology is so firmly entrenched in our social systems as to be ontological. The semiotics of gender, then, is a challenge to the ontological logic of gender/sex ideology through the revelation of its social parameters.

Notes

1. I am quite cognizant that each of the theorists referenced adheres to different feminist positions. However, although each shows variation in feminist orientation, each is very clear that gender and sex are socially constructed categories.

2. I put quotation marks around the word religion as it is a term that separates certain kinds of activities, behaviours, views, knowledge, and so forth from other similar categories and assumes they are somehow different and therefore requiring like kinds of tools and theories, that is, religious, to deal with them. This kind of assumption emerges most explicitly in the work of Mircea Eliade and his followers and is heavily under the influence of Christian theology in terms of favouring ontology over anthropology (Smith 2004, 103). For an extended discussion of this issue see J.Z. Smith (1998), although, unlike myself, he does not resist using the term. See also William Arnal's contribution to the *Guide to the Study of Religion* (2000).

3. Bruce Lincoln terms these sociogonic myths (1989).

4. Lévi-Strauss defined mythemes as "gross constituent units". These units are singular "truths" on the level of the sentence. For Lévi-Strauss, a myth was comprised of mythemes

or its gross constituent units. Studying myth requires that one first identify these units and then examine how they bundle together, or are interrelated, in order to speak mythically (1963, 210–211).

5. An excellent recent example of this myth is the film *The Pursuit of Happiness* produced in 2006. Interestingly, this film combines class difference and race. The protagonist played by Will Smith, rises from poverty and homelessness to become a corporate success story. Smith, along with his son, soars above his "fate" through the application of perseverance, hard work, honesty, and dedication to be rewarded with success. Although this story possibly seeks to positively encode the father-son relationship, it also reinforces the idea that the American capitalist system is just and those crushed by it simply do not try hard enough.

6. Catherine Bell (1992) has sharply criticised the separation of thought and action in ritual studies. She argues that the structuralist theory of ritual, following the work of Ferdinand de Saussure, assumes a dichotomy between action and thought while ritual is seen as action and myth, for example, as thought. In my understanding of ritual such a dichotomy is false insofar as there is no action without thought and no thought without action. Ritual emphasises the body and uses it, or parts of it, to signify meaning. Therefore, I might argue, it is the embodiment of thought.

7. For those authors who take seriously the necessity to study sati with reference to social and historical context see, for example, Hawley 1994; Mani 1998; Banerjee 2003.

8. In the hands of a man, the hoe signals him as feminised. This does not mean that men do not use hoes, rather they do not want to been seen with a hoe in their hands. Hence, Miriam Goheen comments, they will farm far from observing eyes (Goheen 1996, 83).

9. My use of synecdoche, metaphor, and metonymy, toward developing a signing system of gender/sex using myth, ritual, and sign-symbol follows in some small measure George Lakoff's breakdown of metaphor, metonymy, and imagery as "imaginative mechanisms" that he understands are central to how humans "construct categories to make sense of experience" (1987, xii). However, Lakoff is concerned with cognitive science while I am concerned with linguistics. Equally his understanding and use of metonymy reflects my use of synecdoche, but as I indicate in the section on metonymy, although some theorists do not differentiate between the two, I do following Roman Jakobson (2002). See Hayden White who also distinguishes between metonymy and synecdoche (1973, 31–36).

10. For a discussion on homologies see Lincoln 1986 and Juschka 2004.

11. See also the 2006 film *Babel* that refers to this myth in its title to signify the difficulty of clear and unproblematic communication among humans. As much as words and their meaning are the primary means of communication, they are equally the problem of communication.

12. When I speak of "system of belief and practice", I use the term system to indicate a collection of independent but equally interrelated constituents that comprise a unified whole: belief to be any cognitive content held to be true, and practice as a customary and/or traditional way of acting and being. My understanding of the phrase shows some continuity with Niklas Luhmann's conceptualisation of system in that I understand systems to be open to their environments as well as autopoietic (Seidl and Becker 2006, 14–17).

13. I am indebted to Jacques Derrida's (1978, 278–293) reading of *bricolage* which has allowed me to reformulate and apply Claude Lévi-Strauss' concept of *bricolage* within my own theory. Lévi-Strauss' development of *bricolage* sees it as part of the science of the concrete, one that draws upon closed sets in order to construct meaning. The *bricoleur*, he tells us, operates in a closed system and "addresses himself to a collection of oddments left over from human endeavours, that is only a subset of the culture" (Lévi-Strauss 1966, 19). In contradistinction to the *bricoleur* is the engineer who uses a science of the abstract and rather than rearrange signs the engineer uses concepts to attempt to move beyond the closed system: "[the] scientist, on the other hand, whether he is an engineer or physicist, is always on the lookout for *that other message* which might be wrested from an interlocutor in spite of his reticence in pronouncing on questions whose answers have not been rehearsed. Concepts thus appear like operators *opening up* the set being worked with…" (Lévi-Strauss 1966, 20, emphasis original). I would argue, following Derrida, that science, when using language, is equally susceptible to *bricolage*. He comments that "[i]n this sense the engineer is a myth. A subject who supposedly would be the absolute origin of his own discourse and supposedly would construct it "out of nothing", "out of whole cloth", would be the creator of the verb, the verb itself. The notion of the engineer who supposedly breaks with all forms of *bricolage* is therefore a theological idea; and since Lévi-Strauss tells us elsewhere that *bricolage* is mythopoetic, the odds are that the engineer is a myth produced by the *bricoleur*." (Derrida 1978, 285)

14. There has been a long standing discussion concerning myth and ritual as to which precedes and which is dependent (see Csapo 2005, Segal, R. A. 1996 and 1998 and Doniger and Patton 1996). My position is one of privileging the social domain over the metaphysical and biological domains. As myth is linked to the social domain, it is by default privileged as the primary site of production. However, as I see it, myth, sign-symbol, and ritual are interrelated and furthermore I am not interested in arguing which came first, myth or ritual. Rather, myth, ritual, and sign-symbol are all produced in the social domain, although the latter two are ideologically grounded in the biological and metaphysical domains respectively.

15. The myth also indicates that the clitoris prevents the female ancestor from having easy and safe births. The practice is increasingly coming under pressure to cease from local women's groups and NGOs and the global human rights community.

16. The process of developing new interpretations is one by which the rhetorical strategy of metaphor—the polysemy of words—is engaged in order to bring the myth into a current relationship with the present even if myth is always understood to be of the past. An example to demonstrate this is the figure of Jesus in Christian Liberation Theology. In the reinterpretation of liberation theology he *is* the god who opted for the poor, the downtrodden, and the marginalised. In terms of this new myth of Jesus, one notes that he takes on the accoutrements of the communistic revolutionary who rejects systems of domination, capitalism, and class, and in the case of feminist liberation theology, of patriarchy. In this new interpretation the actions and words presented in the Christian gospels are understood to signify Jesus as a twentieth century revolutionary: words such as "the first shall be last and the last shall be first" and actions such as overturning the tables of the money changers become metaphors that say he *is* a revolutionary.

2 Feminist Encounters with Myth
Engaging Angela Carter

Scattered throughout the world and the centuries, however, are instances of religions dominated by women in which women have been leaders, the majority of participants, and in which women's concerns have been central.

Susan Star Sered *Priestess, Mother, Sacred Sister: Religions Dominated by Women* (1994)

Introduction

The intention of this chapter[1] is to think about myth, in particular about mythemes and binarism, and how they figure in gender/sex signing systems. To do this I engage the work of Angela Carter (1940-1992), a poststructuralist[2] feminist writer and theorist. Carter's fictional and non-fictional writings are an imaginative and deconstructive engagement with gender/sex and sexuality. In my own work of engaging myth, ritual, and sign-symbol, I have found Carter's books and articles to be intriguing, thought provoking and uncomfortable as one is never quite sure where to locate her feminist politics. Nonetheless, her work has provoked my own thinking and therefore this chapter asks what it is that Carter saw as central to gender/sex ideology. What is initially apparent, and what I agree with in my own work, is that myth and sign-symbol are integral to a convincing and seductive gender/sex ideology. Noting this, Carter's efforts were to initially demythologise and then remythologise gender/sex (*Heroes and Villains* 1969) and when this failed her efforts were then directed at interrogating gender/sex in light of Freud's theory of the sex-drive, repression, and the unconscious, suggesting that the very social nature of gender/sex and sexuality (*Sadeian Woman* 1979) is obfuscated and mystified when understood within a classical Freudian frame (*The Infernal Desire Machines of Dr Hoffman* 1972).

In my analysis of Carter's work, then, I begin by discussing myth and mythemes, and then move on to engage Carter's non-fictional *Sadeian*

Woman and two of her early fictions, the dystopic *Heroes and Villains* and her post-surrealist novel *The Infernal Desire Machines of Dr. Hoffman*, with myth in mind. Specifically, my intersection with her work begins by examining her politicisation of gender/sex in the *Sadeian Woman*, and then moves on to look at how she links the gender/sex signing system to the establishment of a subjectivity[3] shaped by and through myth, played out in her novels. In her examination of gender/sex through non-fiction and fiction, I would argue that Carter makes very apparent the importance of myth and sign-symbol as integral to the notion of gender/sexed subjectivity in the Eurowest.[4]

Founding and grounding narratives: Power and myth

Often people assume they know what a myth is, that they could easily recognise a myth, and that only ancient and/or pre-scientific peoples, the mythic "primitive" of Eurowestern imagination, and children are those who speak and hear the mythic tongue. Myth is a narrative, but in the Eurowest, under the regime of scientific theory and method, it is often understood to be an ancient narrative, one that has faltered with the onset of history. History in this regime is a record of past events, which, when gathered together, represents a body of knowledge. Myths gathered together under the rubric "mythology" signify unreasoned belief. Although myth and history have the word "story" associated with both, this signals narrated fiction in relation to myth and a record or narrated description of past events in association with history. Equally, myth used in popular parlance suggests untruth and/or naive belief, while history suggests fact and/or reasoned assessment. And finally, myth signifies as irrational, while history is the rational, and it is this dichotomy that infuses history with authority. Michel de Certeau speaks to this understanding of myth and history in the Eurowest:

> In its struggle against genealogical storytelling, the myths and legends of the collective memory, and the meanderings of the normal tradition, historiography establishes a certain distance between itself and common assertion and belief; it locates itself in this difference, which gives it the accreditation of erudition because it is separated from ordinary discourse. (1993, 200)

Myth, it would appear, has little to no exchange value in today's current market of facts. If history has replaced myth in the Eurowest as a repository of certainty, how, one might wonder, can myth be seen as powerful, and powerful in relation to the gender/sex signing system?

Myth is, I would argue, the repressed of history. It is the repressed because it is the unacknowledged sibling of history. Myth works in tandem with history in that, firstly, through the rejection of myth the authority of history upheld, nevertheless secondly, even as myth is rejected, it is taken up and woven into the very fabric of history. The two are entwined and together tell the story of a person, a people, a country, a nation, or a world. In this formulation, then, one cannot separate myth and history other than by unravelling the entire cloth. One cannot distil history from myth as, for example, Rudolph Bultmann and those who followed him would have it. Bultmann's hermeneutical endeavour was to demythologise the New Testament, to separate history from myth, fact from fiction, as if there was a sharp and determinable break between the two (Bultmann 1958). But I would argue there is no clean break between the two as both myth and history are narratives that are typically combined in the majority, if not all, social bodies. It is myth, or the very principle of myth following Roland Barthes, which, "transforms history into nature…mythical speech…is not read as motive, but as reason" (1972, 128).

As the repressed of history, myth has an even greater power than history, for, as Freud noted, what is repressed lies in the unconscious, is thwarted from entering the conscious, and therefore prevents us from having full knowledge of ourselves and our actions (Freud 1991, 327–343). As the unconscious of history, myth is not critically engaged; rather it lurks in and about history establishing a certainty of truth that cannot be seen clearly, cannot be tested, but simply is. In repressing myth and claiming history in the diasporic Eurowest, for example, the very basis of our history is posited on the notion of the eternal human otherwise known as "man". This fixing of man further means, since the late eighteenth century at least, a positing of the eternal female and male (for example man the hunter and woman the gatherer) who stand within an evolutionary history that mirrors too closely the Adam and Eve of hegemonic Christianity. "Man" and "woman" are effectively de-socialised and de-historicised and man and his helpmate remain uncontested figures. In effect the roots of the historical narrative are mystified[5] through its relationship with myth.[6] A significant aspect of myth's power, then, is our unwillingness to see its relationship to history.

If myth's relationship to history is ignored, this is doubly so for mythemes. Mythemes, as I have indicated in chapter one, are elemental themes or singular strands that act as cryptic narratives relating cultural truths. Following Claude Lévi-Strauss, then, mythemes are gross constituent units, but units that are interwoven with the socio-cultural body of knowledge. Mythemes, then, are separable from, and function independently of, the originating myth. These constituent units tend to act as significant and relevant truths that are accepted, rejected or contested within a social body. Mythemes often operate on the level of folk culture, but certainly they can and do operate in bodies of knowledge such as science, economics, politics, education, and so forth. Mythemes are generated and operative in social bodies and impart normative truths shaping what it is we think we know.

Dystopia, surrealism and myth

With the interesting relationship between myth and history in mind and myth's gross constituent unit the mytheme, how might Carter examine myth as it relates to the gender/sex signing system in the Eurowest? What narrative strategies might she engage that would reveal the interweaving of myth and history, and the functional mythemes that shape the gender/sex signing system? There are two she will try: the dystopic narrative[7] with its relentless scepticism; and fantasy within a post-surrealist[8] landscape upon which the binary relationship of myth and history is revealed through Carter's linking them with the unconscious and conscious. Such narrative strategies, Carter hopes, will ultimately challenge the binarism that she sees as primarily produced through myth.

Dystopia is a world that rejects hope. Unlike utopia, which speculates on the imagined possibilities of human nature realised in some idealised frame, dystopia's fantasy is one that undercuts idealism and instead draws on materialism: one cannot escape from the social of social relations. In dystopia an idealised human nature and the essentialised goodness of this nature, taken for granted in utopia, are not assumed.[9] Nor are the socialised aspects of human social relations essentialised as evil: human nature simply cannot be found in any essentialised form be it good or evil. In Carter's dystopic narrative, *Heroes and Villains*, human nature, or that which is produced in nature, is called into question and the social relations of human beings are presented as a continuous never-ending struggle toward the resolution of the present—a present heavily indebted to a sordid past. In the dystopic narrative human nature remains a complex of psychological, physiological, sociological, emotional, and intellectual desires and motivations twisted into a Gordian knot. To cut the knot, as a utopia would have it, is simply to reassert some form of hegemonic power. Played out in a pastoral realm of an unrelenting, hostile, but beautiful nature[10] or in a brooding urban grey landscape of enmeshing social relations, the dystopic narrative forces the reader into a position of full consciousness. Dystopia provides no heroic narrative (a significant mytheme that shapes subjectivity as it is applied to men in the Eurowest,[11] which guarantees self, identity, and security): there is no founding moment that can lift one above the muck and mire of the everyday, and no epiphany which promises a blissful future.

The mythic ground of gender/sex and *The Sadeian Woman*

The deconstruction of gender/sex as a signing system is a complex process. It is not simply a matter of commenting upon the social relations between men and women, although certainly this is a necessary starting point. Social relations are simply one aspect of the gender/sex signing system and the gender/sex ideologies produced therein. The gender/sex signing system is a signifying system that contributes to the construction of social systems in their make-up, organisation, logic, development, identity and orientation. Therefore, to fully grasp any gender/sex signing system requires an examination of its multiple levels of operation.

The gender/sex signing system, or the semiotics of gender, plays out along the lines of the linguistic designators of woman/man, female/male, and feminine/masculine. These linguistic designators operate in a semiotic system that includes, in the majority of Eurowestern social bodies (past and present), binarism or binary logic. Therefore, linked to the gender/sex linguistic designators are a plethora of concepts that function with them in a binary relationship. So, for example, under the influence of Enlightenment logic developed in accord with Aristotelian natural history and philosophy, we see feminine being to irrationality as masculine is to rationality, woman to reproduction as man is to production, and female to weak as male is to strong.[12] In this play of binarism what is obvious is that one half of the pair carries negative social value, while the other carries positive social value. One further notes that the binarisms operative in masculine hegemonies,[13] such as found in the Eurowest, accord negative value to woman/female/feminine and positive value to man/male/masculine. Any concepts linked to the linguistic designators of the gender/sex signing system and developed within the binary logic also acquire, or bring, negative or positive value. What often appears to be fairly predictable in masculine hegemonies that employ binary logic is that, although the conceptual links (e.g. nature linked to female or male, or culture linked to female or male) can and do vary, the valuative function of associating the negative with feminine/woman/female (-) and the positive with masculine/man/male (+) shows considerable continuity.

LIBRARY, UNIVERSITY OF CHESTER

There are feminist theories, for example found in ecological feminism, that argue that the valuative formula in masculine hegemonies is simply a reversal of reality: the truth of binarism is that woman and all the meta-phorically related concepts are the positive side (+) of the formula, while man and all the metaphorically related concepts are the negative side (-). There are still other theories, those oriented to reforming the social body for example, that argue that the valuative aspect is problematic, and instead between women and men is a complementarity of opposites, sometimes termed "equal but different", so that women and men are both seen to make a necessary, but different, contribution to the whole. However, neither of these responses pays attention to the mytheme of the opposition of women and men, operative in the gender/sex signing system since the late eighteenth century, and instead they simply repro-duce it.

The mythic narratives operative in gender/sex signing systems, situ-ated in the social domain and enhanced by the linguistic tool of meta-phor, are the primary site for the generation of social relations between women and men. These are subsequently legitimated and naturalised when further mapped out in the domains of the metaphysical and bio-logical so that masculine and feminine, and female and male, are trans-formed into what is called human nature. This transformation from social being into metaphysical and natural being is accomplished through the metaphoric relations operative in binarism.

Claude Lévi-Strauss (1969) proposed that the most common means of classification among humans is by way of a logic called binary opposition. Although I do not agree that binarism is a universal aspect of human cognition, it is certainly relevant to the Eurowest. Binary opposition is a process whereby categories acquire meaning through the mechanisms of opposition and relationality. What this means is that the two concepts in the binary acquire meaning through their opposition to each other and, furthermore, in this opposition are relationally linked. A good example of this is the savage/civilised binary so frequently found in the myths and mythemes of Eurowestern social bodies. Savage, which takes the nega-tive, has no meaning other than through its oppositional relationship with civilised, which takes the positive. This binary often works in tandem with the feminine/masculine binary in the Eurowest, as some postcolonial theo-rists have argued.[14]

But there is more to binary opposition than this. Binaries also operate in open sets and therefore are able to acquire further meaning from their association with other binaries. These open sets are often incorporated into discursive formations, such as gender/sex, sexuality, race, or geo-political relations. In an open set, concepts are gathered up and linked metaphorically along a vertical axis, and differentially along the horizontal axis. To visualise this see Table 2.1 below:

Table 2.1 Gender/sex binary set

Horizontal axis ↔		
feminine	masculine	
irrational	rational	
woman	man	
passive	active	
female	male	
cold	hot	
etc.	etc.	
		↕ *Vertical axis*

Reading across the table along the horizontal axis the binary terms on the left are seen to be in differential or oppositional relationship to the terms on the right. Therefore feminine and masculine are in differential/ oppositional relationship whereby the differential/opposition allows each term to acquire meaning: feminine is what masculine is not and vice versa. Reading up or down the table along the vertical axis makes apparent the metaphorical relationships wherein feminine is metaphorically related to irrational, woman, passive, female, and cold, while each continues to be in differential/oppositional relationship with its binary partner along the horizontal axis. A further outcome of the vertical and horizontal axes is that any one of the terms can act as a metonymy for the rest of the set. Therefore I can use one half of a binary to evoke the binary itself, for example, cold to evoke the cold/hot binary or I can use one binary to evoke those binaries in metaphorical relationship, for example, along with feminine comes irrational, passive, cold, female, woman, and so forth.

Binary sets are open sets and therefore change is completely possible. Sets are composed of multiple binaries which shift and change over time and can be interlinked such as the binary set related to gender/sex and the set related to Eurowestern colonisation or white settler racism in Canada. By way of the binarism that is inherent to the mythologising of gender/sex, then, human social relations and the understanding of these relations have been mystified or seen to be naturally derived and not a product of social relations. *The Sadeian Woman* lays the groundwork for the analysis of the process of mystification of the gender/sex signing system through binarism and mythemes.

Angela Carter's text on the Marquis de Sade's work is, as she states, "a late-twentieth-century interpretation of some of the problems he raises about the culturally determined nature of women and of the relations between men and women that result from it" (1990, 1). Her intention is a critical engagement through pornography; representations which have, from the late nineteenth century, abstracted the sexual from its social and historical roots (Lee 1997, 10). Carter states that "[f]lesh comes to us out of history; so too does the repression and taboo that govern our experiences of flesh" (1990, 11). We may believe that in our sexual encounters we have stripped ourselves of our "social artifices" as we have stripped ourselves of our clothing, but this is an illusion. She argues that:

> We take to bed with us every aspect of the cultural impedimenta of our social class, our parents' lives, our bank balances … all the bits and pieces of our unique existences…[and] these considerations have limited our choice of partners before we have even got them into the bedroom. (1990, 9)

But why Sade, the most infamous of pornographers, and pornography? How can pornography be put in the service of women, as she argues in *The Sadeian Woman*? To answer the first question, Carter engages Sade's texts because he politicised, and therefore demystified, gender/sex, while the power relations signalled in the sexual act were not concealed. As she argues:

> He describes sexual relations in the context of an unfree society as the expression of pure tyranny, usually by men upon women, sometimes by men upon men, sometimes by women upon men and other women; the one constant to all Sade's monstrous orgies is that the whip hand is always the hand with the real political power and the victim is a person who has little or no power at all….In this schema, male means tyrannous and female means martyrised, no matter what the official gender of the male and female beings. (1990, 24)

As to pornography, its history[15] has shown that it is potentially subversive and politically oriented. Pornography, when it rejects the mythic speech of essentialised sex—the "fringed hole and the probe"—and comments on real relations, provides a critique of current social relations with a view to gender/sex ideology. The moral pornographer's business, argues Carter, "would be the total demystification of the flesh" (1990, 19); in other words, understanding the body or flesh, as socially constructed. The moral pornographer, argues Carter, might not be the enemy of women "perhaps, because he might begin to penetrate to the heart of the contempt for women that distorts our culture even as he entered the realms of true obscenity as he describes it" (1990, 20).

In feminist writings of the late seventies until the early nineties, the issue of pornography had been taken up and argued. These exchanges are referred to as the "feminist sex-wars" and although there was ultimately no resolution ground was given on both sides of this polemical issue. Carter's contribution to the sex wars (seen in *The Sadeian Woman*) was to suggest the idea of moral pornography and then to examine whether or not the Marquis de Sade operated within this frame. She came to the conclusion that it was on the level of the mythic—woman—that Sade's failure to write as a moral pornographer was made apparent.

Sade failed as a revolutionary and/or moral pornographer because he failed to go the distance. The mythic level of the gender/sex signing system was one that Sade did not fully politicise. Although some women are conceived as autonomously and actively sexual in his novels, for example, Juliette, generally these women operate in a mythic frame having been linked by Sade to the figure of the whore. Opposite and definitive to the whore, is the other mythic figure, the virgin, for example Justine, who is neither sexually autonomous nor active. Justine is the passive recipient who, as a normative Eurowestern representation of the female, is fodder for rape. For Sade, the binaries related to the gender/sex signing system of late eighteenth century France remained intact. Although he politicised gender/sex making apparent how social relations are mirrored by sexual relations, the mytheme of gender/sex wherein women are either whore or virgin, Mary Magdalene or Mary Mother of God,[16] remains intact. Carter comments that Sade's adherence to the mytheme of the two natures of women, seen in the figures of Justine as holy virgin and Juliette as profane whore,[17] speaks to his inability to deconstruct the mytheme of women's nature operative in the gender/sex signing system of eighteenth century France (1990, 101). Sade, as Carter argues, fled from his own insights, from the "precipice of freedom" and, instead, resurrected "god, the king, and the law" (1990, 133). Nonetheless, although he failed in this task of moral pornography, Carter engages some of Sade's insights particularly the interconnection of tyranny, sexuality, and social relationships in order to lay bare the mytheme that lies at the core of women's (and men's) subjectivity in the politics of the Eurowestern gender/sex signing systems.

Women's subjectivity and *Heroes and Villains*

As earlier indicated, the textual strategy of Angela Carter's *Heroes and Villains* is one of dystopia. Literally, utopia refers a non-place or no such place, while dystopia refers to an ill, bad or unlucky (*dys*) place (*topos*). Utopia, in order to envision its non-place, rejects the present in its vision of a new and better future. Dystopia, on the other hand, claims the present and carries it into its vision of the future representing the present as the past of this future. By bringing the present as the necessary past of the future, dystopia is able to act as an ideology critique in a way that utopia cannot. This is because, I would argue, utopia represses the past in a desire for a bright new future and is therefore unprepared for, and unable to deal with, the return of the repressed. Although promising a new vision, ultimately any utopia is blind for it does not and cannot know itself.

The use of dystopia as an ideology critique is an aspect of Carter's novel *Heroes and Villains*. In the world of this text a war of the past has altered the social landscape. Only some people had been allowed into deep shelters during the war, and upon emergence the shelter-people had organised themselves into gated villages. Within these villages people were stratified into three distinct classes of professors, soldiers, and workers (farmers). Affiliated with but not representative of any class were women. Beyond the walls of the gated villages were found those who had not been allowed into the shelters: the Barbarians and outcasts (and "their" women and children) otherwise known as *homo praedatrix*, and *homo silvestris*.[18] Therefore, in addition to the village class distinctions were distinctions of a humanity divided into sub-species of men: "*homo faber* [working man], *homo praedatrix* [predatory man], *homo silvestris* [wild man], and various others" (9). The Barbarians, as a means of survival, raided the professor communities, while the outcasts begged at their gates.

Marianne, the heroine of Carter's novel, is the daughter of a history professor and his unnamed wife. For sixteen years Marianne resided with her father in a white tower in the village only seeking escape upon his death. Marianne, unhappy with her life behind the gates of her village, flees the comfort and security of the community. She does this in the company of Jewel, a Barbarian who was injured during a recent raid on her village and whom she rescued and helped to escape.[19] Marianne, unhappy in her tower, resented that as a woman she was both an outsider and insider to her own community. Relegated to the white tower and unable to be an active force in the community, Marianne is incapable of properly expressing her discontent to her fellow villagers: Marianne felt caged and desired to be free. Fleeing with the rescued Jewel, Marianne expects to seek her way in the world, but it is a world she does not know and therefore she cannot protect herself within it. Marianne's freedom is fleeting at best, an interstitial moment between one community and another: her village and the Barbarian band who take her in.

Joining the Barbarians, whose name suggested to Marianne freedom in its linguistic link to wildness, Marianne finds she is given a new non-status: she is no longer insider-outsider, as she had been in her professor village (belonging to the community but unable to carry the identity of that community), but is now outsider-outsider: exterior to both the community and to its social relations.[20] Marianne's status as a woman from outside the group is one of vulnerability and threat. We read in the novel that she is vulnerable to gang rape as she has yet to be claimed by one man, and also vulnerable to burning as a witch. Equally, however, she is powerful because she remains unincorporated into the kinship relations within the new community and therefore is able to elude her commodity status.[21] As a female outsider, like Donally the community's hierophant who is a male outsider, Marianne is feared and it is this fear that becomes the source of her power among the Barbarians.[22]

Marianne's position in the novel is reminiscent of both of Sade's female heroines Justine and Juliette. Justine, orphaned and penniless, was ejected from the convent where she lived and, after several frightening adventures, ended up imprisoned and facing death because she refused to steal for her employer. Rescued from the fate of hanging by La Dubois, the nefarious head of a robber gang she met while in prison, Justine refuses to take up a life of crime with La Dubois and instead holds to a prescribed virtue: a virtue defined by those who continually abuse and exploit her. Justine is ever virgin, and, although she is ever "mindful" of the law, she "unmindfully" obeys the law despite the fact that the law maintains the privilege of men over women and rich over poor. Justine, Carter comments, adheres uncritically to an undisclosed virtue and is subsequently victimised again and again throughout the entirety of Sade's text. It is not, as Carter argues in *The Sadeian Woman*, that Justine holds to a critically engaged virtue; rather she holds to unexamined virtue, regardless that it is this virtue that ensures unjust relations such as those between women and men. To maintain this patriarchal, predetermined, womanly virtue, Justine must remain ever virgin and ever passive—Justine is incapable of agency.

Justine clings to her woman's virtue regardless that her passive adherence meant the death of friend[23] or that it made impossible any sexual encounter other than rape. Justine accepts without resistance the patriarchal precept of virginity as one of the most important virtues of a woman. In order to adhere to this precept, Justine must reject her own sexual autonomy and agency. Carter argues:

> In a world where women are commodities, a woman who refuses to sell herself will have the thing she refuses to sell taken away from her by force. The piety, the gentleness, the honesty, the sensitivity, all the qualities she has learned to admire in herself, are invitations to violence; all her life, she has been groomed for the slaughterhouse. And though she is virtuous, she does not know how to *do* good…. [Justine] is a child who knows how to be good to please daddy; but the

existence of daddy, her god, the abstract virtue to which she constantly refers,
prevents her from acting for herself. (1990, 55, emphasis original)

Marianne, as the professor's daughter, was Justine-like—although certainly not so virtuous, she was, after all, "rather spiteful". However, she
was inactive, a non-agent and simply a commodity whose exchange among
men would allow the phallus to be passed through her from one man to
another. With her escape from the professor's community, Marianne's
character begins to take on more complexity as she moves from the
passive to the active and, Juliette-like, becomes the agent of her own
story.[24] Interestingly, however, as her subjectivity increases the objectivity of those around her increases. The shift here is a subtle one but it is a
shift nonetheless. For example, in the contemporary Eurowest images of
women are typically constructed to invite the gaze. Images of women
(and for the most part these images are the product of masculine fantasies) do not look at the viewer, rather she is to be viewed. Images of
men, however, or at least those men whose bodies have not been
commodified as objects either for commercial, sexual, aesthetic, or
colonialist purposes, meet the viewer's eyes: he is as much gazing at the
viewer as the viewer is gazing at him. In the novel there is a similar shift
in the character of Marianne. She moves from a position of being the
object of the gaze to becoming the objectifying gazer. This suggests that,
as with Sade's Juliette, the claiming of subjectivity and agency in patriarchal relations requires the objectification of some other.

In Carter's dystopic novel, when Marianne views the world, she ratio-
nally assesses it. Walking back to the encampment after she had been
raped by Jewel, enraged and feeling trapped, she encounters Mrs. Green,
a worker-woman who had fled a professor's community many years earlier, and who figures as the "mother" in the Barbarian community. Mrs.
Green, aware that her foster-son Jewel has raped Marianne, chastises
him and consoles Marianne: "'After all, it's not as bad as all that, is it?
He's going to marry you tomorrow'" and again, "'Young men will always
take advantage, dear....And we all have to take what we can get'"
(1993, 58–59). Marianne initially thinks that she "must learn to reconcile
herself to everything from rape to mortality, just as her father had also
told her she would have to do" (1993, 59).

The mytheme of man the hunter who dominates his prey and woman
the subjugated prey who must succumb to his "power" (see also chapter
three of this text) is presented by Mrs. Green, the only mother figure in
the novel, as the normative operation of human relations and existence:
rape is, for women and men, as natural as breathing. Here resides a
mytheme that is pivotal in the construction of women's subjectivity in the
Eurowest; women are the natural prey of men in heterosexual relations

and therefore are normatively, necessarily and innately victims. This is the mytheme that Marianne, like Juliette, rejects. Although Sade maintained the mytheme of natural domination, of the strong over the weak, or as Jewel states, "red in tooth and claw" (18), as if social relations are produced in nature, Juliette is given the option of choosing to be victimiser (whore) or victim (virgin).[25] However, although Marianne may be Juliette-like, she is no Juliette and in Carter's text she acquires the status of the phallic woman (a woman with masculine power). Marianne rejects the mytheme of natural domination and woman as either whore or virgin, and instead reasons her way through the gender/sex signing system, a system which is unequivocally grounded in social relations.

Throughout the text Marianne approaches all social relations as relations of power. She does not sentimentalise her relationship with Jewel because they are husband and wife; she does not sentimentalise her relationship with Mrs. Green the mother figure; she does not sentimentalise her relations with other women of the community because they are, like her, women; she does not sentimentalise her relations with the children because they are deemed innocent (of social relations); she does not sentimentalise her relationship with Donally because they are both from professor communities; and finally she does not sentimentalise her relationship with deity. Marianne, the protagonist of Carter's novel, rejects the idea that human relationships are anything but socially determined. Carter's text, then, undercuts the idea of natural relations between women based on a shared female essence, between men and women based on biology, and between women and children based on instinct, and instead proposes that all human relations are societally constructed, deferred and deployed.

By underscoring the social location of all relationships, Carter implicitly underscores the politicised nature of desire. One notes in the text of *Heroes and Villains* that all of Marianne's relationships are marked by desire, and desire for the other to be fixed in relation to herself: fixed as an object of her desire in order that she may fix her subjectivity.[26] And yet, each relationship, because of the complexity of social interactions, betrays her desire. Furthermore, Marianne recognises that those others also wish to fix her as an object of their desire, and thereby ensure their own subjectivities.[27]

This interplay of subjectivity and objectivity is mapped out in the social relations presented in Carter's novel. Jewel (the male antagonist opposite Marianne) is passionate, momentarily gentle, and sometimes caring, but his subjectivity is a product of his social context and consequently to ensure his own subjectivity he must betray Marianne:

She heard him growl into her throat: 'Conceive you bitch conceive...' 'Why?'
[Marianne asked]. 'Dynastically', he said at last. 'It's a patriarchal system...' 'Give
me another reason' [she responded]. 'Politically. To maintain my status.' [But
Marianne knew there was something more abstract and pushed] 'Revenge,' he
explained. 'Shoving a little me up you, a little me all furred, plaited and bristling
with knives. Then I should have some status in relation to myself' (1993, 90).

In Eurowestern masculine hegemony, to claim subjectivity requires the
domination of women since by definition the system of social relations
privileges all things related to men, masculinity, and maleness. As such,
then, for Jewel to be a subject among the Barbarians he must be a man
and to be a man he must dominate women: his subjectivity is constructed
upon this logic.

Like Jewel, all members of the group reflect their understanding of self
through this prism of social relations and therefore reject Marianne's search
for subjectivity demanding that she maintain the status of object. Marianne's
resistance to objectivity threatens the social structure as a whole for it is
built upon the subjugation of those marked as women. The child Jen,
Mrs. Green's granddaughter, iterates this rejection when she furiously
shouts at Marianne, "'I hope Jewel shows you what's what. I hope he
beats you with his fists, once he's married to you'" (1993, 64). For the
women in community Marianne's desire for subjectivity means she is a
threat to the social system they operate within. Therefore, she can only
be a witch and the reason for the death of their children and the current
ills of their lives. Mrs. Green, also reflecting this concern regarding
Marianne's refusal to be dominated, evokes Sylvia Plath's poem *Daddy*
and lays bare the masculinist romantic narrative which shapes the lives of
the women who "belong" to the Barbarians: "They left the prints of the
heels of their boots on my heart" (1993, 69).[28] Mrs. Green, like all of the
Barbarians, in order to anchor her world upholds this system in spite of
her deeming it unjust to women. For her, as for all the women of the
group, it is simply the way things are and ought to be. Even Donally, the
renegade professor who joined the group and now acts as their hierophant,
rejects Marianne regardless of the fact that they share the language of the
gated professor communities. He too sees her desire for freedom subjugated to his desire for power.

The interplay of the characters of the novel establishes a world of
shifting subjectivities and objectivities. Marianne, Jewel, and Donally, the
central characters of the novel, struggle with the mythemes that weave
and are woven into the fabric of social relations. Carter's efforts are to
envision the possibility of new heterosexual relations in a dystopic landscape. The landscape of bad or ill brings into the future the old tired
relations of masculine domination, but the heroine, Marianne, endeavours

to think about and challenge the binary based mythemes of woman's nature; the whore and the virgin, and the female as prey to the male as hunter. In the novel she ultimately rejects both.

The female subjectivity evinced in the figure of Marianne in Carter's *Heroes and Villains* is a complex mesh between the manifestations of Marianne's own desires and the desire of those others for whom she is simply *other*. In both the professor and the Barbarian communities women are a commodity of exchange and used in order to pass the phallus from one man to the next. But in each of these social formations Marianne resists, incorporates, alters, or rejects the expectations foisted on her, and assesses her own expectations, produced within and by her varying social locations. In this endeavour Marianne faces the problem of women's subjectivity as proposed in a masculine hegemony. Marianne, unlike Justine as found in Sade's text, seeks to be an agent in her own story, and, very much like Juliette, lays claim to her own desires. To do this, however, Marianne rejects woman's subjectivity based on the mythemes of the whore and the virgin and female as prey to male as hunter. Instead, Marianne, the feminist heroine of the novel, creates a new mythic role, that of the tiger lady or the phallic woman who will "rule them [the Barbarians] with a rod of iron" (1993, 150). Carter proposes at this juncture the combining of the binaries to synthesise a new subjectivity for women, the phallic woman. But how useful is this mythic figure, a figure that has gained credence since the publication of this novel in 1969,[29] for women's subjectivity?

Carter, in her text *Heroes and Villains*, attempts to neutralise binaries of object/subject; other/same; villain/hero and female/male. She does this by, firstly, reversing the positive and negative poles (for example in some instances Jewel is the object viewed, Marianne the subject viewing; Jewel is passion, Marianne is reason) and, secondly, by introducing a dialectical play in order to synthesise the binaries. Her point is to think about a subjectivity available to women, but as there are only the mythemes of the virgin and the whore, and woman as prey and man as her hunter in masculine hegemony, Carter must attempt to engage the masculine fantasies of the female/feminine (the dystopic which cannot be eluded), but now through a feminist lens. One notes that in the novel other/same is reversed in relation to woman/man so that the tattooed Jewel stands as *other* to Marianne's *same*. This reversal, engaged by a number of utopian oriented first and second wave feminists,[30] is revealed as problematic by Carter in her effort to envision women's subjectivity within a feminist paradigm. To overcome the binary of whore and virgin, and prey and hunter, Carter proposes a third term the tiger lady, or phallic woman, bringing together the mythemes of women's nature and the proposed phallic power of men's nature. Joining these two she hopes through synthesis to neutralise the binary. However, binaries are also valuative in that each side of the binary carries a value of negative or positive and combining them does not negate the values: one side remains positive, the other negative. In the binarism related to gender/sex signing system, operative in many of the social bodies of the Eurowest, male/men/masculine carries positive valuation and female/women/feminine negative. When these two are synthesised, the negative and positive values are not mitigated and indeed remain operative. It is only the "tiger" or phallic which carries positive value, while "lady" continues to carry the negative. As with Hatshepsut of ancient Egypt (eighteenth dynasty) who wore a false beard to signify she was pharaoh, the masculine remains positive while the feminine remains negative.

Heroes and Villains, Carter's 1969 feminist novel, was not fully successful in conceptualising subjectivity for women. In a novel written three years later, Carter continues her attempt to think about subjectivity, binarism, and masculine hegemony. In this novel, *The Infernal Desire Machines of Doctor Hoffman*, she rejects the notion of synthesis as an answer to the feminist dilemma of binarism in masculine hegemony. Recognising that women's subjectivity is linked to men's, she critically examines the subjectivity of men, turning her mind to wonder how a young man marked by race in a colonised context might be hailed, to use Louis Althusser's (1995) term, as a man.

Men's subjectivity and *The Infernal Desire Machines of Dr. Hoffman*

The surrealist narrative strategy one finds in Carter's *Dr. Hoffman*, published in 1972, is an understanding of surrealism more akin to that of Salvador Dali than the surrealist school under André Breton. Dali's surrealism might be called a post-surrealism since it is one that ironically undercuts André Breton's idealism (LaFountain 1997, 96). When Salvador Dali's work *Endless Enigma*, with its seemingly contrived images, was revealed to the surrealist group his loyalty to Breton's second "Surrealist Manifesto" was questioned: within a year he was expelled from the group.[31] Marc LaFountain (1997, 94) argues that Dali's cynicism concerning the *"signe ascendant*—the hope of Surrealism—a materialisation of truth already available within the universe waiting only for a spark to reveal it" was made manifest in the ironic and rather smug smile on the face in *Endless Enigma*. LaFountain further suggests that Dali proposed in the multivalence of this painting a "transvaluation of the phantom object as phantom meaning", replacing symbol with sign (a foreshadowing of Jacques Derrida's work). In other words, there is no innate truth to symbolise as it is linguistic in nature. By challenging the notion of essentialised and fixed truth, Dali called the entire surrealist project into question. In Dali's work of the 1930s one finds a critique of identity, and of clarity and certainty regarding knowledge of essences and foundations. Dali's work substituted "laterality and *con-fusion* for depth and latency, and deferral and dissemination for identity and totality" (LaFountain 1997, 3, emphasis original).

Interiority and exteriority, within the Dalian frame, are never fixed and certain, neither, then, are the subject or the object. This kind of play is also present in Carter's *Dr. Hoffman*, when representation and reality are disjunctive, conjunctive, and perverted, and where interiority is exteriority and exteriority is interiority. In the novel there is only a constant deferral and a skimming of the surfaces for there are no depths and therefore no essences. The post-surrealist landscape, like the work of Dali, acts as a speculative and critical backdrop whereby the Eurowestern myth of essence, the soul, can be deconstructed.

The narrative strategies of dystopia and post-surrealism challenge mystification and Carter's two novels engaged in this chapter are the means by which the very sociality of human existence is made apparent. Both narrative strategies allow her to challenge Eurowestern myths of human nature, particularly the notion of an inherent gender/sexed nature (prey/hunter) of those groups marked as women and men. In the microcosmic world of dystopia there is no origin, for example Adam and Eve, to be reclaimed, no revelatory event, for example a "falling" in love, and no breaking in from some other "sacred", extra-social, place so that myth can reveal its truth, for example the realm of nature within which human nature is produced. In the post-surrealist world, every aspect of what is known is challenged through perversion, distortion, and/or relocation. The heroic narrative is twisted and distorted, while the romantic narrative, or the myth of heterosexual romance, is presented as the obfuscation of social relationships: desire is equally a determinant of society, and therefore a product of it.

For example, understood economically, desire, as it is manifested in late capitalism, functions in an unending accumulation of surplus, one which ensures the need for more. In this economic frame profit is a continuous process of exchange requiring ever increasing profits. This is equally so for human relations found in capitalism. There can be no realisation of one's desire because desire is something that cannot be realised, as it is in constant abeyance. In *Dr. Hoffman*, then, Carter's commentary on desire and surplus is represented in the name of the hero Desiderio meaning "to, toward, or in desire". There is always a movement toward, but never a realisation of desire. Furthermore, there is no subject of desire, only the object of desire as something always yet to be realised; it is distant and removed. Desire, removed from the realm of ideation to reside in the hand and not the mind, cannot be what one desires, for if it is in one's hand there is no need to desire it. Desire, then, is a signification of lack. In the post-surrealist landscape of Carter's *Dr. Hoffman* there is no possibility for the romantic reification of desire as a thing to be felt, claimed, achieved, or realised; in this landscape desire is simply and utterly lack.

What becomes apparent in Carter's post-surrealist landscape is how men's subjectivity is defined by desire, which is lack, and a never ending process of objectification in an attempt to signify this desire. In the dystopian world of *Heroes and Villains* Marianne's "subjectivity" is bound by the social subjectification (making of the subject) of the gender/sex signing system and hence must negotiate the social ground of her being. "She" has not been the engineer of this social ground and so it neither reflects her nor awards her subjectivity. Instead, she must reflect "his" social ground and the subjectivity "he" offers, taking up the role of the object that has been assigned to her. In the post-surrealist landscape, "laterality and *con-fusion*", and "deferral and dissemination" are offered to the reluctant young hero Desiderio.

Carter's text *The Infernal Desire Machines of Dr. Hoffman*, set in South America, envisions a landscape locked between reality and fantasy with fantasy figuring as the unchained unconscious.[32] Dr. Hoffman's desire machines have instituted a state of chaos where the unconscious of human beings is manifested in the realm of the conscious. The gatekeeper, or the repressive mechanism that Freud conjectures, has been overridden by Hoffman's machines so that the unconscious and conscious function on the same plane. In opposition to Dr. Hoffman is the Minister of Determination, who wages a war with Hoffman over reality, or reality as determined by him who stands as a representative of white Eurowestern men who are the colonial masters of the land. Desiderio, or he who desires, is both the protagonist and narrator of the tale. The story begins with Desiderio, now an old man, recalling his youth for it was a time when he made a choice between two masters, Hoffman and the Minister of Determination. His memories are the basis for the development of the post-surrealist landscape of the novel.[33] The story begins with a slow but gradually mounting interruption[34] of reality. Desiderio reflects:

> Nothing in the city was what it seemed—nothing at all! Because Dr. Hoffman, you see, was waging a massive campaign against human reason itself ....We did

> not understand the means by which the Doctor modified the nature of reality until very much later. We were taken entirely by surprise and chaos supervened immediately. Hallucinations flowed with magical speed in every brain….Dr. Hoffman's gigantic generators sent out a series of seismic vibrations which made great cracks in the hitherto immutable surface of the time and space equation we had informally formulated in order to realise our city. (1994, 11, 17)

Into the mix of reality and fantasy enters Desiderio who sardonically assumes the role of hero; a hero whose actions will bring an abrupt end to the infernal desire machines of Dr. Hoffman.

Up against Hoffman is the Minister of Determination and his reality machines, the latest of which is a computer programme that fixes a thing by its name and a name by the thing. According to the Minister's "theory of functions and names", "the criterion of reality was that a thing was determinate and the identity of a thing lay only in the extent to which it resembled itself" (1994, 23). The Minister sought to fix meaning to the object and the object to meaning never allowing slippage between the two.

The struggle between the encyclopaedist, the Minister of Determination, and the poet, Dr. Hoffman (1994, 24) is not a matter of a struggle for freedom as their orientations might suggest. Both the Minister and Hoffman sought to articulate a paradigm for reality and by doing so lay claim to the power of naming, for whoever names it claims it; such is the logic of colonisation. Two kinds of ideology, logical-positivism—what I apprehend I know, and what I know I master: *cogito ergo sum*—and metaphysics—what I desire I ideate, and what I ideate I master: *desidero ergo sum*—are represented by the figures of the Minister of Determination and Dr. Hoffman respectively. Their contestation appears to be one of order versus chaos, but there is more than this for central to their struggle is a desire for power.

Desiderio enters the melee between the two, an agent of the Minister of Determination who has been sent in search of Hoffman. But Desiderio has his own desires the like of which determines the various landscapes he encounters throughout the novel. As an agent for the Minister his quest was determined in advance: to destroy Hoffman's machines. But internal to his quest, its engine, are two of his most ardent desires that will, in the end, come into conflict: his desire for his beloved, the Beatrice-like Albertina, and his desire for a master, someone who, father-like, might show him the proper path to masculine hegemony. The contestation is between the mother and the father, or the imaginary and the symbolic to use Lacan's terms (1988).

Desiderio is a young man born of a woman who earned her bread by selling her body. His unknown father, one of the many men who had purchased her, was of Indian extraction and Desiderio describes himself as a slip up of business and a mix between races. This positing of Desiderio as a man with only a matrilineal genealogy but with the "genetic imprint" of his Indian father locates him on the margins of the white hegemonic power that rules his city. Like most masculine heroic figures in Eurowestern myth his parentage is in question, and like most other heroes, immortality is conferred upon completion of the quest. This is the gift of masculine hegemony to those who would claim and assume its dominant form. However, unlike most heroes, Desiderio's insider/outsider status, his racial marking, allows Carter to complicate and subsequently question the subjectivity proposed in a white masculine hegemony.

Desiderio is a cynical romantic, longing for something but bored by everything he finds. Throughout the movement of the novel and across differing landscapes Desiderio seeks his heart's desire, Albertina, daughter of Hoffman. She first emerges in his dreams, and throughout his quest he encounters her in a variety of guises. However, each guise or form is in part a manifestation of Desiderio's desire (1994, 204). Often, however, he does not recognise her, since he does not know his own desire, and when she does finally assume what might be her own form she is first raped by the Centaurs of Nebulous Time, and later murdered by Desiderio.

In the novel the rape of Albertina was not motivated by a desire for pleasure; rather it was motivated by a grim desire to punish the female/feminine. Raping Albertina the centaurs "...showed neither enthusiasm nor gratification. It was only some form of ritual, another invocation of the Sacred Horse" (1994, 180). At the centre of the centaurs' existence was a divine drama, a myth of betrayal wherein the Bridal Mare betrayed the Divine Stallion, the sun horse, and this betrayal, then, shaped every movement, action, and aspect of their lives. The female in any manifestation must be ritually, socially, daily denigrated, while she must labour excessively and submit to any and every male. So rigid was the effort to hold to the myth of betrayal, that Albertina, clearly not a centaur, was nonetheless raped because she was marked by them and Desiderio as female/feminine.

In the world of the centaurs their gender/sex binary set structures their existence. Other binaries that function in this set with female/ male, woman/man, and feminine/masculine are mortal/ divine, profane/ sacred, evil/good, impure/pure, and human/horse. In this gender/sex ideology, the centaurs were the profane to the sacred of the Divine Stallion and the Bridal Mare. They were profane because of the adultery committed by the Bridal Mare, the mate of the Divine Stallion, and so the centaurs were cursed with humanness and endured a split human/horse nature. In their system of belief and practice, their horse nature was an aspect of the divine, while their humanness was an aspect of their mortality, and this mortality signalled their sin. In this frame, the excrement from their horse behinds was a sacred offering but their human skin they mortified by tattooing it ritually, painfully and extensively (1994, 178). Their human flesh marked their sinful state so that ecstasy was found in the infliction of pain on the human flesh of their bodies. Framed in this fashion the rape of Albertina was, in equal measure, a punishment and a gift. In the masochistic world of the centaurs pain was ultimately joy. Reflecting on the rape during their stay with the centaurs, Albertina suggests that the rape may have been the product of her unconscious (1994, 186), but Desiderio knew it was a product of his.[35]

Desiderio's desire, in equal measures, sublates and subjugates Albertina. Albertina, like Beatrice of Dante's *Divine Comedy,* is but an ideation. Offered the bliss of fulfilled desire; his and Albertina's eternal embrace, Desiderio falters in the face of it. If he should consummate endlessly his desire with Albertina in a mesh cubicle powering the doctor's infernal desire machines, he would become as nameless and faceless as those others locked in eternal embrace in their cubicles. Offered power through matrilineal descent (1994, 197), Desiderio rejects the offer: he would be feminised and become nothing more than an object of desire, much as Albertina, or any woman. Desiderio, instead, chooses to kill Doctor Hoffman and Albertina in the name of the Minister of Determination. He would, as he claimed, become a hero rather than a lover. Having killed Albertina, Desiderio tucks into his breast pocket a handkerchief stained with her blood "where it looked like a rose" (1994, 218). Dead, she no longer threatens his subjectivity for she has returned to the status of ideation. Desiderio can once again begin to long for Albertina as his heart's desire: "And so I identified at last the flavour of my daily bread; it was and would be that of regret. Not, you understand, of remorse; only of regret, that insatiable regret with which we acknowledge that the impossible is, *per se,* impossible." (1994, 221)

When we look for a delineation of men's subjectivity in Carter's *Dr. Hoffman,* it becomes apparent that it is a slippery concept moving between unreason and reason. Because Carter is concerned with gender/sex ideology she wishes to understand the very odd relationship between women and men; that of the object to the subject. Albertina, as the object of Desiderio's desire, figures as the something which fantasy projects in order that the masculine subject can locate himself. Jacques Lacan suggests that "Desire is a relation of being to lack. This lack is the lack of being properly speaking. It isn't the lack of this or that, but lack of being whereby the being exists." (Second Seminar, 223 quoted in Silverman

1992, 20) In order to fill the gap, the hole which is the centre of subjectivity, a fictive object is posited. This positing of the object, then, allows for subjectivity in and of itself. Fantasy, as Kaja Silverman notes, "conjures forth a fictive object for a fundamentally a-objectal desire ... [i]t translates the desire for nothing into the desire for something" and that something is the self, the self as lack (symbolic castration) which recoups being through the object (that which mediates the passing of the phallus) and which then, as Silverman argues following Lacan, "fills the void at the center of subjectivity with an illusory plenitude" (1992, 4–5).

Throughout the text Albertina remains ever present but always distant; she is far enough away so that she does not threaten Desiderio's subjectivity. At a distance she remains a fictive object of Desiderio's desire. Once in the caves underneath the mountain behind the castle of Dr. Hoffman, her father, the reality of the fantasy becomes apparent to Desiderio. Desiderio would not receive the phallus from Dr. Hoffman mediated by Albertina since within the realm of the imaginary the unconscious, which Dr. Hoffman ruled, Desiderio's subjectivity as full was unmasked and he saw himself as lack, as absence—something his name foreshadowed. The "subject of the unconscious" (Desiderio in Dr. Hoffman's freed unconscious) as Silverman states, reading Lacan, "is 'acephalic'—that is 'headless', or, to be more precise, devoid of 'self'." She goes on to say: "This subject, which Lacan calls the 'je', is devoid both of form and of object; it can perhaps best be defined as pure lack, and hence as 'desiring nothing'." (1992, 4) In order to reinstall fantasy in the service of reality, rather than the reverse, Desiderio kills the father and the daughter, and in this reinstates the illusion for his master the Minister of Determination. In doing such Desiderio ensures that his desire once more has a fictive object forever ensuring his subjectivity.

Desiderio's killing of Dr. Hoffman is a variant of the oedipal drama, a masculine myth best articulated in the work of Sigmund Freud. In this myth the son harbours a secret desire for the mother (his first object of desire), but the father stands in his way. In order to claim the mother and usurp the father, he must of necessity kill him to lay claim to the phallus. Although Hoffman is no father to Desiderio; we do not know his father and many of the "masterful" men he meets on his journey, the Minister of Determination, the sadistic Count, the bay stallion, leader of the centaurs, and Dr. Hoffman are all possible fathers. As Desiderio comments, he was a young man in search of a master.

Desiderio, by claiming the Minister of Determination over and against Dr. Hoffman and Albertina (a matrilineal system), returns a hero, the ideal of the masculine in a masculine hegemony and so assumes his subjectivity—regardless of the cost:

...perhaps I was indeed looking for a master—perhaps the whole history of my adventure could be titled 'Desiderio in Search of a Master'. But I only wanted to find a master, the Minister, the Count, the bay, so that I could lean on him at first and then, after a while, jeer. (1994, 190)[36]

But there is more to this subjectivity of men. There is of course the ideological contestation between the Minister of Determination and Dr. Hoffman. Two realms, the conscious and the unconscious—but also named the logical-positivistic and the metaphysical or, as Sally Robinson (1998) has stated, "the throne and the altar", struggle to determine the rules of the game with Desiderio, the potential son, as the prize. Some feminists have questioned why Carter allows reason to win out over unreason in the play of the novel. Some have contended that she demonstrates that a choice between philosophy and poetry is always a hopeless one (Gamble 1997, 115) and I would agree in part, but Carter's work is never so simple. When we look at Desiderio we see a subject trapped between two warring figures each using the *bricolage* of the current cultural economy in order to establish the hegemony of his own ideology. Desiderio is the interpellated subject, the marginalised male/masculine subject who demonstrates to us the process of interpellation, and in this instance the construction of a masculine subjectivity offered to men marked by race, class and/or geopolitical location. To find his identity Desiderio must respond to a "you" by which he has been hailed, and the "you" he will respond to is the one that most comfortably assimilates the *bricolage* of the current cultural economy that he, as a product of this system, has already internalised and therefore is the one that commands his belief. As Silverman argues, drawing upon Althusser and Lacan, "it is only by successfully defining what passes for 'reality' at the level of the psyche that ideology can be said to command the subject's belief" (1992, 21).

The set of samples, the *bricolage* of Dr. Hoffman, defined a reality that Desiderio could not in the end believe because it revealed to him a "self" as lack and the headlessness of his own subjectivity. On the other hand, the *bricolage* produced by the Minister's computers held a masculine subjectivity, the hero, which Desiderio misrecognised as his own, and so it was the ideology of logical-positivism that best misrepresented to Desiderio the reality that commanded his belief. Desiderio, although contemptuous of the Minister's reality, was bound to it for in the end he was a product of the Minister of Determination's ideology although marginalised and resistant to it. Ideological belief may, as Althusser suggests, "have little to do with consciously held ideals, 'kneel down, move your lips in prayer, and you will believe'" (Althusser in Silverman 1992, 17). As much as Marianne was apprehended by her social system and forced to negotiate its binaries and mythemes in order to claim her role as object, so too

Desiderio was apprehended by his social system and forced to negotiate it in order to claim his role as subject, albeit his racialisation in a Eurowestern masculine hegemony suggests that the subjectivity he would claim could only be problematic: he was now the Indian son of a white father in a world were Indian was synonymous with the feminine and unreason.

The subject contested

The subject contested brings an end to this chapter. The mythemes that reside at the centre of subjectivity are called into question throughout Carter's work. We note that both protagonists are marginal to their social systems: Marianne is the white daughter of the ruling, if not controlling, class of professors, while Desiderio lacks a male genealogy and is racially marked as an Indian in colonialist South America. We begin, then, with negative subjectivities attempting to find a positive subjectivity in a hegemony that from the outset denies them normative human status: racial, sexual, and/or class differences have set them apart. The Eurowestern mytheme of a fixed and certain human nature, Adam followed by Abraham, Jacob, Isaac, Joseph, Moses, David and Jesus, establishes a subjectivity that already situates both protagonists as variant forms of the "other": only the white Christian (even if he is secular) man can epitomise and therefore represent true human nature, the universal human, or the "Subject" of Lacan's theorising. Marianne and Desiderio reside in social systems that locate at their foundations the mytheme of human nature, but human nature depends upon difference, be it sexual, racial or class, in order to guarantee its truth. Both Marianne and Desiderio struggle against this mytheme with greater or lesser degrees of success.

What Carter's novels and text undercut, then, is an essentialised subject, the eternal human, and what they underscore is a constructed subject who in turn constructs her/his world. Revealed in her work is that the subject, in and of itself, depends upon the category of object to exist. In the struggle for subject status, then, her work makes apparent the binary that upholds the notion of subject and allows it to carry meaning. This binary relies upon the mytheme of a fixed human nature devoid of such markings as gender/sex, race, or class, and it is this fixed human nature that is problematic for the "other" who wishes to lay claim to it. To lay claim to subjectivity in the Eurowest means engaging the binary and laying claim to the mythemes, and consequently one must allow the already-there ideology to command one's belief, "they must kneel down, move their lips in prayer, and they will believe".

However, neither is Carter asserting that one should lay claim to the position of object any more than she suggested that one lay claim to the position of subject. Rather she demystifies both subject and object locations and, in this, reveals the binarism and mythemes that operate as part of our philosophy and history. Her first move in *Heroes and Villains* is to propose a dialectic to solve this problem through the bringing together of chaos and order in service of the social. These binaries emerged from the social and were shown as such, but, problematically, the binarism was not fully demystified by the engagement of dialectics. In *Dr. Hoffman* Carter drew within her analysis semiotics in order to further reveal what Silverman calls the "dominant fiction" of the Eurowest wherein

> …'exemplary' male subjectivity cannot be thought apart from ideology, not only because ideology holds out the mirror within which that subjectivity is constructed, but because the latter depends upon a kind of collective make-believe in the commensurability of penis and phallus…within our dominant fiction the phallus/penis equation occupies absolute pride of place. Indeed, that question is so central to the *vraisemblance* [verisimilitude] that at those historical moments when the prototypical male subject is unable to recognise "himself" within its conjuration of masculine sufficiency our society suffers from a profound sense of "ideology fatigue". Our entire "world", then, depends upon the alignment of phallus and penis. (1992, 15–16)

Throughout her work Carter does not resolve the dominant fiction of commensurability of the phallus and the penis. Rather she demonstrates the social and psychical operations of binarism and mythemes that ground the uterus and phallus in nature. Silverman emphatically argues that "'Male' and 'Female' constitute our dominant fiction's most fundamental binary opposition" (1992, 34–35). Carter, too, intent upon demystifying the mythic grounds of women and men's subjectivity, and ultimately subjectivity itself, makes apparent the marriage between mythic speech and binarism in order to cut out the ground from beneath the subject and illustrate the *bricolage* that is used to construct it.

Notes

1. This chapter is a significantly altered version of "The Fantasy of Gender/Sex: Angela Carter and Mythmaking", from *The Influence of Imagination: Essays on Science Fiction and Fantasy as Agents of Social Change* © 2008 Lee Easton and Randy Schroeder by permission of McFarland & Company, Inc., Box 611, Jefferson NC 28640. www.mcfarlandpub.com. I wish also to thank William E. Arnal, Stephan Dobson and Kenneth MacKendrick for their helpful comments.

2. In the many analyses of Carter's work she is labelled a postmodernist writer. See, for example, Tucker (1998); Lee (1997); Michael (1996); Bristow and Broughton (1997); and Müller (1997). I place Carter in the poststructuralist camp because of her emphasis on the structural aspects of language and its signification; her use of intertextuality; her engagement with the works of French theorists such as Michel Foucault, Jacques Lacan, Roland Barthes, and Claude Lévi-Strauss; her play with binary opposition; her focus on lifting up and examining mythological structures; her constant problematising of the "I" of identity; her socialisation and historicisation of any discourse; and her constant focussing on how power is central to the subject/object divide. Although postmodernism and poststructuralism can and do intersect, postmodernism tends more toward an engagement with philosophy and aesthetics while poststructuralism engages linguistics structures, and signifying systems. For my differentiation between poststructuralism and postmodernism I am beholden to Judith Butler (1992).

3. Subjectivity and objectivity, as I am using them in this chapter, reflects Carter's usage. Carter's effort is to keep the unconscious in mind when thinking about identity and its construction.

4. Although the texts of Carter's that I engage were written two and three decades ago, and certainly feminist theorising has shifted since then, I would argue that current issues in twenty-first century, issues related to women's innate motherlessness, gender/sex and sexuality, class, and race continue to require investigation.

5. "Mystification is [within the Barthean frame] a sinister, conspiratorial force, whose quite immoral purpose is to endow historical or cultural phenomena with all the appearance of natural ones." (Sturrock 1979, 59)

6. Even more problematically, as Hayden White observed (1973), how could history even exist without the positing of this subject "man" through whom everything else is known?

7. George Orwell's *1984: A novel* (1949) is a well known example of the dystopic novel.

8. I also think that Carter was in some measure tapping into magical realism (also known as magic realism and/or marvellous realism) by establishing the scene for her novel in South America but *Dr. Hoffman* appears to me at least to lean more toward fantasy. In this novel Carter tends to focus on the unconscious and conscious, and the imagination as tools by which to question the gender/sex signing system in the Eurowest. Magical realism combines magic and the ordinary in order to comment on Eurowestern philosophy and to visualise another way to conceptualise human existence (Bowers 2004). A well known and significant novel in this genre is Gabriel García Márquez's *One Hundred Years of Solitude* (1972). Carter's novels *Wise Children* (1992) and *Nights at the Circus* (1994) are recognised as belonging to the genre of magical realism.

9. As Dragan Klaić (1991, 3) argues, dystopia is not a negative utopia or even a counter-utopia for these terms imply an opposite or mirror image of utopia. Dystopia is "an unexpected and aborted outcome of utopian strivings, a mismatched result of utopian efforts—not only a state of fallen utopia but the very process of its distortion and degeneration as well". I do not agree completely with Klaić's interpretation of dystopia but I do agree that the terms "counter" or "anti" do not capture the intention of the "bad" or "ill" that the *dys* of dystopia proposes.

10. In *Heroes and Villains*, nature is beautiful: "These roses opened flat as plates and from them drifted the faintest and most tremulous of scents, like that of apples. Though this scent was so fragile, still it seemed the real breath of a wholly new and vegetable world…" (1993, 22). But it is equally hostile: "They had reached a region where the hedgerows were composed solely of those plants with cutting leaves whose fruits were globes of poison. The riders cuffed the heads of their inquisitive mounts away from the sides of the road but the plants grew in the roadway, also, and cruelly cut open bare feet and also the legs and underparts of the horses." (1993, 101) And ultimately it is relentless: "This house was a gigantic memory of rotten stone, a compilation of innumerable forgotten styles now given some green unity by the devouring web of creeper, fur of moss and fungoid growth of rot….The forest perched upon the tumbled roofs in the shapes of yellow and purple weeds rooted in the gapped tiles, besides a few small trees and bushes. The windows gaped or sprouted internal foliage, as if the forest were as well already camped inside, there gathering strength for a green eruption which would one day burst the walls sky high back to nature." (1993, 31–32)

11. The heroic narrative is one of the more significant mythemes of men's subjectivity in the Eurowest and elsewhere. It is of course adaptable to women, hence heroine.

12. The binary play in Eurowestern social bodies is nicely developed in Sherry Ortner's early article "Is Female to Male as Nature is to Culture?" first published in Rosaldo and Lamphere's *Women, Culture, Society* (1974). Although her thesis came under criticism for its lack of attention to differing social bodies wherein such binaries do not play out, nonetheless it is an apt description of the gender/sex binary set as it plays out in the Eurowest under the influence of classical Greek thought wherein oppositional thinking is a central logic. See G. Lloyd (1979; 1966) for an insightful and useful analysis of classical Greek thought.

13. Masculine hegemony is a web of interlocking political, social, and cultural forces circling around and valuing above all things maleness and masculinity. Drawing on the work of Antonio Gramsci restated in Raymond Williams: "It is a whole body of practices and expectations over the whole of living: our senses and assignments of energy, our shaping perceptions of ourselves and our world. It is a lived system of meanings and values—constitutive and constituting—which as they are experienced as practices appear as reciprocally confirming." (1977, 110) In other words, masculine hegemony is both the (typically but not always male) rulers and its masculine ideology, which is understood to be the way things are, and those ruled within the system understand themselves as part of the system. Hegemony, and masculine hegemony therein, constitutes a sense of reality so that experiencing reality outside that frame is for many quite impossible. Hegemony, and masculine therein, is culture and all its operatives and its hierarchies and classes, while its formation grounds that culture in a reality of its own construction.

14. For postcolonial work that examines the savage/civilised binary see, among others, Edward Said 1994, while postcolonial work that links the savage/civilised and feminine/masculine binaries is Anne McClintock's *Imperial Leather* 1995. A significant aspect of postcolonial analysis is working through Eurowestern binary logic toward understanding the representation of people and cultures perceived as "other"; the latter of which itself is a part of the other/same, or alterity/ipseity, binary. See also Juschka 2003b.

15. For an extended conversation on the history of pornography, see Lynn Hunt's edited text *The Invention of Pornography* (1993).

16. Mary Magdalene was not a whore in the New Testament texts; rather she had been possessed by seven demons, which Jesus, according to Mark 16:9, then cast out. (Luke 8:2 refers to the possession as well, but does not clearly state that Jesus cast out the demons, although certainly the assumption is present in the text considering Jesus is the subject of the sentence.) However, since demons, possession, the female and sexuality have been linked in Christianity since at least the Middle Ages, Mary Magdalene tended to be figured as either a prostitute or whore.

17. The placing together of the two Marys around the figure of Jesus in Christianity can be found as early as the second century CE and as late as the sixteenth century CE. The figures of Juliette and Justine, the first the whore and the second the virgin, appear to be Sade's refiguring of this binary pair. As Sade was an anti-Christian living in a Christian paradigm, he may have unconsciously mirrored this mythic figuring of "woman." That Sade's protagonists, Juliette and Justine, are two dimensional and either whore or a virgin but never both and never more than just the one is a clear indication of his mapping out of women's subjectivity within this mythic frame.

18. Although not clearly stated, there is some suggestion that those in the professor communities, who were those allowed in the shelters, are privileged white folks, while those various others living outside of the walls of the professor villages are lower class whites, and racially designated peoples. Although this is not spelled out we do find out that Jewel's father, of the Bradleys, was black while his mother was a Lee. The Lees we are told were Old Believers, who were clannish but had class.

19. Jewel is the same barbarian Marianne had seen kill her brother ten years earlier.

20. In the novel, as in all patriarchal and patrilineal social formations, women belong to a group but do not pass along membership in the group. This ambivalent identity that women often carry explains in some measure their status as the enemy within. A telling example of this positioning of women as the enemy within is the European witch-craze of the late Medieval and early modern periods. See chapter four for further discussion of this phenomenon along with the work of Anne Barstow (1994) and Bram Dijkstra (1996).

21. For an insightful discussion of women's commodification see Galye Rubin (1975).

22. Donally, a renegade professor who lords over and controls the barbarians in much the same way as Kurtz is a despotic ruler in the *Heart of Darkness* (Gass 1998), attempts to nullify Marianne's potential power by incorporating her into the community through marriage to, and impregnation by, Jewel, the most beautiful of the barbarians. Working within these parameters, then, Jewel rapes Marianne when she tries to escape. After the rape Marianne challenges Jewel regarding his actions and he replies; "'It's a necessary wound,' he assured her. 'It won't last long....' [Marianne pushes the question further] 'Why did you do it to me?' He appeared to consider this question seriously. 'There's the matter of our traditional hatred. And, besides, I'm very frightened of you.' 'I have the advantage of you there,' said Marianne, pushing him away and endeavouring to cover herself. 'Don't be too sure.' he replied. 'I've got to marry you, haven't I? That's why I've got to take you back....''Donally says...Swallow you up and incorporate you, see. Dr. Donally says. Social psychology. I've nailed you on necessity, you poor bitch.'" (Carter 1993, 55–56)

23. For example Justine's uncritical adherence to one aspect of women's virtue in eighteenth century France, passivity, meant that even though she pitied the wife of the vampiric Count de Gernande, whom he tortured and ultimately murdered, Justine cannot envision a means to assist this woman, and instead assists the Count first by undressing his wife in preparation for torture and then in bringing her to him. Justine comments that "In spite of the horrors…I had no choice but to submit with the utmost resignation". (Sade in Carter 1990, 52)

24. This movement from the passive to the active is represented in the novel in a rhetorical shift of looking at Marianne (object) to looking through Marianne's eyes (subject).

25. Sade, as Carter argued, conceptualised two natures for women, the whore and the virgin. In patriarchal relations it is only the virgin who can become a legitimate mother.

26. Carter's effort is to ask the reader to think about the construction of the gendered subject in Eurowestern social formations. To her mind, this construction of subjectivity, or self, is produced in and through the social body and is enacted both consciously and unconsciously. Ultimately, however, subjectivity, or the subject, acquires meaning in binary relationship with that which is given the status of object.

27. Desire, then, is not innocent of politics. In other words it is not simply a "raw" human emotion or instinct. Indeed, Carter might well argue that the discursive framing of desire makes it a significant engine of power in the Eurowest. For example, in this location proper women are to be altruistic, without desire, unless that desire is manifested as instinctually oriented toward the survival of her offspring or potential offspring. Therefore she must desire for others and not for herself or she is, much like Juliette, an improper woman or the whore. A good example of the playing out of the mytheme of proper women's altruism can be seen in the media's fascination with the mother who fights a wild animal to protect a child or who lifts up a car single-handedly in order to save her child. The media is also interested in the opposite of the altruistic "good mother", or the selfish improper woman, who abandons her child to ensure her own well-being. The representation of the bad mother works equally well to uphold and legitimate the mytheme of the altruistic woman. In this binary play between the bad mother (whore) and the good mother (virgin) we note how subjectivity and objectivity are developed, and how, with regard to gender/sex, such a mythic construction and symbolic formulation continue to ensure that women *qua* woman (the good and bad mother) remain objects fixed in the field of cultural desire. The woman who must and would be a mother lives for others and never for herself and therefore she has no autonomy.

28. The lines I am referring to are "Every woman adores a Fascist/The boot in the face, the brute/Brute heart of a brute like you" (Plath 1965).

29. There are numerous version of the phallic woman found in film, novel, and video. Examples of her range from Ripley in the *Alien* series, Lara in *Lara Croft: Tomb Raider*, Anna Valerious in *Van Helsing*, or Jane Whitefield of the Thomas Perry mystery novels.

30. There are numerous examples of feminists using reversal to deal with gender/sex binarism in their utopian novels but two who are quite representational are Charlotte Perkins Gilman (first wave feminism) with her novel *Herland* (1979) and Sally Miller

Gearhart (second wave feminism) and her novel *Wanderground: Stories of the Hill Women* (1978).

31. Salvador Dali joined the Surrealist group with André Breton at its centre in 1929. He is credited with contributing to the notion of the surrealist object or the phantom object, and developing the paranoiac-critical method. Dali was expelled from the Surrealist group in 1939, shortly after the completion of his painting *Endless Enigma* (1938). For a discussion of Dali's participation in the surrealist group see LaFountain 1997, 49–70.

32. Following Sigmund Freud, Jacques Lacan, and psychoanalytic theory in general, Carter uses the term unconscious rather than subconscious.

33. We read at the outset of the novel, "Because I am so old and famous, they have told me that I must write down all my memories of the Great War, since, after all, I remember everything" (1994, 11). But of course since fantasy has been engaged in the text the 'I' of the narrator is called into question "...for I was a great hero in my own time though now I am an old man and no longer the 'I' of my own story..." (1994, 14).

34. I use the word interruption intentionally in an effort to capture both notions of "a breaking into" and "a break with".

35. Desiderio, who had been held in check by a centaur as he watched the rape of Albertina, recalls, "I could not remember when or where I had seen it, such a horrible thing; but it was the most graphic and haunting of memories and a voice in my mind, the cracked, hoarse, drunken voice of the dead peep-show proprietor, told me that I was somehow, all unknowing, the instigator of this horror. My pain and agitation increased beyond all measure." (1994, 180)

36. See also David Fincher's 1999 film *Fight Club* which also engages the motif of the young male adrift in a capitalist (feminine?) world lacking phallic guidance.

3 The Agon of Men
Masculinity and Warfare

This notion of a gender specific ideology has roots, not in the generic prehistory of men and women, but in western European social institutions which may have emerged during the Industrial Revolution of the nineteenth century; mainly the nuclear family, and a gender-based division of labour.

Judith Stevenson, "Shaman images in San rock art:
a question of gender" (2000, 45)

Actualistic research shows that the record reflects the operation of many processes, both human and nonhuman. It also shows that the human related elements are inconsistent with modern hunter-gatherer patterns of settlement and subsistence. Support for contingent inferences about big game hunting, home bases, nuclear families and paternal provisioning—all key elements of the Washburn-Isaac model—disappears accordingly.

J. F. O'Connell, et al. "Male strategies and
Plio-Pleistocene archaeology" (2002, 862)

Introduction: the mythic discourse of warfare

In what follows in this chapter, I discuss a general mythology of warfare and masculinity in the Eurowest and conjecture on why the mytheme of man the warrior has become one of the most powerful determinants of Eurowestern mainstream masculinity in the gender/sexed signing system. Further, following Bruce Lincoln (1989) and Maurice Bloch (1986; 1992) and applying their theories of ideology related to myth, ritual, and sign-symbol, it is my general position that these three categories of human endeavour allow for the mystification of the actual messiness and negative,[1] zero,[2] limited,[3] or abstract[4] return from warfare for those (primarily men, but all must be masculine) who embark upon it. It is my argument that the mytheme of man the warrior acts as a potent draught that befuddles the minds of those who willingly join the battle taking up the role of the sacrifice.

However, rather than engage the actual events or instances of warfare; to write a history of Eurowestern warfare using armed conflicts as
case studies and then seeking common patterns, I want to speak about
the mythic discourse of masculine warfare and its warriors. To do this I
engage Homer's *Iliad* and *Odyssey*, but I also make reference to other
narratives and ritualistic moments of warfare. By such references I do not
wish to imply that warfare does not change in relation to time and space.
Rather, I draw upon ancient Greek and Roman texts because they, with
their science, maths, philosophy, law, and bureaucracy, act as a foundation myth for the "enlightened" Eurowest. The texts I draw upon either
fully engage and propagate or ironically make apparent the ideals of warfare as glorious, necessary, and, ultimately, a masculine heroic tragedy.
Such ideals divorce warfare from the squalid, brutal, and tedious repetition of human slaughter. Numerous war films since the Vietnam war,
from *Apocalypse Now* (1979) to *Jarhead* (2005), have sought to think
about war differently and to critically engage it, raising such issues as the
two poles of terror and boredom that soldiers move between or even the
absolute absurdity of war (*Catch 22*, 1970). Nonetheless, warfare continues to be couched in terms of a masculine heroic tragedy. Here tragedy
stands as, following Hayden White, a mode of emplotment or a way by
which a history, story, event, and so forth is told. Tragedy from the outset
assumes a state of division within humans; unfallen and fallen. The unfallen
state resides in some long removed past, and now humanity, all of it,
exists in the fallen state. Within this mode, then, is the struggle of human
beings to cope with this immutable and eternally divided state. As White
comments, in tragedy there is a resignation

> of men [sic] to the conditions under which they must labor in the world. These
> conditions, in turn, are asserted to be unalterable and eternal, and the implica-
> tion is that man [sic] cannot change them but must work within them. They set the
> limits on what may be aspired to and what may be legitimately aimed at in the
> quest for security and sanity in the world. (1973, 9)

There have been numerous studies of warfare.[5] However, often the approach taken assumes that warfare is both natural and inevitable; an un-
avoidable tragedy of human existence and socialisation. The belief is that
from time immemorial humanity has engaged in warfare as a necessary
strategy of existence. This assumption is not difficult to understand considering the place that warfare (ritually or symbolically enacted, or real)
has had in the mostly masculinist telling of prehistories and histories of
the Eurowest. In an effort to challenge this assumption, Barbara Ehrenreich
in her text *Blood Rites* (1997) seeks to undermine the notion of an innate
biological basis for male violence and warfare, and examines the links

between warfare, blood sacrifice, and hunting. These three bloody activities she links through violent death and subsequently grounds them in an inferred archaic experience of human predation both as prey and predator.

Linking hunting—either as the hunted or taking up the role of hunter —blood sacrifice and warfare, Ehrenreich argues that skittering around the edges of hunting is the opposition of prey and predator (1997, 7–97). It is this opposition of prey and predator that she uses to tease out her theory that humans came to the knowledge of hunting and warfare through the use of defensive tactics such as mobbing. However, Ehrenreich's argument is problematic from the outset in that there are two assumptions that operate in and support her analysis. The first is the assumption that the mytheme of man the hunter is an expression of an evolutionary truth. Although I also engage hunting and link it to warfare in this chapter, what I endeavour to do is engage the concept of hunting in terms of its mythic formation in Eurowestern systems of belief and practice. Secondly, Ehrenreich holds an unexamined belief in the facticity of male-female sexual difference, and one that is based upon the model of female-male sex opposition, a model Thomas Laqueur had convincingly called into question (1992). The latter assumption is made apparent when she takes the position that predation led men to respond by taking up weapons (fight?), while women apparently did not respond at all (flight?). Why, I might ask, would women not equally take up weapons in response to this speculated archaic experience? What could reside at the core of this assumption other than the gender/sex binary set wherein female/woman/feminine are linked to the passive and male/man/masculine are linked to active?

I would agree with Ehrenreich that the prey/predator opposition is significant, albeit I want to take it in a different direction and argue that it is a binary, one that has been evoked in relation to, and linked with, gender/sex difference rather than a residual, unconscious, and collective human memory. I might further suggest that the prey/predator binary is central to linking the categories of masculinity, hunting, and warfare. In other words, it is the prey/predator binary that links the mytheme of man the hunter with the mytheme of man the warrior (both of which are gender/sexed coded). Therefore, rather than propose an indeterminable real experience of predation in the misty past maintained in a so-called collective unconscious (Ehrenreich draws on both Joseph Campbell and Carl Jung), I would propose that the prey/predator binary is what brings masculinity, hunting, and warfare into metaphorical relationship operating as they do in the Eurowestern gender/sex binary set. Further to this, then, and ensuring that predator is metaphorically linked with male/man/

masculine are female/woman/feminine and their linkage with the category prey: in a binary system both sides of the equation are necessary in
order that the binary functions in any meaningful way.

The prey/predator binary

In hunting, one is, or hopes to be, the predator, a condition that humans
may not have always shared with other carnivorous mammals and rep-
tiles. That is to say, for a long period of time humans, with their limited
natural defences, may well have been prey more often than they were
predator. It is here, Ehrenreich argues, that humans learned defensive
measures in order to survive the life and death drama enacted daily on
the African savannah. Here is where mobbing as a tactic may have been
employed teaching humans, she argues, that numbers could overwhelm
a lone attacker (1997, 52–67). Yet in this tactic there are always risks as
some may die, and yet all must be willing to take the risk so that each has
a fighting chance to live. This, she argues, is the transition point that
marks humanity's shift from the category of prey/scavenger to scavenger/
predator.

Thereafter, Ehrenreich continues, with the increase in the size of the
brain, attributed by some anthropologists and evolutionary theorists to
the eating of meat[6] (which of course brings one to the man the hunter
mytheme), and the ability to manipulate objects strategically, humans
made a dramatic shift from being primarily prey to primarily predator.
Humans begin by occupying the category of prey[7] but then shift to the
category of predator as made manifest in the mytheme of man the hunter.

Whether there is a biological experiential memory of being prey, or
there was a shift from prey to predator, as Ehrenreich argues, is immate-
rial insofar as neither can be any more than speculation and both take for
granted the mytheme man the hunter which is so prevalent in the Eurowest.
What is of interest to me, then, is how the prey/predator binary works in
relation to the man the hunter mytheme. In the binary system, following
Claude Lévi-Strauss (1963, 206–241), hunting mediates the prey/preda-
tor binary and allows the metonymical migration of the human from one
side of the binary (prey) to the other (predator). This metonymical shift is
signified by the new binary hunted/hunter. This new binary demonstrates
a shift in conceptualisation of relations whereby one is removed from the
whole of the group to stand over it. In other words, as predator one is
part of the group "animals" and culling it, while as hunter one is set apart
from the group and hunting it (see also Bloch 1992, 8–23).

The prey/predator binary and the mytheme of man the hunter

The mytheme of man the hunter is one that resonates powerfully through-out Eurowestern social bodies and is founded upon several ideas, aside from being signified as masculine which I will consider in a moment. The mytheme takes within its meaning frame several ideas: the idea of co-operation, so that some have suggested that hunting led to human social formation (Ehrenreich 1997, 36ff; Stanford 1999; Kaplan *et al.* 2000; Leakey and Lewin 1992; Barkow, *et al.* (eds.) 1992); that the prey sought in the hunt was a large animal whose struggle may have meant the death or injury of some of the group; that man the hunter gives death, but this is in order to ensure the life of the members of the group; and that hunting activities were shrouded in secret ritual (see especially Eliade 1964; 1985).

It is impossible to say if hunting as a contribution to survival of the group was always and everywhere a masculine preserve. Certainly in hunting and gathering societies (as well as among some men in industrial societies) hunting large animals appears to be an arena where men have had an opportunity to establish or challenge status among other men (O'Connell, *et al.* 2002, 832–833), but women equally hunt small ani-mals, and men also gather food (Ember 1978 and Shapiro 1998). Hunting would not have been cut off from other kinds of subsistence labour as it often is in Eurowestern representations, and this separation from other kinds of food acquisition is one aspect of the man the hunter mytheme that makes apparent that it is a mytheme. In the Eurowest men are hunt-ers even when they are not and women are gatherers even when they do not.[8]

What is evident here is that the activity of hunting, which mediates or acts as a middle term for the binary prey/predator and subsequently pro-duces the binary hunted/hunter, is linked to the female-woman and male-man binaries. Therefore, man is metaphorically linked to hunter and predator while woman is metaphorically linked to hunted and prey. How this is achieved is via a link made to the mytheme of man the hunter, which has its own binary partner, woman the gatherer. Within this binary set, as she is gatherer and he is hunter, she is situated in the position of hunted/prey while he maintains the hunter/predator position. Hunting produces the binary hunted/hunter and since man is hunter (predator), woman must of necessity be the hunted (prey). The table below provides a visual of the binary play.

If, following Claude Lévi-Strauss, we think of hunting as a mediating category for the prey/predator binary, as hunting is that which distinguishes between prey and predator, we note that a new binary emerges, that of

Table 3.1 Man the hunter/woman the gatherer binary set

Category 1	Category 2	Mediation
Prey (-)	Predator (+)	Hunting
Hunted (-)	Hunter (+)	Death
Death (-)	Life (+)	Birth
Reproduction (-)	Production (+)	Gathering
Gathering (-)	Hunting (+)	Domestication
Female (-)	Male (+)	Child
Descendants (-)	Ancestors (+)	Deity (ies)

hunted and hunter. This binary is subsequently mediated by the category of death, one gives death and the other receives death, and we can shift to the next pair in the binary set. In the next row we begin with death which stands in a binary relationship with life both of which are mediated by birth since birth is the threshold between life and death. This then leads us to reproduction and its binary partner production, which is mediated by gathering. Gathering is an occupation that depends on the reproduction of plants and the storing, and cooking of collected foodstuffs. Gathering is linked to hunting in a binary relationship, which is mediated by domestication (pastoral activities and farming activities). This binary is linked to the woman/man binary and it is mediated by the category of child (child is a potential woman or man), which then produces the descendant/ancestor binary. This last binary is itself mediated by the category deity(ies).

I could continue to produce more binaries, however, my point is that through a chain of binary associations male-man is associated with predator, hunter, life, production, hunting and ancestors, while female-woman is associate with prey, hunted, death, reproduction, gathering, and descendants. You will note that one half of the binary stands in negative relation to the other half of the binary. This is not the result of "natural elements" inherent to any of the binaries. Rather, it relates to the positive valuation of male/men/masculine in masculine hegemonies, and currently all Eurowestern social formations are masculine hegemonies[9] and have been such throughout most of history.

Mythemes: man the hunter and man the warrior

Whether organised and cooperative hunting preceded warfare or warfare preceded organised and cooperative hunting is difficult to say. One could make an argument for both cases, although symbolic and mythic representation could be read as suggesting hunting was prior to warfare. However, this in itself may suggest that the mytheme man the hunter is simply more entrenched and used to support the ideology of warfare. Regardless of chickens and eggs, what is important here is that hunting brings to mind the binary of prey/predator, and this binary could be equally mediated by warfare, for in warfare one occupies both positions of predator *and* prey. And secondly, warfare is typically gender/sex coded so that even when women have armed themselves and fought for the survival of the group, have gone to war as combatants or in support of combatants, or joined and fought in resistance groups, their presence is typically erased or diminished, for example women said to be camp followers and nothing more. Women, as female and feminine, do not signify as warriors, and if they do, as in some mythic cases such as the Amazons of ancient Greece, such figuring is mapped out in relation to the idea of monstrosity either as the phallic female or the butch lesbian. In Angela Carter's novel *The Infernal Desire Machines of Doctor Hoffman*, we meet such women who, through necessity have each "earned her rank by devouring alive, first gnawing limb from limb and sucking the marrow from its bones, her first-born child. So she earns her colours. To a woman, they are absolutely ruthless. They have passed beyond all human feeling." (1994, 160)[10] A woman who embraces death, as a soldier must, is, in the current gender/sex ideology of the Eurowest, a monstrous feminine whose vagina and womb consume rather than produce.

One-to-one combat

Battle, which is linked to warfare, is one-to-one combat and can be understood as an agonistic rite or a rite of competition and combativeness. Battle of course took place in the idealised past between two opponents, for example, Paris and Menelaos before the gates of Troy, while one's brothers watched in close proximity and others, including women such as Helen, viewed from the heights of the wall. On the level of the microcosm we have two opponents who come against each other wherein, most likely, one will lose and one will win. In single combat typically two opponents are prepared by others to come against each other. They will be dressed in appropriate garb and they will have made the necessary sacrifices and/or prayers ensuring that they have properly prepared themselves for the agonistic event. For example, among gladiators of ancient Rome where this kind of agonistic ritual was central to the ideology of warfare, combatants swore an oath "to be burned by fire, bound in chains, to be beaten, to die by the sword" (Kyle 1998, 87) and participated in an initiation wherein the individual was struck with a rod, the act of which

signified his (or her) willingness to submit to the rules of gladiatorial combat in the arena.

Once prepared, the individuals entered the field or amphitheatre where
there would be spectators.[11] The two combatants came or were brought
to the space of combativeness whereupon names were announced, deeds
recited, and acknowledgements of opponents or some other formal greet-
ing and/or introduction enacted. When indicated the two combatants, or
however many sets of two, engaged in battle. There would be cheering,
yelling, exclamations, curses, and so forth from the spectators. In the end
there were losers, left shamed and alive, or shamed and dead. The winner acquired prestige, possibly increased status—a long-term gain—and
often material goods of some sort.

When larger warfare (and equally preparation for long-term assault) is
engaged soldiers require a longer process of preparation in order to be
ritually indoctrinated. One has to prepare the group targeted to be soldiers, those marked as males/men, in order to inculcate fighting, combativeness, and a willingness to risk one's life for the larger community. A
sense of affinity, to draw on Bruce Lincoln (1989, 8–11), within the
social group must be engendered, while a sense of potential threat
from those groups marked as enemies or potential enemies must be
constructed. A social border must be demarcated in order that one is
hailed, to draw upon Louis Althusser (1995), as belonging to the group.
One's life is worth less than the group, and therefore one's life can be
sacrificed for the group. As a part one must be willing to be sacrificed for
the whole.

The achievement of this process, to be willing to die, is through initiation into the role of warrior or soldier. This initiation, and subsequent
relations within the group as one of them, creates a new identity. As has
been argued (for example Arnold van Gennep 1960; Victor Turner 1969;
Ronald Grimes 1982; Elaine Combs-Schilling 1991; Maurice Bloch 1992;
and Carol Delaney 1995), when one is initiated one moves from one way
of being to another way of being. Related to war, then, the undefined
youth becomes a warrior or soldier.

In the instance of the warrior it may be his first raid, first kill, or survival
of a combat that completes the initiation; in the instance of the soldier,
the initiation is longer and requires fuller submission to the social body at
large. The warrior (unless defending his own property or holdings) may be
made to join an army, such as Odysseus or Achilles in Greek myth, and
may submit to the rules of combat, but it is the soldier who must submit
to the rules of the social aggregate and protect it over and above his own
life. The warrior seeks increased prestige and status, along with goods;
the soldier is inculcated with seeking the betterment of the social body,

which may well entail conquering others. The soldier must be willing to sacrifice himself to become one of the many unnamed who died or will die in battle for some higher ideal held by his people, country or empire, but always it is the ideology of the ruling elite. He must be, then, inculcated into the myth and ritual of warfare.

Telling tales: Homeric warfare and the *Iliad*

The *Iliad* is a snapshot of the story of a ten year war between the Trojans and the Achaeans purportedly over Helen having fled to Troy with Paris. In this snapshot the Achaeans have been camped outside the walls of Troy for ten years with the story itself circling around the conflict between Agamemnon, the king of kings, and Achilles, the warrior of warriors. In Homer's epic Agamemnon publicly shamed Achilles, and Achilles, in his wrath, withdrew to his tent and was no longer willing to engage in battle on behalf of the Achaeans. The prideful actions of both Agamemnon and Achilles put the entire Achaean campaign at risk. However, for the purposes of this chapter I do not engage Homer's epic tale in full or its central theme; rather I draw upon stories related to several of the players and refer to a few scenes that further the analysis of the mytheme man the warrior.

In the ancient world there were many who thought and wrote about the heroes found in the *Iliad*. Two such heroes who drew attention from ancient Greeks were Achilles and Odysseus, due in some measure to the hero cults that had grown up around their names and deeds. Interestingly, there are several stories that speak to the reluctance of both Odysseus and Achilles to join the attack on Troy. Odysseus was bound by the oath imposed on all Helen's suitors, at his suggestion, to attack any who kidnapped her from Menelaos. Achilles, however, being somewhat younger, was not bound by the same oath and yet he too was drawn into the war through a ruse of the wily Odysseus since it had been foretold that the Achaeans could not win if he did not join them. The stories of the reluctance of both heroes to go to war, then, represent instances of narrative resistance to war.

When Menelaos and Agamemnon arrived on the island of Ithaka, home of Odysseus, they found Odysseus, felt hat on his head, ploughing the sand with a horse and bull yoked to his plough. Odysseus did not wish to honour his oath to Menelaos and sought a means to get out of it without losing honour. His idea was to feign madness, hence the ploughing of the sand. Palamedes, who had accompanied Menelaos and Agamemnon, guessed that Odysseus was seeking to deceive them and so placed Telemachos, the new-born son of Odysseus, in the path of the plough. Odysseus stopped and his ruse was revealed (Hyginus[12] 95 in Trzaskoma, Smith and Brunet 2004, 244). Odysseus, caught out and bound by oath, reluctantly agreed to join the attack on Troy.

In the story that relates Achilles' resistance,[13] Achilles was also aware that he was to be conscripted into the war against Troy. To avoid this he was sent by his mother to the court of King Lycomedes on the island of Scyros. Here he was dressed in feminine garb and put in the company of the king's young daughters.[14] According to the story, Odysseus, sensing the ruse, flushed Achilles out from amongst the women by including a spear and shield among the gifts deemed appropriate to girls which had been laid out in the king's courtyard. Odysseus then had an alarm sounded and Achilles, believing there to be an attack, ripped from his body the feminine garb and took up the spear and shield (Hyginus 96 in Trzaskoma, et al. 2004, 244–245). The moral of the two stories might be that all men are not equally indoctrinated and some do indeed resist sacrificing themselves for the larger aggregate or an aggregate for which they do not feel any particular affinity. However, that the mythic resistance of two heroes has managed to survive, and survive in terms of having signification, through the many fractured centuries so that I and others can read it, suggests that it is about more than individual resisters to warfare; it speaks to an awareness of the effort it takes to convince men to go to war.

In the *Iliad* there are many scenes where men must be encouraged to go into, or to stay in, battle. Often times the narrator presents individual cases of resistance or resistance by many. In all instances shame and obedience to authority are used in equal measure as means by which to keep the man or men in place. For example, in one scene, early in the story, Agamemnon has decided to test the loyalty of the soldiers and so proposes that he will tell them to retreat to the ships.[15] The commanders are to hold them back and speak to each in turn. Odysseus moves among the men haranguing both soldier and noble, clouting the former and speaking convincingly to the latter. His method of persuasion is to use authority, force and shame.[16]

In the situation of armed conflict and overcoming the resistance of some men to engage in war or coercing those who flee from war, force and persuasion are used in equal measure. Odysseus takes the staff of Agamemnon, the latter's symbol of authority, and uses it both to persuade, drawing on Agamemnon's authority through the staff, and to cudgel, using the staff as a weapon. Equally he names the resisters as cowards and/or women—"weak sister"—invoking a gender/sex ideology wherein women signify as naturally weak and to name a man as such is to shame him.

We see, then, that engendering the will to kill requires persuasion and force. Warriors or soldiers who desire to withdraw from battle risk being named deserters and traitors, and force is used not only to punish the perpetrator, but to discipline the rest of the troops. In ancient Rome, according to Polybius, if a unit of soldiers was considered disobedient lots were drawn and one of every ten men marked by lot (a black pebble) was bludgeoned to death (force) by the other "luckier" members of his unit. This ritual killing, or possibly sacrifice, was called *decimatio* (Polybius, *Histories* 6.38 in Hopkins 1983, 1). Those who were not killed, but were the killers, were then put on rations of barley, rather than wheat, and forced to camp outside the safety of the camp wall (shame). The soldier could be fined, flogged, beaten with a cudgel or killed depending on his infraction. The soldier, although a citizen, was one who of necessity was required to act as if his life belonged to another: his unit, unit leader (centurion), lieutenant (tribune) general (praetor), Rome and emperor. Although the soldier was a free man during his time of service his oath put him in a position analogous to that of a slave.

In the *Iliad* Hector, brother of Paris and eldest son of Priam king of Troy, castigates Paris for his cowardly behaviour. When the Achaeans and Trojans have come together in battle, each facing the other, Paris stepped forward as if to be the first to engage battle. Menelaos, deserted husband of Helen, then stepped forward to take up Paris' challenge. Seeing this Paris withdrew from his forward position and took refuge among the mass of soldiers. Hector, seeing this, upbraided Paris.[17] In open battle to be willing to kill (predator and hunter) is to be willing to be killed (prey and hunted). Force, persuasion, and shame are some of the means by which to engender the desire for battle in he who would be warrior.

Internal boundaries and hierarchical formations

In the agonistic play of war, internal boundaries are created and enforced. There are those who will be the high priests of war, otherwise known as the generals who define the means and ways that warfare is enacted. Agamemnon and Hector are the primary generals on either side of the conflict in the *Iliad*. Secondary to them are those who are regarded as sub-commanders such as Odysseus among the Achaeans and Sarpedon among Troy's allies. These leaders brought their own troops, primarily common men, whom they oversee. Within the social construction of armed conflict, a hierarchy is formed that is deemed both natural, normative, and very necessary. Each player has been indoctrinated to understand himself as merely a part of the whole and therefore obedient to the whole.[18]

The boundaries drawn around the communities are equally rigid. There are the Trojans and the Achaeans each of whom operates in a different sphere. In the *Iliad,* as in any conflict, affinity is shared amongst the groups, while estrangement is operative between groups: differences are underscored and similarities underemphasised (see also Lincoln 1994). For example, Paris enters the battlefield wearing a cowl of a leopard skin, suggesting berserker behaviour, and roars at the enemy. Of course this is the scene where Paris flees, retreating to the arms of Helen when challenged by Menelaos. The opening of Book Three, from which the above scene is drawn, relates the coming together of the two armies with Homer writing

> The Trojan squadrons flanked by officers / drew up and sortied, in a din of arms / and shouting voices—wave on wave, like cranes / in clamorous lines before the face of heaven, / beating away from winter's gloom and storms,... The Akhaians for their part came on in silence, / raging under their breath, shoulder to shoulder sworn. (Homer 1974a, 67)

Trojans are signified as non-human, the other, and Achaeans as human signalling the author's use of the binary other/same, and where some of his sympathies lie.

Prior to the battle, there is the preparation, the offerings to the gods, the feasting, the dressing, and the sharpening of weapons. The engagement of battle is a ritual process wherein the ordinary man is removed from his ordinary life in order to take up the role of predator and prey. His affinity is made with the brothers in his squadron, the men of other squadrons, the officers, and commanders. Those whom he will kill are not like him for they are not Achaeans. In order for him to see the world in this light, the rite of sacrifice or the offering to the gods prior to battle, initiates a process whereby he is shifted from being human to being a soldier. In the field he cannot feel love, compassionate, pity—he cannot look into the eyes of the man he has just mortally wounded for it would "unman him". To be a man in this setting is to be brutal, cruel, and filled with rage, much like the hero Achilles. It is also to be fearful, but rather than succumb one makes the fear work for one such as Odysseus does. One must set aside thought, morality and rationality with regard to what one is doing. The ritual prepares the ground for the altered state of being[19] that must be engaged in order to become both prey and predator.

The seduction of the heroic narrative and the requisite sacrifice of men: the cases of Patroklos' death and Achilles' shade in Hades

Throughout the *Iliad*, as in many other tales of war, two narratives are woven together to form a whole. One is the heroic narrative wherein the hero will overcome and survive all obstacles placed in his path. The other narrative is the tragic tale circling around those heroes overcome by the obstacles, and such men, then, signify as a sacrifice. The two together form a seductive narrative evoking as it does masculine coded ideals such as courage, loyalty, steadfastness, intelligence, power, and nobility. The narrative seduces the unwitting to engage warfare in order that he may acquire and attach such superlatives to his name. To fight to the death is to acquire status—status among one's family and community, but most particularly among the newly constituted group to which one now belongs, one's soldier brethren.

This combined narrative of heroic tragedy continues to function in stories of modern warfare. For example, WWI saw the predominance of this narrative taken up by the entire social aggregate (women passed out white feathers to those able-bodied men who did not enlist) and was particularly strong among soldiers (the horror and the heroics of trench warfare such as found in the novel *All Quiet on the Western Front* (1929)).

The author of the *Iliad* was not, I think, so naive, but played the scene of Patroklos' death ironically. The death of Patroklos, which is one of the most clearly evinced instances of warrior/soldier as sacrifice in the epic, is a scene that arguably represents the author's ironic engagement with warfare, regardless that the entire epic is devoted to war. In this particular scene, Patroklos, lover and friend of Achilles, dons the armour of the sulking Achilles when the Achaeans are particularly hard pressed by the Trojans:

> 'Akhilleus!....Lend me your gear to strap over my shoulders; / Trojans then may take me for yourself / and break off battle, giving our worn-out men / a chance to breathe....' So he petitioned, / witless as a child that what he begged for / was his own death, hard death and doom. (Homer 1974a, 378–379)

The armour of Achilles marks his warrior status and Patroklos when putting on the armour of Achilles can be seen to be metaphorically putting on the warrior. Patroklos, a young man and certainly subordinate to Achilles, puts on the boots of another and those boots are just a little too big. When Patroklos is killed, the illusion of Patroklos as warrior also dies. Also laid bare with the death of Patroklos is another illusion; that warfare is somehow ennobling. Patroklos dies, his soul now bereft of a body "bemoaning severance from youth and manhood, / slipped to be wafted to the underworld" (Homer 1974a, 403).

Upon the death of Patroklos, Achilles joins the battle but in due time he oversees the proper mourning, wailing, sacrifices, and feast for Patroklos. Again, in case we did not get it the first time, the ironical position of Homer is made apparent when burned with Patroklos on his funeral pyre are twelve young Trojan men who were sacrificed as part of the funeral rite. Many have speculated on this reference of explicit human sacrifice; but could it not mirror and make a comment on the sacrifice of men, often young men, in warfare? Patroklos obeyed the idealised rules of warfare and was sacrificed, while Achilles shamed and enraged soon shares his friend's fate when he too becomes a sacrifice.

In the *Odyssey* (the tale of Odysseus' ten year journey home) we meet Achilles in Hades. The great warrior who secured prestige and status through warfare was, in death, nothing but a simple man. No ideology, no heroic tragic narrative can reconcile a man to his death when he is dead; the mytheme only works for the living. In Hades, Achilles and Odysseus meet when the dead are summoned by Odysseus pouring the blood of a sacrificed black ox into a pit. After Achilles drinks the blood, Odysseus lauds him

> But was there ever a man more blest by fortune / than you Akhilleus? Can there ever be? We ranked you with immortals in your lifetime, / we Argives did, and here your power is royal/ among the dead men's shades. Think, then Akhilleus:/ you need not be so pained by death.'

Achilles replies,

> 'Let me hear no smooth talk / of death from you, Odysseus, light of councils. / Better, I say, to break sod as a farm hand / for some poor country man, on iron rations, / than lord it over all the exhausted dead.' (Homer 1974b, 190)

Heroic narratives are meaningful only to the living as the dead hero is simply that, dead.

Modern warfare

Having discussed the sacrifice of the male for the continued good of the social aggregate, and the seductive mythic narrative, man the warrior, which acts as a call of the S(s)iren drawing men to their deaths, I wish to make some brief comments on modern warfare and the continuance of the mytheme of man the warrior. It is this mytheme that acts as a metaphor transforming a boy and/or a problematic, possibly even feminine, man into a soldier, a war hero, and one who would sacrifice himself for his masculine brethren and country. In many ways the mythic narrative of hero and sacrifice continues to function in the ideology of warfare. This narrative was very powerful in WWI. The famous poem "In Flanders Fields" evinces the tragic heroic narrative of man the warrior figured now as a soldier. The last lines in particular address this mytheme:

> To you from failing hands we throw
> The torch; be yours to hold it high.
> If ye break faith with us who die
> We shall not sleep, though poppies grow
> In Flanders Fields. (McCrae 1919)

In modern warfare, from the nineteenth century until the present, however, where death is mass produced, the narrative of the warrior as a singular figure is less in evidence. Instead, the narrative shifts and continues to allude to heroism, but a heroism of the one as part of the many. The "we" and the plural "you" of the above poem speak to this group identity. The "man as warrior" is too egotistical and singular to function in modern of warfare. The willingness to risk one's life continues to be rewarded in ceremony and with medals, but, as most of the soldiers in modern warfare are found among the non-elite, a different set of ideological tools are linked to the narrative in order that it bring about a similar effect: the willingness to be killed or to kill; to be prey and predator.

A significant component of the narrative of war is love of one's country, or nationalism, wherein one is willing to sacrifice one's life for a concept more often than not generated by the elite of the social body. Within nationalism is a well developed sense of affinity; we are Canadian, American, British, French, and so forth (and I particularly use Eurowestern countries as nationalism emerged from these locations). Those who are marked as the enemy, Germans, Japanese, North Koreans, and North Vietnamese, Taliban or al Qaeda, or whoever, are designated as a threat, are typically otherfied: they are "krauts", "nips", "gooks", "hajji", and so on, but what they are not are human beings. Again and again, visible signs of their inherent evilness or otherness are constructed in order to make of them a *thing* necessary to kill. They are signified as monstrous, uncivilised, and barbarous in order that their destruction, by any means, is understood to be rational, necessary, and inevitable. Marking of those who would be the enemy is also internally applied to those perceived as having links with the enemy, for example Canadians of Japanese descent during WWII or, currently, those perceived as Arab and/or Muslim, particularly in the United States. Often their citizen rights and movable wealth are stripped from them while their land is taken: they are gathered up under the sign of pariah and threat, and imprisoned. Those marked as enemy are made alien and otherfied so that they are no longer understood, and all that they do is a mystery. Their affinity, previously operative, is no longer signified. Framed in this fashion, the "enemy" is the alien who can be found within and without the social borders, and must be annihilated and/or contained in order to secure the safety of the social body.

Estrangement makes of the enemy the other, but it does not necessarily engender the will to be killed and to kill. This is where the second part of the narrative emerges. As I indicated, modern warfare draws upon primarily middle and lower class peoples and/or people of colour, otherwise known as the "common" people, for the majority of its soldiers. Stan Goff reports a comment that:

> A quick look at U.S. military history shows that the Department of Defense doesn't give a rat's ass about a soldier once they are done with him or her. In fact, sometimes we're expendable even before our tour of duty is complete. Not expendable in combat. We expect that. But to experiment on us with atomic weapons, administer hallucinogens, or just plain ignore the danger of that stuff we walked through in Vietnam that killed every leaf, every ant, every cricket, and turned a cacophonous mountain rainforest into a rolling corridor of dead brown silence. (2004, 119)

In modern contestations of warfare, up to and including Vietnam, one threw as many live bodies as possible against the enemy: the more living male/masculine bodies that could be thrown at the "enemy", the better the chances of winning.

The storming of the beaches of Normandy and their defence is a fine example of throwing living persons against an enemy with little thought as to how many will die. The point of this sacrificial act was to land on the coast and from here to make inroads into German occupied France, regardless of the cost of human lives (over seventy-five days 40,000 soldiers of the Allied forces were killed and nearly 240,000 German soldiers).[20] These are "common" lives and not the noble or elite lives of those who fought from horse, chariot or jeep. How does one develop the heroic tragic narrative to include the mass of common men who must become willing sacrifices for their nations? One draws upon the notion of the inherent nobility of the masculine warrior to say to the common man in war 'you will be ennobled'—not in the sense of individuality, but in the sense of masculinity and its qualities:

> During the mid-Victorian period, 'manliness' was most commonly used to mean courage and independence, but by the end of the century it had come to refer to a wide range of virtues: honour, fair play, forthrightness, vigorous physical

activity, chivalry, courage, ambition, toughness, pluck, sacrifice and self-reliance, decisiveness, determination. (Moss 2001, 29)

This was the ideal and dominant masculinity typically espoused by the bourgeoisie. Others, lower class men, men marked by race, intersect with this dominant masculinity, an ideal, accepting and conforming, altering and drawing upon components of it and so forth; but they are never unaffected by it, particularly when functioning within, or in association with, such institutional state apparatuses as schools, team sports,[21] the boy scouts, cadets, and the armed services.[22] This new heroic narrative intertwines nationalism and masculine ennoblement drawn from the mytheme of man the warrior.[23] As Mark Moss comments in his text, at this juncture in time manliness was to contain and transform modernity and its threats by adhering to ancient ideals of masculinity such as chivalry and vigorous physical activity (ancient Greeks) but translating them within the modern period as inherently linked to nation state. Manliness became increasingly closely identified with the defining images and ideals of the nation. Among those ideals were "'spiritual and material vitality, being part of the team, [and] loyalty to group and country.' Courage, physical strength, and military discipline became paramount dimensions of manliness in the years after 1870." (Moss 2001, 29)

How is it that these men (and some woman—but the ritual of warfare and its mythological narrative is masculine and primarily hails those who misrecognise themselves as men) are able to overcome their will to live and their learned moral behaviour not to kill? One rite of passage is of course boot camp. Boot camp is a rite of initiation that removes the man from his mundane environment wherein he understands himself as, say, Bernard, high school graduate, worker at the GM plant, weekend ball player, buddy of George and Stan, son of Sarah and Greg, and possibly boyfriend to Jane (or Jeff, although this latter is an anathema in the army— properly masculine men are heterosexual). In boot camp he will be renamed, possibly becoming Bernie, and will have been reshaped and remoulded into a soldier. A young man drafted into the Vietnam War and interviewed by Ray Raphael comments that:

'You go through this real heavy anonymity orientation. You begin by following a yellow line through this building, six or seven hours of standing in line for tests and shots. They do a whole physical trip on your body....you spend the whole day walking through this building naked. Eventually they get around to cutting your hair and giving you clothes, the same color clothes, everything the same....They try and plug into you right away that your are all the same and that you will conform to this new system. And uniformity is the code of the system.' (1988, 28)

He is taught to obey without question and to use tools of violence. He learns that he is a man and that he is but one part of the machine of his regiment or platoon, and if he should fail in his unflagging support of his masculine brethren, he not only imperils his own life and masculinity, but also the lives and masculinity of his brothers. He must always act with them in mind, and behind "them" can be found his nation.

Those initiated in boot camp learn to ideally move, act, eat, think, and sleep as one. Ideally, they are one. Together, they are a force to be reckoned with, while individually they are nothing. Together they evince the impenetrable masculinity of their nation state. They will die for their nation and will become ennobled, and therefore are properly masculine men in their willingness to die. They are trained and taught as masculine men to ignore pain, and to feel little other than ebullience at the successes of lessons learned and killing skills acquired. They are transformed from questionable men to properly masculine men with promises of a heroic destiny:

> In a young country like Canada, the most potent heroes were often military men. War meant 'suffering together'....Rallying young men to become soldiers and imposing a patriotic frame of mind led them to accept the idea of sacrificing themselves for the country....This willingness to die for one's country was vital, fostering a sense of pride among those making the sacrifice. (Moss 2001, 55–56)

And, when it is all said and done, and if the soldier survives, there are no rituals of reintroduction in Eurowestern nations such as one finds among the Maori. Among the Maori warriors could not participate in celebrations of victory until the priests had roasted the hearts of slain enemies, offered some of this to the warrior deity Tu, had eaten some themselves, and then shouted spells to remove the blood curse allowing warriors to return to their mundane lives (Ehrenreich 1997, 12). Instead soldiers returning from war must pick up their civilian lives as if nothing has happened. There is no consideration of the after-effects of war, such as post-traumatic distress disorder, for these men are properly masculine, and blood, sweat, and tears are part of their daily normative fare. These men, having risked being killed and killing, and having acted as prey and predator, live with the knowledge of the death that missed them and the deaths they meted out. But more, since they are not dead, they cannot be properly masculine men, the proper hero, for such a man within the confines of the heroic tragic narrative has ultimately refused the role offered to him, that of sacrifice.

Concluding comments: Predator and prey

I have brought together several ideas with regard to warfare and the sacrifice of men, particularly young men. I began by thinking about hunting and the binary of prey and predator and how this binary brings together the mythemes of man the hunter and man the warrior both of which act as guiding principles of warfare. Warfare in the ancient and modern world uses the heroic tragic narrative in order to convince men to take up the role of sacrifice and sacrificer.

One notes that many of those who would be and are soldiers *cum* warriors are young men. These young men anticipate the cold embrace of death for ideals, for kings, for causes, and for nations. They will bleed out their life's blood as one more sacrifice for the good of the whole. They are the sons (of "lesser" men) who are willing sacrifices for the fathers. It is the fathers, as political and military leaders, who send them into war knowing that many will not return. It is the fathers' ideals that the young men learn and ultimately uphold with the sacrifice of their lives. It is not, as Sigmund Freud thought, that the son wishes to kill his father; rather, I would argue, it is the father who seeks to kill his son. The fate of Jesus in Christian systems of belief and practice is a fine example of this impulse.

The Vietnam War was a war where out and out resistance to conscription was engaged. At this moment of time, there was a refusal to be manipulated by force and persuasion, and a rejection of the seductive heroic tragic narrative of masculinity and ennoblement. Some young men rejected the formulation of warfare as ennobling and indeed pointed to the war-mongering manipulations of the ruling elite as actions that served only the interests of the ruling class. Some young men of this time, then, refused the war offered them by the fathers of their nation. As for the men who did go, there would be no grave for the unnamed soldier, no poppies row upon row; instead there would be erasure, denial and shame. They would be in the end betrayed by the masculine heroic narrative of war. As Achilles was made to comment in the long distant past, "Better I say, to break sod as a farm hand/for some poor country man, on iron rations,/than lord it over all the exhausted dead." (Homer 1974b, 190)

Notes

1. One loses his/her life or physical well-being, such as loss of limbs or bodily functions.

2. One returns home largely undamaged.

3. There is some minimal gain with regard to status or economics.

4. One's country is enriched through the occupation of conquered lands and therefore one's standard of living is maintained or even improved.

5. For example, some few nonfiction texts on war and warfare published by the first month of 2007 are Watson 2007; Challans 2007; Bell, D. A. 2007; Robb 2007; Flavell and Conway 2007; Hama 2007; Green and Brown 2007; Neimeyer 2007; Cowen and Gilbert 2007; Showalter and Astore 2007; Black 2007; Helm 2007.

6. There have been a number of theorists who have argued for a causal link between large human brain size, hunting and the consumption of meat. See for example, following O'Connell *et al* (2002) Tooby and DeVore 1987; Barkow *et al*. (eds.); Leakey and Lewin 1992; Stanley 1996; Deacon 1997; Stanford 1999; Stanford and Bunn 2001. This hypothesis, for it is a hypothesis, has been popularly used to shore up the view that the human is a "natural" carnivore and predator and not normatively a vegetarian, to establish men as the *primary* movers of human evolution, and as a touchstone for normative maleness and masculinity (in the binary system men are active while women are passive). But, as Robert Foley has commented, "[t]he causes of human evolution in the early stages may well have been increased hunting, but the unintended consequences for both the drastic expansion of the human population and the global changes in the environment are the product of change in a herbivorous strategy" (1995, 84). This is aside from the problem of seeking a key factor (prime mover) that then requires one to discount or ignore all other possible and contingent factors. As Foley argues: "Prime mover models must result in an irresolvable paradox concerning continuity versus uniqueness. In evolution we always seek continuity, because this is what is implied by the notion of descent with modification. But when we find it, we are disappointed, because we have lost the distinction that seemed to have made us unique, and therefore lost explanatory power." (Foley 1995, 69) For a thorough and articulate challenge to "man the hunter" as the primary mover of human evolution see O'Connell, *et al*. 2002.

7. And humans continue to occupy this place of prey in some locations where there are large predators such as cougars, lions, tigers, grizzly bears, komodo dragons, crocodiles, sharks and so forth.

8. So, for example, in a 2002 programme entitled *The Power of Play*, based on the work of David Elkind (2007), when approaching a new game, girls will "gather" knowledge prior to engaging in the game, while boys immediately jumped in demonstrating, according to the narrator, their "hunting" orientation.

9. As indicated more fully in chapter two, masculine hegemony is a web of interlocking political, social and cultural forces circling around and valuing above all things maleness, men and masculinity.

10. This particular chapter in Carter's novel is entitled "The Coast of Africa" and the Amazons referred to are in the service of the despotic ruler who is figured as the Count's black twin in that both the white Count, the latter a fictionalised Marquis de Sade, and the black despot are one and the same, while both signify as aberrant masculinities that shape and determine white masculinity. The Amazons are equally black, and also old women, and the cannibalism that they practise presents another fantasy of white Europeans in the face of the so-called native women who, according to some sixteenth century travel accounts, dined on the flesh of men. See Michel de Certeau (1988, 209–243).

11. The space of combat is marked off from other space and often it was encircled by seating for spectators. Decorated poles further marked off the space, while at one end of the field was typically found a shrine. The determination of the space of the gladiatorial arena is discussed in more detail in chapter five.

12. Hyginus' *Fabulae*, which relates both stories of Achilles and Odysseus, is dated to the fourth or fifth century CE.

13. For other references to this story see *Scholia Iliad* (first century BCE–second century CE) (Erbse 1969–1977, 19.326), Statius (d. 96 CE) (Mozley J. H. 1928, 1.849–50) or Pausanias (second century CE) (Jones 1918, 1.22.6).

14. It has been argued that this story records ancient male initiation as seen in the Athenian festival the Oschophoria. The Oschophoria consisted of a procession out of the city to the seashore whereupon a sacrifice ensued at the end of which was a festive return to the city. The procession was led by two elite young men from the island of Salamis who were dressed in women's clothing. See Cyrino (1995) for the link between Achilles and this festival, Seaford (1994, 240 and 271), for reference to the festival, and Osborne (1994, 158–159), for a discussion of how this festival was important for the ritual iteration of Athenian political borders.

15. Bruce Lincoln also refers to this story in his text *Authority: Construction and corrosion* (1994, 14–27).

16. To the noble he said "It isn't like you to desert the field / the way some coward would!" To the common man Odysseus said: "bawling still", he drove him back, he swung / upon him with his staff and told him / "go back, sit down, listen to better men— / unfit for soldiering as you are, weak sister, / counting for nothing in battle or in council!" (Homer 1974a, 50)

17. "You bad-luck charm! / Paris, the great lover, a gallant sight! You should have had no seed and died unmarried. / Would to god you had! / Better than living this way in dishonour / in everyone's contempt./ Now they can laugh. Akhaians / who thought you were a first-rate man, a champion,/Going by looks—and no backbone, no staying/ power is in you" (Homer 1974a, 69).

18. Of course, in the *Iliad* the tension between Agamemnon and Achilles is over Achilles' refusal to accord Agamemnon the authority and respect the latter thinks is his due. To emphasise this, Agamemnon asserts his dominance by taking Briseis, a woman given to Achilles by his men when the spoils of conflict were divided. Achilles would have none of this assertion of dominance and so withdraw from the battle to his tent.

19. Ken Russell's 1980 film *Altered States* comes to mind.

20. In another example related to this battle, Stephen Powers comments that: "For the next month Lieutenant General Omar N. Bradley's First United States Army pushed slowly south, reaching a line along the St.-Lo-Périers road on 18 July, absorbing forty thousand casualties in its costly twenty-mile advance." (1992, 456)

21. As Varda Burstyn comments on in her text *The Rites of Men: Manhood, politics and the culture of sport* (1999, 165): "'Sport is the human activity closest to war that isn't lethal,' said former U.S. president Ronald Regan in 1991. The similarities between sport and war consist of a shared culture of combat and the competitive deployment of force and violence."

22. See Mark Moss's *Manliness and militarism: Education Young boys in Ontario for War* (2001) for a close examination of the institutionalisation of masculinity in Ontario

Canada in the period immediate to WWI. See also Cynthia Enloe's work wherein she argues that it "requires more than just one form of masculinity and more than one form of femininity to make militarization work in each setting" (1989, 122).

23. Femininity is of course central to this production of masculinity. Femininity is the binary partner and therefore the feminine carries all that is opposite and marks the territory properly masculine men should not traverse.

4 Signifying Demons
Gender and the Ritualised Performance of Possession and Exorcism

Sacrifice is a religious act which, through the consecration of a victim, modifies the condition of the moral person who accomplishes it or that of certain objects with which he is concerned.

Henri Hubert and Marcel Mauss, *Sacrifice* (1964, 13)

Prelude

Where chapter one laid out the theory of a semiotics of gender in relation to myth, ritual, and sign-symbol, the following two chapters focussed largely on myth and its intersection with gender/sex. My intention was to examine how myth is a significant means by which to code social bodies. Myth operates both macrocosmically and microcosmically to speak about existence, humans in existence, the proper form of existence and so forth. Myth is a powerful medium by which to legitimise and generate gender/sex ideology. Angela Carter, intent upon untying the Gordian knot of gender/sex, realised that even if undone it will quickly be redone. Gender/sex is a primary category of human social relations, and seeking ground exterior to gender/sex is as futile as seeking ground exterior to the notion of being human: we cannot know ourselves outside of these categories. But this does not mean we are at the whim of the category of gender/sex, for we have created the category itself and so are in the position to challenge, endorse, resist, and alter it. It is not that gender/sex necessarily precedes the human; rather gender/sex is a primary category for the Eurowestern conceptualisation of what being human means. Therefore, as commented on in chapter three, we have narratives from all areas of knowledge in the Eurowest that come together to establish a discursive frame by which we know ourselves as gender/sexed and what being gender/sexed entails, such as the necessity for young men to sacrifice their lives in order to know themselves as "real" men. In this current chapter and the next, the intention is to engage ritual and its intersection with the body to speak the "truth" about gender/sex. Ritual is, as Maurice Bloch (1986) and Bruce Lincoln (1991) have argued, a powerful mechanism for the legitimation and deployment of ideology and, in the instance of gender/sex, the most powerful mechanism, since ritual deploys in and through the body.

Introduction

The subject of witchcraft trials has been of great interest to feminists since the early 1970s, if not earlier. Initially, a number feminists in the fields of history, sociology, psychology, religious studies, and anthropology described this period as the holocaust of women. Some, such as Mary Daly in her book *Gyn/ecology* (1978), proposed that hundreds of thousands and possibly millions of women and girls were tortured and burned at the stake (or hung), with Andrea Dworkin (1974) having suggested a figure of nine million. Although certainly these are high estimates, some of what these feminists were responding to was the erasure of women as a gender/sexed group in the histories thus far on the subject of witchcraft and its trials in the early modern period of the Eurowest. Since their work other feminist-oriented historians such as Anne Llewellyn Barstow (1994) have sought to provide more accurate figures. In her text, *The Witchcraze*, she has proposed an approximate figure of two hundred thousand charged,[1] with eighty percent of these being female; and of those charged approximately fifty percent were executed for the crime of witchcraft with eighty-five percent of these persons being female (a figure of about 80,000 executed with 65,000 of these being female) (1994, 25). Barstow coincides with Brian Levack's (2006)[2] totals, but argues these totals may well be too conservative as those charged with witchcraft (informally as well as formally) also died at the hands of their neighbours, died during their incarceration due to disease and malnourishment, committed suicide to avoid torture and burning, or died during torture and therefore were not necessarily included in the legal records of the time (1994, 22–23).

Some have argued against the witch hunt as gender/sex coded, claiming, for example, that the terms witch and sorcerer are used interchangeably in the records of witchcraft trials and therefore men as well as women faced torture and death as witches. This is certainly true, but it does not by any means change the gender/sex coding of what occurred (either related to female or male), and nor does it change the obvious fact that the categories of the female and feminine were intimately linked to the devil, demons, and witchcraft and therefore more women than men would have been targeted due to the very nature of the discourse itself. Henricus Institoris and Jacobus Sprenger[3] propound as Question Six "why a larger number of sorcerers is found among the delicate female sex than among men" (2006b, 111–125), and in the sixteenth and seventeenth centuries Nicolas Remy (1970, 56), Martín del Rio (2000, 135 n.2), Jean Bodin (2001, 49), and Johann Weyer (1991, 314) either directly or indirectly refer to female weakness, curiosity, and natural deceitfulness as the cause of women's greater susceptibility to witchcraft and/or possession. Nevertheless, William Monter does point out that in Northern France at least half of the victims were men and, of interest to this chapter, there appears to be an over-representation of shepherds and clerics who comprise at least half of all men charged in Northern France (2002, 42–43). Loudun, the location of the event that this chapter engages, is not in the geographic area analysed by Monter but the incidence of male clerics charged and executed reflects this phenomenon.

It is evident, however, from the texts of the period that speak to demonology and witchcraft (those referred to above and Pierre de Lancre in the seventeenth century), along with trial records, that women were over-represented as a group among witches. Indeed, the tendency current even now is to equate the concept of witch with the female and feminine, while the devil and demons are understood to be male and masculine—albeit problematically, something that will be of importance to the conceptualisation of possession and exorcism. From the outset, then, the discursive play that delineates witchcraft is gender/sex coded.

But this chapter is not about witchcraft *per se* although certainly narratives of witchcraft and witch trials enter the discussion. Instead, in this chapter I am interested in examining possession and exorcism and their gender/sex play in the early modern period of France, with a particular focus on Loudun. I became interested in Loudun after having seen *The Devils* (1971) directed by Ken Russell and having subsequently read Michel de Certeau's superb text *The Possession at Loudun* (1996). Certeau was keenly interested in the discursive play of possession and how it registered shifting political and religious powers, and epistemological change. In his text Certeau is very much aware of gender/sex in the variegate narratives of Jeanne des Anges (the possessed mother superior of the Ursuline convent in Loudun) and Urbain Grandier (the Loudun priest she and her possessing demons accused of sorcery), but his examination is not focussed on the semiotics of gender/sex, the matter I am interested in.

Certainly the pitting against each other of the "voices" of Anges and Grandier, the primary players in this ritualised drama, is a simplification of the event that played out between them since there were numerous actors. Involved were the Huguenots and Catholics, priests, nuns and lay persons, secular and religious, the king and cardinal, lawyers, doctors, foes, family, and friends of both Anges and Grandier. Still, these two players can be read as sign-symbols that signified possession and witchcraft when contained within the ritual drama, and, more broadly, the struggle between Catholic and Protestant, tradition and modernity, rural and urban, and women and men in early modern France.

In her text, *Discerning Spirits* (2003), Nancy Caciola comments that in the Middle Ages there was category confusion between mystics, demoniacs, and witches, particularly as they related to women, while the juxtaposing of malign and benign spirit possessions "led to an epistemological conundrum for the mediaeval Church on both the local community level and the translocal, institutional level" (2003, 33). This conundrum persists in some measure in the early modern period but typically women who evinced symptoms of spirit possession were perceived as having either succumbed to possession by demons (victim) or were witches (assailant) and therefore wilfully in league with the devil. "Woman" as mystic was a phenomena of the Middle Ages but it was one that was being replaced with woman as possessed or woman as witch in the early modern period. Differentiation between woman as victim or assailant continued to be important, but in cases of possession it was necessary to differentiate between those who suffered from a medical problem such as melancholia, those who dissembled, and those truly possessed. In order to ascertain the "truth" or authenticity of a possession a bevy of specialists; physicians, representatives of the parlement (court of law) and/or king, exorcists, clergy, and of course members of the community, either officials or simply town or village folk, were involved. As Philip Benedict has commented:

> ...neighbourhoods thus had many stable residents, and these people knew a great deal about one another, for work, play, and conflict all regularly spilled out of cramped shops and houses into the street. Furthermore, residential proximity entailed obligations of mutual assistance, obligations that are attested to by numerous court cases which show town dwellers interceding in quarrels to protect their neighbours 'as a good neighbour should'. (1992, 16–27)

The discursive formation[4] of possession, exorcism, and witchcraft evidences an over-representation of women, while the confluent juridical, philosophical, theological, and medical discourses used to contain and control possession and witchcraft demonstrate an over-representation of men. In their most basic discursive structures, then, possession and exorcism, and witchcraft and punishment were gender/sex coded from the outset. Although this gender/sex coding was deployed in possession and exorcism, and witchcraft and punishment, its efficaciousness was dependent upon ritual. Ritual was a significant medium by which the body of the possessed or the witch was made to speak the truth; not just about gender/sex and possession, but also about the existence of demons and angels, and the devil and god. Possession and exorcism, and their attendant ritual, then, signified beyond the current possession-exorcism event to a larger truth, and it was this truth that the Catholic Church in the face of Protestant dissent wished to lay claim to. Ritual, then, is of key importance for understanding not only possession, exorcism, and witchcraft but also their gender/sex coding.

The body was (and continues to be) central to gender/sex coding, possession, exorcism, and ritual. Flexible, pliant, resistant, and mysterious, the body was a primary site for the struggle between heaven and earth. Michel Foucault developed a conceptual frame by which to understand the body as the site of ideological deployment (and resistance to this deployment). Naming the force that shapes and controls the body as biopower, Foucault suggested that there are two kinds of power asserted, disciplinary and regulatory. Disciplinary power is that which establishes the knowledge of and power over the individual body and its capacities, gestures, movements, location and behaviours; while regulatory power is that which is inscribed in policies and interventions that govern the population. Regulatory power is, he argued, focused on the "species body" or the body that serves as the basis of biological processes affecting birth, death, the level of health and longevity. Regulatory power is accomplished by state intervention through such mediums as demography, public health agencies, economics and so forth. Foucault argued that Eurowestern biopower emerged in concrete terms at the beginning of the seventeenth century whereupon it was delineated in its two forms of disciplinary and regulatory powers (1980, 135–159). The body, individual and species, then, became a primary site of struggle.

The body, as Lisa Silverman (2001) articulates in her text *Tortured Subjects*, was throughout most of the early modern period in France considered to be a vehicle of truth. The body in its gestures, regularities, contortions, grimaces, illnesses, and affects would not dissemble as the self might do. And more particularly, the body could be made to speak the truth through the medium of pain. In the judicial system torture was perceived as a normative means by which to access the truth. Pain enveloping the body would force the truth from the mouth of the accused.[5] Silverman argues that:

> Belief in the bodily location of evidence is reflected in the formulaic phrase employed in the sentences that sought confessions of crimes....Truth and the act

> of knowing are consistently connected with the physical body rather than with
> the act of speaking or telling….Truth and the body appear to be virtually insepa-
> rable through the lens of these sentences. The embodiment of truth, its physical
> reality and location, are not merely assumed but expressed in the sentences.
> Torture is thus the means of revealing the intimate connection of truth and the
> body and then severing that tie. (2001, 80)

Believed to be the site of truth, the body was central to the determination of possession and witchcraft, and central to the efficacy of exorcism
and torture. Unable to lie, the body revealed the truth in its fleshy contortions, grimaces, and marks of the devil. Urbain Grandier, like all sorceresses and sorcerers in early modern France, was stripped and shaved in
order to find the markings on his body that spoke of his relationship with
the devil.[6] Certainly such action shamed, and was meant to shame, the
individual, but more specifically the body was used as the medium of
truth (Silverman 2001, 81). It was the pain of torture that forced a confession from Grandier's mouth. The body, however, could not tell the
truth unless properly enclosed by ritual. Ritual not only normalised and
legitimated possession, exorcism, torture, and execution; it also ensured
that each was perceived as rational and/or effective. Furthermore, and
most importantly, it provided a means for the public performance of possession, exorcism, and execution.

The context, which I will address in the following section, is complex.
At this very interesting moment in time the struggle between Catholic
and Protestant (the Huguenots in France), was fully engaged, although
the French religious wars had ended in 1598 with the Edict of Nantes.
Regardless, strife would continue and surface again with the thirty year
war of 1618–1648 (direct French involvement from 1636 until 1648) the
Fronde (1648–1653), and the revocation of the Edict of Nantes in 1685
by Louis XIV. Throughout this very tumultuous time there were, as Philip
Benedict comments, "periods of prolonged crisis and eras of recovery
and expansion" (1992, 27).[7]

Reflecting the complexity of the early modern French context, this
chapter draws upon various materials from the period: theological or theo-
logically oriented sources that include a tract written for the king of
England by a Huguenot, Nicolas Aubin (witness to the events in Loudun),
the *Malleus Maleficarum* (penned a century or so earlier by two Dominican friars and that dominated the thinking of the time), the writings of a
Spanish Jesuit Martín del Rio, and the autobiographical writing of sister
Jeanne des Anges; from legal or legally oriented sources I draw upon the
writings of Catholic lawyers, Jean Bodin and Pierre de Lancre, and finally
from medical sources I use the work of Johann Weyer the Dutch-German
physician. My effort here is to bring together a number of primary sources

drawn from three important areas; theology, law, and medicine (albeit philosophy is never absent from any of these sources), in order to think about the intersection of gender/sex, the body, and ritual with possession, exorcism, and demonological and witchcraft narratives of early modern France.

Early modern France: The context

Early modern France was, as mentioned, a complex and chaotic period. Although certainly there were periods of quiet, these were interspersed among longer and more frequent periods ranging from general unrest to complete upheaval and destruction. As the possession event I examine in this chapter falls in the first third of the seventeenth century, I begin my brief excursus into the social and historical context of early modern France in sixteenth century and the rise of the absolute state. However, I certainly cannot do justice to the immensity of the history of early modern France over this 150 year period, so my intention in this chapter is to intersect with what I consider to be key historical themes that are useful for thinking about possession and exorcism in this context. Furthermore, my intersections with these moments are not linear; rather I present the period contextually.

The political landscape of early modern France saw the introduction of what has been called the absolute state. Perry Anderson (1979) in *Lineages of the Absolute State* contends that it was in the course of the sixteenth century that the absolute state began to emerge throughout Europe. Anderson argues that the feudal system had basically established a hierarchy of groups with common interests, topped by the ruling group of nobles. In the absolute state this ruling group was transformed into a political class at the top of which was the absolute ruler or monarch. Until the demise of this institution the monarch would distribute power, particularly political power, among nobles who ensured, but not without elements of resistance, the absolutism of that ruling monarch.

The rise of the absolute state, Anderson argues, was a means to ensure the continuation of the nobles' power, which had been challenged by the gradual disappearance of serfdom. Serfdom had ensured the control of the rural masses—peasants—via their linkage to the land and the lord in the feudal mode of production. Peasants owed their lord dues made manifest by the goods they produced. However, this changed and dues became money rents rather than the goods produced by the land and, with this change to money rents, came the weakening of the nobles'

power over the peasant. The result was, Anderson argues "a displace-
ment of politico-legal coercion upwards towards a centralised, militarised
summit, or the Absolute State" (1979, 19). The primary political rationale for the emergence and existence of the absolute state was, according to Anderson, the subordination and control of the lower classes, peasant
and plebeian, in the social hierarchy.

The mercantile bourgeoisie had emerged in mediaeval towns and they
also represented a threat to monarchical and aristocratic power. In towns
merchants had gained wealth through commodity exchange and it was in
towns that technological (e.g. movable type which brought the advent of
printing) and commercial (e.g. the rise of the banking system) advances
occurred. Because of this wealth the mercantile bourgeoisie were also
able to lend money to the aristocracy who, without large scale mercantile
ventures, did not have a strong enough base of wealth necessary to hold
political power. Merchants, then, with their wealth were able to lend
money to, and therefore obligate, these nobles. Through this exchange,
merchants were able to access limited power and increase their wealth.
These powerful merchants, in conjunction with barons and princes, were
able to fortify their towns, building walls for protection. This meant that
towns and the powerful families, the rich merchants and the nobles affiliated with them, began to represent a threat to the king who was working
to centralise power in the monarchy. But as threatening as town and city
power was, it equally enriched the king allowing him to hold power externally in relation to other early modern states. At the bottom of this
social heap were the peasant and plebeian groups whose appropriated
and controlled labour power brought them into conflict with the monarch, aristocrats, and merchants, although uneasy political alliances did
arise between the merchant and plebeian groups when resisting nobles
and the centralisation of power in the monarchy.

The last several decades of the sixteenth century in France were fraught
with military and social conflict. The religious wars had raged for thirty-six
years and ended with the signing of the Edict of Nantes in 1598. These
wars, however, did not simply reflect conflict between Catholic and Protestant but also represented a struggle for power between the monarchy
and noble families, between monarchy and fortified cities, between southern and northern France, between the king and the Catholic League,
between the Catholic League and Protestant leaders to control the
monarchical power after the murder of Henry III in 1589, between peasant and noble, and between Spain and France (1594–1598) (Anderson
1979, 91–93). It was the end of the religious wars that allowed for the
solidification of a royal state, one that would, under Louis XIII (1601–
1643) and Cardinal Richelieu (1585–1642), seek to centralise power in

the monarchy and ensure that, for example, southern France, dominated by Huguenots, no longer represented a threat to the crown. Certainly, this was an important political subtext that was played out in Loudun during the period of the possession. As Michel de Certeau comments: "[i]n November 1631 the baron de Laubardemont received a royal commission to raze the castle and outer walls and towers [of Loudun], as he had already done to the castle of Mirebeau (1629) and the citadel of Royan (1630)" (1996, 26). Laubardemont was numbered among the nuns' most avid supporters and Grandier's most insistent persecutors.

Another important thread to the story of possession and exorcism was the emergence of the plague in France. Although the plague had visited France regularly since its devastating appearance as the Black Death in the fourteenth century, it returned to France as a pandemic once again in 1628. Michel de Certeau opens his story of the Loudun possession by referencing the plague, referring to it as "a physics of evil" and noting that it was understood to "possess" a city through the "infection of the air" (1996, 11). The aetiology of the plague was not understood at this time, but efforts to control its spread, if not find its cure, had begun to be implemented in France. Certainly in the past, in cities and areas affected by outbreaks of the plague those who could flee did, while those who could not, the poor, in large measure, died in droves. In urban locations assemblies were cancelled and people hid in their homes, or if plague was in a house then both it and its occupants were boarded up. This kind of quarantine had been rather *ad hoc*, but under the jurisdiction of the state, effected through the offices of the attendants, a more systematic quarantine was developed (Brockless and Jones 1997, 69, 351). In 1631 the Parlement of Paris decreed that "every locality within its jurisdiction [was] to establish a health council (*conseil de santé*) to oversee the health and well-being of city under the threat of the plague" (1997, 351).This more systematic response was an outcome of the pandemic of 1628–1631 and central to its rationale was the notion of sealing off and erecting firm boundaries (*cordons sanitaires)* to separate the plague-ridden from the plague free (1997, 351). This porousness and sealing is something I will return to when discussing the female body, but first a comment on physicians, some of whom stood their ground and remained in afflicted cities in the face of the human devastation wrought by the bubonic plague.

Not all those who could flee a plague ridden city did. Some religious stayed and attempted to provide some relief to the dying and minister to the dead. Urbain Grandier, it was said, had been such a priest. Some few physicians were also numbered among those who stayed and ministered to the dying. Physicians had various theories and beliefs about the plague, all of them generally erroneous. In large measure, still under the sway of a cosmology wherein the plague was a *peste* sent to punish humankind, the plague was met with various apotropaic responses such as mass processions, collective penitence, pilgrimage, public prayer, the ringing of church bells,[8] and of course the time honoured scapegoating and murder of Jews, itinerant groups such as gypsies, and (in the fifteenth through to the eighteenth centuries) witches, all of whom were seen to be instrumental in bringing on the plague. Physicians, particularly those in the employ of the state—the *médicin de santé*—would verify plague as the cause of death and provide advice regarding hygiene (Brockless, *et al.* 1997, 69). Although physicians had been around for quite some time, their importance to the state was increasing in the face of pandemic illnesses such as the plague, typhus, syphilis, and tuberculosis—and, of course, as specialists who could legally determine the truth of possession and witchcraft.

Roman law, as distinct from Canon law, had two distinct sectors, civil law and political law. The former, called *jus*, regulated economic transactions between citizens, while the latter, *lex*, "governed political relations between the State and its subjects" (Anderson 1979, 27). Roman law, rediscovered as early as the eleventh century in Bologna, was operative in the south of France and was largely adopted by the king and the French Parlements by at least the sixteenth century (Irvin 1992, 109–114).[9] The French Parlements, as administrators of the law, were established in large cities in France beginning with the Parlement of Paris in 1307, and then the Parlement of Toulouse in 1437 (Silverman 2001, 40), while thereafter other cities such as Dijon, Aix, or Grenoble were granted parlements by the king. The Parlements were the highest of the ordinary courts and heard cases related to both civil and criminal justice. The Parlement was the court one would appeal to regarding sentencing from the lower courts of the *capitoulat* (town council), the *sénéchaussé* (court of the *Sénéchal* or the King's representative), and the *bailliage* (the King's representative particularly in the North of France) (Silverman 2001, xiii). In instances of possession and witchcraft, then, although the religious of the Catholic Church assisted in determining authenticity regarding possession and witchcraft, they, as representatives of the Catholic Church, did not punish those who pretended to be possessed or execute those found guilty of necromancy or witchcraft. Instead, it was the secular apparatus of government that saw to their punishment. However, there was certainly an expectation on the part of the religious who concurred on the authenticity of the case that the secular arm should properly punish the accused, either by public whipping in the instance of pretended possession or burning at the stake in the case of witchcraft. The Dominican friar Henricus Institoris, the co-author of the *Malleus Maleficarum* and a practising inquisitor in Germany, lamented that judges did not punish thoroughly or consistently enough those many sorceresses and some few sorcerers who plagued the land. Typically in cases of possession and witchcraft joint action was carried out between the religious and lay authorities. As seen in Loudun there was a joining of forces between lay and religious to determine the authenticity of the possession and the guilt of Urbain Grandier as a sorcerer.

As a normative aspect of Roman law, torture was a means by which to ascertain the truth in instances were truth was uncertain. In France when guilt was unclear and a confession was required prior to sentencing, or when information on accomplices was sought from the condemned by the court, the accused was put to either the *question préparatoire*, in the instance of the former, or the *question préalable* in the instance of the latter, although certainly both could be used (Hunt 2004, 45; Silverman 2001, 42). However, the use of torture as a means to gather evidence in the court case was beginning to be questioned in seventeenth century France, and even at the time of the events in Loudun it was not a regular mechanism used by the justice system. Silverman comments that the seventeenth century saw a decline in the use of torture, and this was, she argues, because there was a shift in the understanding of pain as a means to truth. Still, it would take another hundred years for torture as a norma-tive judiciary practice to be abolished: 1780 for the *question préparatoire* and 1788 for the *question préalable* (Silverman 2001, 63–64).

Historians have argued that torture was in large measure a means to frighten the accused into a confession of guilt. Indeed there is some justification for this position as often times a ruling of *question préparatoire* or *question préalable* would have an attached *retentum*[10] to the sentence requiring that the accused be first *presented* with the instruments of tor-ture and then asked to confess and/or to provide information on possible accomplices. Torture apparently did not recognise social differences be-tween peasant, religious, merchant, man, woman, youth, or noble as any one of these groups could be tortured. Only the prepubescent, the sick, the mad, the deaf, the dumb, the pregnant, and the recently delivered woman (up to 40 days after delivery) were exempt from torture (Silverman 2001, 43). Enacted or presented, torture was a terrifying reality of the justice system, and certainly one many sought to avoid.

Women and men in early modern France, although both equally sub-ject to the possibility of torture, and certainly the *presentation* of torture, were not necessarily faced with the same kind of torture. Silverman has noted that in Toulouse, at least, there is a clear indication that torture itself was gender/sex coded. There were several general kinds of torture in France used during the *question*: the *estrapade*, the *question ordinaire*, and the *question d'eau* and the *brodequins* or *des mordaches*, both *questions extraordinaire*. The *estrapade* was applied equally to men and women and consisted of lifting the person on a rope by their tied wrists, which were behind their back. Pulled up several feet off the ground by a pulley they were suddenly dropped. This was done repeatedly resulting in dislocated shoulders, and sometimes permanent injury. The *question d'eau*, applied to men, consisted of stretching the person and then forcing a large amount of water (three buckets) into the stomach of the accused. The *mordaches* (a variant version of the *brodequins*—see below), applied to women, consisted of the bending of the leg until the heel touched the thigh whereupon the leg was enclosed in a vice-like binding over the knee and thigh. Pressure was then applied by the tightening of a screw (Silverman 2001, xv, 97–98).

The gender/sex coding of torture, at least in Toulouse, suggests an understanding of bodies as first and foremost gender/sexed. Men and women require different forms of torture and therefore torture itself was gender/sex coded. In other words, torture was shaped by gender/sex and therefore signified gender/sex. Just how the *question d'eau* signified male and the *mordaches* signified female is unclear, but the logic appears to be inversionary since pressure to the male body was applied to his interior, and pressure to the female body was applied to her exterior (see also Silverman 2001, 97–98). The application of torture inverted the Aristotelian norm of male outside and female inside and might suggest proper punishment for an accused who crossed the gender/sex line, that is, the male was too feminine and the female too masculine. In order to deal with such transgression, then, her masculinity (signified by exteriority) is neutralised when her legs are shattered. He, on the other hand, traversed the feminine road and so his interiority, which marked him as feminised, is further penetrated as water is poured into his gut. His gender/sexed torture pushes him even further into the feminine through penetration and increased moisture as the female was conceived, under the influence of Aristotelian anthropology, as wet and cold. His torture, then, moved him further into this state.

However, when Urbain Grandier was tortured, he had been sentenced to the *questions ordinaire* and *extraordinaire* (he was put to the *question préalable* in order to determine accomplices), he was subjected to the *brodequins*, a possible feminine torture in Toulouse according to Silverman. Nicolas Aubin does not appear surprised concerning the kind of torture applied to Grandier and instead comments upon its severity. According to Aubin, the self-claimed witness of the Loudun possessions and execution of Grandier, the *question extraordinaire* in Loudun consisted of tying wooden planks around the legs of the person between which, legs and planks, wedges were lodged. The number of wedges were used appears to be dependent upon the crime, but Aubin tells the reader that Grandier was given two more wedges than was the norm. The wedges were then struck repeatedly with a hammer until "the bones of the legs do crack and fall to pieces" while in the case of Grandier "when his legs were shattered, and they saw the marrow come forth, they gave over the torture, took him out, and laid him on the pavement" (Aubin 1705, 149).[11] Grandier supplied no names.

Silverman notes this anomaly in Grandier's torture and suggests that it and another case where a woman was put to the *question d'eau* may indicate that the gender/sexing of torture might be not be certain (2001, 98). However, that torture may have been gender/sexed does not seem too far-fetched, although how that gender/sexing is understood may not have been standardised across France. If the body is to speak the truth, then certainly the gender/sexed body may well have required different methods to secure such ends. Why Grandier was put to a possible feminine torture is unclear, unless of course, as Pierre de Lancre[12] commented twenty-two years earlier, "the priest who celebrates mass at the [witches'] Sabbath is the true succubus of the blessing that God has placed in his hand" (2006, 475). A succubus is a demon that takes female form, and Grandier feminised through his relationship with the devil possibly deserved to be tortured as female. But this remains speculative.

Gender/sex and the body in early modern France

Like the complexity of the social and political context of early modern France, gender/sex ideology was a complex affair demonstrating variation within classes, between rural and urban locations, religious and lay, and men and women. And yet, regardless of this variance, there was, as is now, a dominant gender/sex ideology that was a basis for determining proper and improper actions, dress, assumptions, roles and behaviour. This gender/sex ideology, or normative gender/sex relations, was typically disseminated by the elite, religious and lay, and is evidenced in their writings. Not all agreed with the dominant gender/sex ideology and some contested it (e.g. menstruation meant the female was stronger than the male since her body naturally bled itself), some agreed with it but found the need to nuance it (women were weaker, but as weaker were a more appropriate vessel for deity's work), while others accepted it wholeheartedly. In many instances, however, gender/sex was an assumed category, one perceived to be created and imbued by deity in and through nature.

However, in early modern France narratives concerning demonology and possession, as well as those relating to theology, medicine and law, as elsewhere across Europe, operated within and contributed to the formation of the dominant understanding of gender/sex wherein women were perceived as both physically and spiritually weaker than men, and subsequently more vulnerable to the devil. This did not mean men were not possessed, they were, as in the case of Jean-Joseph Surin the priest who came to Loudun to rid Jeanne des Anges of her demons. However, women were predominant among the possessed (and those accused of witchcraft), while those men who succumbed to possession and sorcery may well have been suspect with regard to their masculinity. What was it that led to the widespread belief that the female was more susceptible to possession (and witchcraft) than the male?

Prior to 1800, within Eurowestern social bodies, the dominant view of the gender/sexed body was under the influence of Aristotelian theory, both from Aristotle himself, and also through Galen, a second to third century CE physician of the Roman Empire. In this theory of gender/sex and the body, played out in relation with the mediaeval theory of humors that dominated all forms of western European knowledge at this time, the male was hot and dry and the female cold and wet (Lindemann 1999, 8–37). As women were cold and wet, they were seen to be more susceptible to, for example, melancholia, a disease brought on by an imbalance of black bile. Although certainly some men, particularly scholars and mystics, were also prey to melancholia, melancholia was a feminine disease, and, according the sixteenth century physician Johann Weyer, the devil gravitated toward black bile, particularly if there was an excess of it. Weyer, in support of this theory, relates in his book the story of the possession of Margaret, a twenty year old woman living in the village of Levensteet whose possession he chalked up to her youthful age, female sex, and a long term fever that had produced an "excess of heavy bitter, melancholic humor [that had] putrefied within the body" (Weyer 1991, 314).

Central to this formulation of the female and male in the gender/sex ideology worked out in the domain of the biological, as per the semiotics of gender, are two key points. The first is the idea of opposition so that if men are hot and dry then of necessity women must be cold and wet. The second is value is given to each side of the opposition so that the female is given negative value and the male positive value. Furthermore, under the influence of Aristotle, the female body was understood to be an inversion of the male body so that while his genitals were properly located on the exterior of the body, hers were improperly located on the interior of the body. As the inverted male, the female was a misbegotten male and therefore problematic from the outset. She was an inversion of the norm, much as the festival of carnival and the ritual of charivari were inversions of the norm. And although these inversionary ritual activities were embraced suggesting acceptance of difference or alterity, their acceptance was rather a gesture toward what was deemed the proper order of things.[13] Likewise the female's alterity gestured toward the human norm, the male.

The notion that the female is an inversion of the male is called a one-sex and two-gender model and was, as Thomas Laqueur (1992) has so convincingly argued, the dominant gender/sex ideology in early modern Europe.[14] As I have indicated above, then, the female is perceived as weaker in terms of her physical and mental states, and this is understood to be a natural outcome of her wet and cold nature, and her bodily inversion of normative exterior genitalia seen in the male. But what of the spiritual? The myth found in the second Genesis story concerning Adam and Eve completed the narrative of the weakness of women. In this myth, as it was interpreted at this juncture in time, Eve demonstrated her weaker nature when she spoke to the serpent having succumbed to curiosity and naiveté. For this she was punished by the deity with painful childbirth. Adam, on the other hand, did not speak to the serpent, but nonetheless allowed himself to be led astray by Eve when he did not control her actions. He was punished with manual labour. As Pierre de Lancre comments when discussing the issue of the greater propensity of female sorcerers:

> It is very true that the Evil Spirit draws women's flighty minds much more easily toward superstition and idolatry than those of men. That is why one reads in the great book of Genesis that the diabolical teachings were from the beginning of the world taught to Eve rather than to Adam; and furthermore, that she rather than he was seduced by Satan in the form of the serpent....God wanted to weaken Satan more, which he did, and this occurs first in establishing his reign, and by giving him power over creatures of less dignity, such as serpents; and over the weakest creatures, such as insects; then over the other wild beasts, rather than over humankind, then over women, then over men who live like beasts rather than over the others who live like human beings. (de Lancre 2006, 82)

Further adding to the "problem" of the feminine and her incredulous and curious nature, was the permeable boundary, or the porousness, of the female body. Reflected in attitudes toward bathing in the early modern period of Europe was the problem of porousness, which was understood to make the body more vulnerable to invasion by disease, both physical and spiritual. During the mediaeval period bathhouses had been common, but under the sway of religion, morality, and medicine bathhouses were understood to promote licentious behaviour and, more importantly for this analysis, bathing was understood to open the pores of the body making the individual vulnerable to invasion. Lawrence Brockless and Colin Jones comment that:

> Medical reasoning buttressed this critique: the opening of pores allowed ingress, it was held, to epidemic diseases, plague, and syphilis not least….A greater sense of bodily containment and boundedness emerged, particularly in books of manners from the Renaissance onwards, although these did not exhibit overmuch anxiety about body-washing. (1997, 49)

Sara Matthews-Grieco further comments that:

> Slowly baths became a medical rather than a pleasurable or hygienic practice, accompanied by the use of cupping-glasses to draw off harmful humors and inevitably surrounded by a series of precautionary measures. The body was considered "open" and vulnerable when wet, "closed" and protected when dry. (1993, 49)

The natural porousness of the female body was central to the logic of girls and women's vulnerability to possession.

The female, of no will of her own, leaked blood from her vagina and milk from her breasts. This leakage suggested that she was porous and open on a fundamental level: fundamental because she had no control over it. Wet and cold by her innate nature and open and without control, the female body was susceptible to invasion by a demon. Weyer comments in Book Four, Chapter XV, that some physicians had argued that the devil could gain entrance into the body through the pores, which are stretched by him to allow the insertion of odd objects that have no place in the body such as knives, straw, nails, stones, hair, thorns, fish bones, and so forth. Weyer argued against this idea insisting it was an illusion since deity had narrowly constricted the pores from the beginning allowing the passage of only the "thinnest liquid, such sweat and vapour and nothing thicker and more solid" (1991, 319).

Along with the tendency of the female toward susceptibility of melancholia and credulity, and equally linked to the porousness of the female body—her permeable boundary—was also the problem of the uterus and the female's subjugation to it, particularly girls and women, such as nuns, who had not given birth. Commenting on this latter, Weyer argued that instances of so-called possession could be the result of a number of natural causes such as the rising up of the uterus in the young girl, which causes suffocation, or melancholia due to excess black bile.[15] Although certainly his diagnoses were problematic, having followed Hippocrates and Galen on this subject, nonetheless it is clear that his view of female and male physiology, like the majority of physicians throughout Europe, was greatly informed by Classical Greek physiology and medicine. Under the influence of Hippocrates, Aristotle, and Galen, the perception was that women were particularly vulnerable both to an excess of black bile leading to melancholia and to the restless womb. In the *De praestigiis daemonum* Weyer relates the tale of Antonio Benivieni (1443–1502), a physician he respected, who was faced with an instance of possible possession:

> A sixteen-year-old woman's hands became contorted when pain arose in the lower part of her abdomen. As she broke into a terrible scream, her whole stomach immediately swelled so greatly that one would have thought her eight months pregnant. When her voice gave out, she hurled herself hither and thither all around the bedroom, sometimes touching the soles of her feet to her neck, and then leaping back to her feet, and once again falling forward and jumping back up. She kept doing this over and over until she gradually came to her senses and recovered to an extent. Upon being asked what she had done, she was totally unaware of her behaviour. Seeking the causes of the disease, we thought that the illness stemmed from a stifling or suffocation of the womb and from evil vapours carried upwards and repeatedly striking the heart and brain. But when no progress was achieved by our medications, she became even more fierce; staring about with wild eyes she finally broke into vomiting and cast forth rather long curved nails and brass needles together with wax and tangles of hair, and finally a piece from her breakfast, so large that no one could have swallowed it down his throat. And since she had often repeated this action right before my eyes, I thought that she was in the power of an evil spirit who blinded the eyes of the spectators while carrying out these activities. She was therefore turned over to Ecclesiastical "physicians", and she confirmed the truth of the matter by even clearer signs and proofs. We heard of her prophesy, and in addition saw her do things which surprised all powers of disease, and even exceeds human capacity.[16] (1991, 297)

The above description of this young woman and her possession is quite intriguing insofar as it is a fairly typical narrative of the phenomenon, or the symptomatology, of possession in the early modern period, including the possessed nuns of Loudun over one hundred years later. Also evidenced in this passage are both notions of the female body discussed above; its porousness representing a lack of firm bodily boundaries (external objects located inside the body, a phenomenon I will return to later) and the restless womb.

If the normative female body was understood to be soft and porous, the normative male body was understood to be hard and impenetrable. This oppositional formulation might suggest that the male body could not be possessed, but this was certainly not the case. Some men were indeed subject to possession by demons, however, those males possessed tended to be numbered among boys, male youth,[17] male peasants, and priests of the Catholic Church such as Jean-Joseph Surin.[18] Although the proper male body was understood to be sealed, hot, and dry and the proper female body to be porous, cold, and wet there were always exceptions that proved the rule: some men were not properly masculine and male and equally for women. Therefore, as not all women were possessed by demons or involved in witchcraft, regardless that they were seen to be female, so too not all men were impervious to demon attack and some were also among those gathered up and executed in the witchcraft trials. Those men who succumbed to the devil, either through possession or witchcraft, were either young enough that their bodily boundaries had not been properly sealed, poor enough that lack of social status and the engagement of bodily labour stigmatised them and associated them with the feminine, or were too inclined toward the melancholic and therefore perilously oriented toward the feminine since an overabundance of this humor was understood to be a malady of the female.

Proper masculinity was constructed in relation to the notion of a firm boundary between the feminine and masculine and female and male. The monstrous feminine threatened masculinity with contagion, particularly in light of the conquest and colonisation that had taken off in the sixteenth century. As Michel de Certeau has demonstrated in his text *The Writing of History* (1988), there was a concern with the so-called native whose inversion and monstrosity represented a threat to those who journeyed into and returned home from the "edge" of the world. Men who had contact with these "others", particularly through sexual relations, risked contamination. The "other" found in these far away worlds of the west and east, with Europe marked as the centre, were represented in travelogues as firmly and irrevocably rooted in nature, *adversus* to culture, seduced by the devil and, like the female/feminine, marked a boundary between "them" and "us".[19] Certeau comments: "What travel literature really fabricates is the primitive as *a body of pleasure*." (1988, 226, emphasis original) Certeau examines in detail the travelogue of Jean de Léry, a sixteenth century Calvinist who travelled to and along the coast of Brazil, and notes the binary system that provided a template for this young man's view of the world he finds *over there*. The binary system that Certeau lays out based on Léry's travelogue (Table 4.1) is useful for thinking about European masculinity perceived to be potentially at risk (1988, 228).

One binary that I include, and which Certeau did not (marked by the square brackets), is female-feminine/male-masculine binary. This binary clearly fits comfortably in the set that undergirds much Eurowestern early modern thought and proved eminently useful in order to exploit and savage those countries and their indigenous occupants as the "other". The problem, however, of feminising the category of the other meant

Table 4.1 Eurowestern binarism

Primitive	vs.	Civilised
nudity	vs.	clothing
(festival) ornament	vs.	finery (stylishness)
hobby, leisure, festival	vs.	work (occupation)
unanimity, proximity,	vs.	division, distance
pleasure	vs.	ethics
[female-feminine]	vs.	[male-masculine]

that men marked as other were also feminised and this, I would argue, was a basis for the anxiety that required the delineation of proper masculinity (and of course proper femininity). Mitchell Greenberg (2002), reading Molière's *L'Avare* (1668) and *Le Malade Imaginaire* (1673), argues that both plays comically undercut the operative ideal of the "patriarch" who represents the ideal human. Molière's method, Greenberg argues, is to embody the patriarch who in the end, regardless of his efforts, is subject to the body—his own body. Jumping off from Greenberg, then, one could argue that it was the anus that marked *the* place of potential invasion and loss of control of the male body. The orifice of the anus undercut the idea of control when it became apparent that humans must develop bodily control to regulate defecation and that under certain conditions such as illness, fear, excitement, and death such control was illusory. The anus and its vulnerability to loss of control and penetration brought the male perilously close the feminine. Such fear of contagion may well have been an element of why it was so necessary to control the female-feminine; for to control "her" was ultimately to have control of self; self from the perspective of the male.

Ritual, the female body, and possession

The body is central to the concept of possession and there are a number of reasons for this, some more obvious than others. In most Christian systems of belief and practice both negative and positive supernatural powers, which operate in a binary relationship, are able to act in the realm of humans. This realm is perceived as corporeal and at the centre of this corporeality is the embodied human. This embodied human is, more or less, the site of the struggle between evil and good. We read in the *Malleus Maleficarum* (1486) that:

> We may therefore say that demons can harm and possess humans at the insistence of sorceresses, in the same five ways that they can do so by themselves without sorceresses, because in that case greater power to act savagely against humans through sorceresses is permitted to the demon since God is more offended.....the reasons why God permits humans to be possessed....Sometimes a person is possessed for his greater merit, sometimes for someone else's trivial misdeed, sometimes for his own venial sin, sometimes for someone else's serious sin, and sometimes for his own great crime. (Institoris and Sprenger 2006b, 296–297)

Deity and demon are understood to engage each other in the human realm, although clearly the devil knows his master and engages in such play in order to test the hearts of women and men; was this not the case in the myth of Job, an often included biblical reference in discussions of obsession and possession? But more to the point, to deny that the devil acted without the permission of deity was to take a heretical position on the subject. Deity and demon were not in a struggle for power over the human realm; rather the demon was allowed to possess the individual for the ultimate glory of deity.

The soul was not considered to be the site of possession, although the soul was understood to be located in the body. The demon inhabited the body[20] and indeed he apparently opted for particular parts of the body; the leg, arm, stomach, and so forth (the demon was always referred to in the masculine, although it was believed he could take female form as a succubus). Jeanne des Anges was possessed by seven demons, and when made to verbally commit herself to deity by Pierre Barré, canon of the Church of Chinon, during the initial days of her possession, she was only able to commend her soul and heart "without constraint", and not her body. Aubin commented that "but when he bid her say, that she gave her body, she made resistance and seemed not to obey, but by force; as if she were willing to say, the devil possessed her body but not her soul" (1705, 29). Her body was like a "diabolical atlas", comments Michel de Certeau, with Léviathan lodged in the "middle of her forehead", Isacaron lodged "below the last rib of the right side", Balam "lodged in the second rib of her right side", and Behemoth "lodged in her stomach", while Aman and Asmodaeus, two other demons, are not given a explicit bodily location (Certeau 1996, 90–91). The body was normatively understood as fragmented in the early modern period with individual parts, in some measure, understood as wholes unto themselves (Vickers 1997). This conceptualisation of the body, then, was translated into the knowledge of possession, which is not surprising considering that physicians often played a central role in diagnosis and treatment of the possessed and the identification of witches.

The body, then, is central to possession as it is the stage, both the interior and exterior of the body, where the drama of possession is played out. But the kind of body most susceptible to penetration by the devil was the female body since it was "known" to be cold and moist, and therefore susceptible to the black bile of melancholia, a substance that Weyer argues demons prefer (Weyer 1991, 315). The female body was also known to be porous and therefore problematically open to potentially possessing demons, while the female's nature, dominated by credulity and curiosity, combined with the former to make women more vulnerable to possession. But what does the ritual of possession-exorcism look like?

As with the concreteness of the body, possession was thought to be instigated by some concrete object that gave the demon access to the potential victim. In the possession case of the cloistered nuns at Weret, for example, they were first obsessed[21] by the demon, so they claimed, after a "poor old woman" borrowed from them three pounds of salt at Lent and then repaid them "almost double the amount at Eastertime".[22] Thereafter, according to Weyer's telling of their tale, "little white spheres were found in the dormitory, like sugar-covered seeds but salty to the taste..." (Weyer 1991, 304). The possession of the nuns of Loudun also included material objects said to signal the presence of demons. There were two apparitions that appeared; their deceased confessor and a man seen from the back who was later identified by them as Grandier. In between these two manifestations, on 23rd September 1632, a small black ball was said to have rolled across the floor of the refectory. Another spectre appears, this time with a book and then a spectral black globe appeared which threw Sister Marthe to the floor and pushed Jeanne des Anges into a chair (Certeau 1996, 15–16). On 1st October Jeanne des Anges, "reclining with the candles lit, and having seven or eight of her sisters around her to help her in particular because the attacks she was having, felt a hand, though seeing nothing, which, closing on her hand, left in it three thorns of a hawthorn..." (Certeau 1996, 16). These were burned by Anges under the direction of the exorcists as they were felt to be indicative of a demon's exterior presence (obsession).[23]

Following obsession is possession and once odd objects such as nails, hair, cloth, stones, and other material were ejected from the body, then it was understood that the demon had moved from the exterior to the interior of the body.[24] The nuns of Loudun, like other possession cases of the time, expelled odd objects from their mouths: Jeanne des Anges ejected first a feather quill, "about a finger's length", and later a silk button (Aubin 1705, 106–107). And, although certainly the three thorns of hawthorn and then later roses (also burned) were interpreted as signs of a pact with the devil on the part of Grandier, they also acted as sign-symbols that spoke of the presence of demons. In possession cases, as well as witchcraft trials, evidence, as it was interpreted, took concrete material form: for possession (and subsequently possible charges of witch-craft) objects such as nails, stones, hair, salt, thread, and so forth found on the premises, under beds, and underneath (or above) thresholds were understood as the initial mechanism that allowed the demon to gain en-trance to the abode of the victim, while similar objects expelled from the body, usually through the mouth, were understood to signify that the demon had gained entrance into the body. The necessity to find physical signs of the devil and his minions was also a central aspect of the witch-craft trail when prosecutors sought the mark of the devil on the body of the sorceress or sorcerer. Writers of the time, Institoris and Sprenger, Bodin, del Rio, Lancre, and other demonologists and witch-hunters all agreed that the devil made a visible mark on the body, although finding the mark could prove difficult.

The mark of the devil was something engraved upon the body by the devil during a ritual wherein allegiance was sworn. Such a ritual was gen-erally understood to have taken place during the witches' sabbath. Pos-session too was a ritualised affair that typically took the form of public spectacle, as it did in Loudun. Possession began with a sign, a concrete sign, but soon became a performance, one that was enacted primarily by the possessed and the exorcists, although those assisting, government officials and representatives such as Jean Martin de Laubardemont the king's counsellor and physician, played their role as well. No public ritual is efficacious without an attendant audience, and observing in Loudun were many people: local and regional, peasant, merchant, and noble, and even "foreigners" from as far away as Scotland.

Every aspect of the bodies of the possessed women were examined minutely for traces of the demons, while every sound, grimace, gesture, and contortion was observed in order that the demons be identified. Aubin, who later fled Loudun and France with the reassertion of intoler-ance for those of the "reformed religion", described the possessions in his book, although certainly he considered them to be a fake; an elaborate ruse put into play by Urbain Grandier's enemies. He paid attention to the bodies, gestures, and grimaces of the nuns, seeking not for proof of pos-session, but rather deceit. The Huguenots were wise to the politics of possession and how too often the devil would preach to those in atten-dance at the exorcism the truth of Catholicism and the deviltry of the reformed religion. The possession of Nicole Obry and the miracle of Laon as it was called (1566) is an excellent case in point. This possession-exorcism ritual was a thoroughly public affair, staged in part in the

Cathedral in Laon, wherein the devil claimed the Huguenots as his own (Walker 1981, 23). It was believed that, although the devil was a liar, he could not lie when compelled by the priest with the host in his hand. Aubin, writing of Loudun, tells the reader that

> the superior (Anges) had no sooner discovered the two magistrates [Protestants], but she had violent commotions, and performed strange actions; she made a noise which was like that of a pig, she sunk down into the bed, and contracted herself into the postures and grimaces of a person who is out of his wits; a Carmelite friar was at her right hand, and Mignon[25] at her left, the last of these put his two fingers in her mouth and presupposing she was possessed, used many conjurations, and spake to the devil, who answered him after this manner in their first dialogue. (1705, 23)

On 18th October, 1632 two Loudun doctors, a master surgeon and a doctor of medicine, attested after examining Anges and Sister Claire that their "bodily extortions", "involuntary movements throughout their members", "yellow faces and eyes rolling upward", the "stopping of the pulse during said rigors", and an evident lack of exertion even when violently convulsing were the proper signs that spoke of authentic possession (Certeau 1996, 49).

The masculine devils had penetrated the bodies of the female possessed. They ravished the nuns and caused them to writhe, twist, and wriggle in shocking and wanton ways; all this as the male exorcists, priests, civil servants, local townspeople, Catholic and Protestant, watched in fascination. Certainly some women were there to watch, but primarily it was men who watched as both the masculine demons and male exorcists tormented the female flesh of the possessed. Like some pornographic S&M film, all were enthralled by the bodily torture: torn hair and flesh, broken teeth, gagging and vomiting, choking, slapping, punching, crawling, begging, twisting and thrashing bodies, and always central to this abjection of the female flesh was its subjugation: initially by masculine demons and then by male exorcists and priests. The misogyny of the age was played out on the stage of possession. It was through the flesh of the female and their mouths that the demon spoke. He used their long, blackened tongues, a typical sign of possession (phallic one might say), to blaspheme.[26] The demon had no fleshy body, therefore no mouth or tongue of its own for it was a spirit (Institoris and Sprenger 2006b, 73–85). The demon stole (possessed) the body of Jeanne des Anges, along with nine of her Ursuline sisters and seven non-religious (eight religious and three non-religious were also obsessed), and made it perform in patterned and procedural ways initiating, once again, the rite of possession-exorcism (Certeau 1996, 91–93). As Certeau comments: "But from the outset the demon expresses himself in another language, which in Loudun becomes much more essential: a body language. Grimaces, contortions, rolling of the eyes, and so forth, little by little constitute the devil's lexicon." (Certeau 1996, 44)

The ritual of possession-exorcism, a ritual that signalled possession, marking it off from melancholia and madness, consisted of unnatural locomotion, bodily insensibility, convulsions, and bodily contortions such as heels bowed to the back of the head. There were swellings and bulging of the body, while the eyes often rolled back into the head. Facial grimaces contorted into fierce and frightening expressions that often included an extended and lolling tongue—"prodigiously great, long, and hanging" (Aubin 1705, 203). The skin was discoloured with strange and inexplicable marks such as wounds and writing. There was a wretched smell exuding from the mouth of the possessed while rude and non-human vocalisations emanated from it. Demoniacs had unusual strength and responded phobically to religious apparatus, be it prayer or items such as the cross, host, and holy water. The possessed exhibited inappropriate behaviour usually of a sexual nature and showed contempt for, and arrogance toward, social superiors. There was a speaking in an unfamiliar language, usually Latin, Greek or Hebrew and knowledge of events and secrets beyond the possessed's ken. And finally there was sermonising, a speaking of proposed spiritual truths: the demon using Anges' tongue cried out "that there were Huguenots there..." (Aubin 1705, 54). Such signs of possession had been catalogued over time and became the means by which possession could be ritually performed, but equally the means used by doctors and theologians to judge a case of possession as "authentic"; in other words, a case of "true" possession and not a situation of malice, political or economic machination, or fraud.

Encircled by the exorcising priests, along with many curious spectators, female flesh was made to speak of the dangers of existence. The bubonic plague of 1628–1631 had contaminated and ravished Loudun, as it did France taking an estimated 750,000–1,150,000 lives (Brockless, *et al.* 1997, 39). The last plague victim in Loudun succumbed to the disease just days before the first act of the ritual drama ensured. The bodily signs of the plague mirror the bodily signs of possession. Below Jacques Roland, writing at the end of the 1631 pandemic, describes the bodily symptoms of the bubonic plague:

> ...he experiences continual vomiting and retching, a strange lack of appetite, an extreme fever; the insides, even the head, seem to be burning with pain; while the external parts are all frozen, the lower belly is all swollen, the stomach tight. He is seized with anxiety and cannot sleep and yet is endlessly drowsy. His face changes completely, the eyes become red and wild, his temples are drawn, his nostrils enlarged, the end of his nose becomes pointed, the mouth, from which

> exudes a cadaverous odour, hangs open, his tongue goes dry and black, his lips turn leaden. He is afflicted by great bouts of thirst, he finds breathing difficult, his skin becomes spotted with red, violet, and black pustules and marks and he is tortured by abscesses in several spots as his body becomes covered by buboes or painful tumours and other horrible symptoms. (in Brockless, et al. 1997, 37)

Similarly, the possessed, when exhibiting signs of demonic possession, suffered rigidity and swellings of the body while a foul odour exuded from the mouth. The eyes bulged, and the skin was either livid or yellow, and great tumours appear on the body, as with Jeanne des Anges when a tumour appeared in her armpit when the demon Astaroth appeared (Aubin 1705, 206).

There was a conceptual link between the plague and demonic possession. For example, Weyer comments that the possession of the nuns of the convent of Nazareth at Cologne (Germany) was a "plague" that spread like a contagion (1991, 311). This is not surprising in light of the belief that the plague was deity punishing the people for their sin (see above); much as demonic possession was used to punish the individual or someone close to her (or him). The plague penetrated the social body bringing to the surface the disease that was insidious to it. To fight it required several tactics: the multiple social bodies, represented by heterogeneous cities and towns, must be controlled, contained, and hedged in by purifying circles, the *cordons*, which allowed a sealing up of the fragmented social body; second, the disease itself must be fought and so purifying fumigations, street cleaning, burial and disinfection services, and ritual actions such as ringing church bells,[27] prayer, procession, and pilgrimage were used to deal head-on with the illness and in order to purge it from, thereby purifying, the social body.

This was equally so for the possessed of Loudun and the possessed throughout the early modern period. Possession with its clearly demarcated signs provided visual cues that allowed for the implementation of exorcism. As Arnold van Gennep (1960) argued many years ago, a ritual has three stages consisting of separation, transition (liminality), and incorporation. Separation marks the first stage of the ritual, wherein those (the obsessed and potentially possessed) who would participate in it were set apart. Secondly, the fully possessed participants entered the transitional or liminal stage where they are betwixt and between, or in a threshold stage being neither fully human nor fully demon, but both. In the liminal stage, the ritual participants enacted their apartness through visible signs of possession; of necessity they must embrace this second part of the ritual in order to arrive at the third stage of incorporation, or restoration to humanity, through the exorcising of the demons.

The ritual of possession-exorcism, then, begins when the individual is set apart, in this instance when it was determined the nuns were possessed. This separation established a boundary between those who were contaminated and those who were not, much like the efforts to control the plague wherein towns were cordoned off. The nuns then entered a state of liminality where the rite of exorcism was enacted in order to maintain and secure the boundary between impure and pure, but more importantly to purge the female flesh of its occupying masculine demons. Through fumigation, prayer, punishment, religious song, pilgrimage, and seeking deity's forgiveness and protection the female bodies of the nuns were cleansed of the plague of demons. Having been cleansed, the possessed were incorporated back into the social body with some evincing a new status such as Jeanne des Anges who went on to become an influential mystic whose left hand had been engraved with the names of Jesus, Maria (Mary), Joseph, and F.D. Salles[28] upon the departure of her demons.

Between the body politic and the female body there was a conceptual link; the female body acted as a metonymy for the social body, something both the state and the church wished to control. The disciplining, purging, and sealing of the female body was a mirror for, and a ritual-symbolic enactment of, the proper containment and sealing of the heterogeneous social body in early modern France.

Ritual, the male body, and exorcism

But what of the male body and possession, since it is gender/sex that concerns this chapter? Men, particularly young men, peasants, and clerics appear to be those who number among the possessed, although certainly their numbers were significantly lower than women. As I have argued, a cultural aspect of the early modern period was the logical understanding that the female was susceptible to possession due to a moist, malleable, and porous body, and a weak spiritual and mental nature. The exorcism scripts again and again struggle with gender/sexed pronouns, and, as Caciola comments,

> For I know of no group of mediaeval sources other than manuals of exorcism that commonly uses gender-inclusive pronouns....[And] even more strikingly, many texts that begin inclusively, or with masculine pronouns, switch to *exclusively* feminine usage as the script progresses. (2003, 251, emphasis original)

The male, however, was less susceptible due to his dry, firm, and sealed body, and a normative strong mental and spiritual nature. But this did not mean that men could not be possessed, for men, like women, did not always evince the idealised gender/sex attributes. Indeed that some men, like Jean-Joseph Surin, were obsessed and risked possession proved the rule of female-feminine susceptibility. As Genesis was interpreted by many at this time, Adam, the first male, was created by deity from the dust and into his nostrils deity breathed the "breath of life" (Gen. 2: 7), and although Adam had been seduced by Eve, he had not been seduced by the serpent (Gen. 3: 2–7). Eve, however, was created from a part of Adam but, much like the animals created before Adam, deity did not breath into her the "breath of life" (Gen 2:22).

Within the Christian paradigm, both Catholic and Protestant, Adam was the ideal male human while Eve was a female copy of this ideal. Not all men, however, lived up to this ideal as vice and sin shifted them from the ideal, leaving them open to the wiles of the devil and his minions. For example, when men became enamoured of things of the flesh or desirous of power or wealth, when men were too curious and sought secret and esoteric knowledge, or when men were too sympathetic to the female, then they were susceptible to the devil as they had become in some measure feminised. Jean-Joseph Surin, Jeanne des Anges' last exorcist, belonged to this last group, being oriented toward the mystical and sympathetic to the plight of the female.[29]

However, although some men may be susceptible, the proper male was not. Instead, men numbered among the exorcists, inquisitors, lawyers, judges, and executioners (all ritual specialists) who took on the devil in order to protect women, who were typically assumed to be the responsibility of men. Caciola argues that the ritual of exorcism showed a marked shift in the middle of the fifteenth century toward systematisation and textuality. She comments that:

> Indeed it is precisely in the fifteenth century, the period Goddu posits as a nadir of the exorcistic activity, that exorcisms suddenly achieved a striking visibility in other documents in European archives. Manuals of exorcism, produced for the first time in large numbers in the fifteenth century as portable pocket books, demonstrated that exorcism had not become a "failure" at all. It had simply mutated, ceased to be an improvised public spectacle at a saint's tomb, and instead becomes a liturgical performance....These new exorcisms were scripted liturgies, rather than spontaneous healings: hieratic in tone, repetitive in form, and eschatological in doctrinal scope. (2003, 236)

The ritual of exorcism took on new importance in the fifteenth century as the men of various Christianities,[30] locating themselves in the war camp of deity, took up arms to battle the devil (and each other of course). The masculine demon (typically referred to as "he" in exorcism scripts and in tales of possession)[31] had taken up lodging in the female (or feminised) body and must be forced out by the masculine exorcist. Literate, the proper exorcist (typically a cleric) belongs to the elite estate in France. His elite status is marked by his knowledge of demonology (e.g. Institoris and Sprenger, Bodin, Lancre, and del Rio) and his ability to read and properly speak the exorcist text. His ritual efficacy allowed him to force the demon(s) to name himself (themselves) and once named the exorcist was able, with his ritual virility, to draw on the power of deity to command the demon(s). Equally, the exorcist mercilessly and brutally demanded obedience from the possessed, and, through (usually) her, the demon, regardless how torturous the exorcism. We read in Certeau's text of the purging, bleeding, and fumigation with sulphur[32] and other noxious substances enacted on the possessed nuns. When the exorcists wished the demons to appear, particularly if important people were in attendance, then fumigation was employed:

> For anger and to sour the humor of the possessed woman, he would use smoke produced by lighted candles of pitch resin, of dwarf elder sulphur, and similar things, having the possessed woman's face held over the smoke until, unable to withstand it longer and losing patience by the excess of pain, Satan appeared in her. (1996, 128)

If the devil didn't kill them, then certainly the ministrations of the exorcists might.

The ability to cordon off a demon marked the exorcist as properly masculine and his ritual as efficacious. Surin, who spent just over two years seeking to exorcise Jeanne des Anges, did not use the above techniques. Instead, he sought to model piety to Anges, to avoid commanding her, to avoid public spectacles of the exorcism, and to exorcise her through song and prayer. Anges writes in her autobiography, composed seven years after her public pilgrimage across France to the tomb of Saint François de Salles in 1637:

> The Father, not only in the beginning but also through all of his conduct, kept to the practice of not ordering her to do anything; and although she was very obedient and though he saw what she needed, he never said directly to her: Do this; and he never told her that he wanted anything from her. (Goldsmith 2001, 51)

In the end, Surin himself, questionably masculine, was obsessed by the demon within three weeks of wrestling it, and himself, at times unable to speak, was later committed in 1644 to an asylum for those suffering from melancholia. He, like Anges, remained suspect: he for his feminine leanings, and she regarding the legitimacy of her possession, a possession that resulted in an accusation of witchcraft directed at a fellow religious, Urbain Grandier.

The sorceress and sorcerer

As earlier indicated, men were also implicated in the witchcraft trials across Europe, particularly in the Northern regions. According to William Monter (2002, 42) and Bengt Ankarloo (2002, 73, 93), among others, in Northern France (the largest cluster from Normandy), Iceland, Finland, and Livonia men were over-represented in the numbers of those charged with witchcraft. However, this over-representation can be reversed as was the case in Finland. During the sixteenth century sixty percent of those charged with sorcery were men, while in the seventeenth century over sixty percent charged were women (Ankarloo 2002, 71). Clearly gender/sex does figure, but not in a straightforward fashion. Rather, the gender/sex ideology of social location, for example Northern Europe, inter-sects with cultural narratives and ultimately shapes phenomena such as the European witch hunts of the sixteenth, seventeenth and eighteenth centuries. Ankarloo, cognizant of gender/sex ideology, comments that in Finland and Iceland those who trafficked in magic were men (2002, 71). In Normandy shepherds and clerics loomed large as two groups of men charged with and executed for witchcraft. Lancre, in his efforts to purify the Basque territory of France, implicated eight priests, three of whom were burned alive in Paris. Prior to Loudun, and indeed commented upon by Father Mignon (confessor of the possessed Ursuline nuns and one of their early exorcists) was the case of the execution of a priest in Aix-en-Provence (1609–1611) (Certeau 1996, 4, 22). Why were clerics targeted among men? Why does Jean Bodin state rather matter-of-factly that "it has been found in countless trails that witches very often are priests, or they have secret dealings with priests" (2001, 216)? It certainly could be argued that it was this particular group who numbered among those very interested in books of necromancy. Richard Kieckhefer comments on how in the early fourteenth century "possession and use of magical writings becomes a recurrent theme in the records of prosecution" (1998, 1). What is of significance here is that the emphasis was on books of magic so that books are central to the determination of necromancy, rather than, as with sorcery trials focussed on women, paraphernalia such as salt, stones, concoctions, and the like which were central to determining their guilt.

Linked specifically to men and the figure of the sorcerer, then, are the texts used to conjure and expel demons, cast spells, find wealth, or dis-cover secret knowledge. Books of necromancy, unlike other books, were understood to be in and of themselves containers of evil. There was a strong sense that books of necromancy held demons and, indeed, were alive with demons. This idea is not so far removed from the cultural imagination of Eurowestern twentieth century and can still be seen in such popular media as the 1997 television series *Buffy the Vampire Slayer* and Roman Polanski's 1999 film *The Ninth Gate*. As Kieckhefer relates:

> The archbishop recognised that the book was full of incantations, and formulas and signs belonging to the wicked magical arts. So one day…he had fire brought in an earthen vessel, and he set fire to the book. Immediately the air was so darkened that the citizens were afraid and clung to the archbishop. (1998, 5)

The demons which inhabited the book were burned along with it.

When Grandier was formally accused of witchcraft his home was searched and it was at this time that the tract against celibacy, said to be written by him, along with, according to Aubin, Weyer's book *De praestigiis daemonum* were found. The former was burnt with Grandier on 18th August, 1634, while the latter was frowned upon by the Church, particularly after the publication of Bodin's demonology text. Men, masculinity, books and writing were conceptually linked in the early modern period, and therefore necromancy tended to be a crime of men rather than women. Furthermore, it was a crime of the literate, a group to which many clerics belonged. Grandier was by all accounts an intelligent man. His knowledge, his litigation skills, his charisma, youth, and attractiveness, his liaisons with several women in Loudun,[33] and his lack of animosity for Huguenots in many ways fit the bill of the archer sorcerer, a being Institoris and Sprenger write of in *Malleus Maleficarum*.

There are three kinds of sorcerers, according to this work: the archer sorcerer,[34] the sorcerer who enchants weapons to ensure they cannot be wounded,[35] and those carrying books and enchantments for protection or to cure people, particularly those who have borne the brunt of a sorcerer's curse (2006b, 339–349). They contend that the worst of these three groups was the archer sorcerer as his intentions were malicious and his crimes deadly. It was, they comment, the archer sorcerer who had intimate relations with the devil giving over his body and soul to him. He was perceived as the most malignant as he practised *maleficum* (malfeasance) against deity, the Church, and the people. Sorcerers and sorceresses proved to have used magic to harm others received no mercy from the courts.

Grandier, because he was accused of sending demons to obsess and possess the Ursuline nuns, was named an archer sorcerer and so died, like some of his fellow clergy, in the unforgiving flames of Christian politics. And like the possessed nuns, Grandier was hemmed in by ritual: first the standard narrative wherein pacts, three in this instance, thorns, roses, and water, were used to link him with the devil; second, the appeal process whereby Grandier attempted to secure the intervention of the secular court and halt the exorcisms; third, a formal charge was brought against Grandier so that his property was confiscated; fourth, his confinement and examination for the devil's mark (three were found, but Anges said there were five); fifth, he was brought into the presence of possessed nuns in order to exorcise them, whereupon he was attacked by them;[36] sixth, he was put to the *question préparatoire* in order that he confess; seventh, he gave a written confession; eighth, he was put to the *question préalable* concerning accomplices; ninth, he was lead through the streets of Loudun in a wagon stopping first at his church and then the Ursuline convent where he declared his sin and asked for deity's forgiveness; tenth, he was publicly condemned and burned alive; and eleventh, his ashes (or at least those not collected by the crowd) were scattered to the winds. Ritual was the pre-eminent method by which to establish, legitimise, and confirm not only the dominant Catholic cosmology, but the veracity of the actions that the officials took regarding the nuns' possession and Grandier's condemnation and execution. Moreover, the process of the *question* was highly ritualised (Silverman 2001, 91–95) and this further hemmed him in.

The masculinity of the sorcerer, unlike the obliquely feminised possessed priest,[37] is a hyper-masculinity. As hyper-masculine, it is overabundant, excessive, and, significantly, not in the service of the ruling institutions. Hyper-masculinity, because of its excess generally signified through sexuality, also approaches the feminine but this time from a different direction. Within the Christian paradigm, the sorcerer was excessively embodied due to his lust and desire for material joy rather than spiritual joy. He sought power, wealth, and sexual gratification taking what was not his and harming others in the process. According to Bodin, the sorcerer could change his shape and take the form of a wolf, and he gives the example of two men, Michel Verdun and Pierre Burgot, who were charged with sorcery. In this form the sorcerer ate human flesh, usually children, and copulated with she-wolves. These two sorcerers (shepherds from Northern France) were said to have used their powers to kill people (Bodin 2001, 122–123).

The figure of the werewolf is ithyphallic; in other words, understood to have an enormous sexual appetite and genitals to match. Bodin also comments on a sorcerer priest Benoît Bern, who at eighty years of age confessed to having sexual relations "with a demon disguised as a woman" for more than forty years (2001, 132). Bounded by fleshiness brought on by his relationship with the devil, and signalled by his sexual excess, his excessive curiosity and desire for material gain, esoteric knowledge, and the desire for power, the sorcerer was in alliance with the sorceress in their devotion to evil. His excessive desire, represented at times by his lycanthropy, and his arrogance in turning away from deity to the devil marked him as hyper-masculine, and therefore he too was feminised.[38]

Grandier, who was said to have sent the demons that penetrated the nuns' bodies and who seduced Anges in her dreams, evinced a demonic masculinity.[39] Martín del Rio comments that:

> it is clear that the assembly and association of magician with the evil spirit is like that of two brigands. One [magician] wanders openly in a wood while the other [demon] lurks secretly in ambush. The first attracts the attention of a traveller by means of a hiss or a sign, and the second pierces him through with a treacherous arrow. (2000, 73)

With such a conception of the magician, as a brigand, in mind, it is not surprising that so-called good and proper men must deal with those such as sorcerers and werewolves who evince an aberrant masculinity.

Conclusion

As the late Mary Douglas argued four decades ago: "The body is a model which can stand for any bounded system. Its boundaries can represent any boundaries which are threatened or precarious." (1966, 115) I would further contend that it is the female body that is most amenable to this kind of modelling in early modern France (and this continues to be so in many social and cultural locations). The female body was conceptually linked to the inert social body and/or geo-political body. This kind of representation of country and state is visible in the figures of Britannia, blind justice, the Statue of Liberty, or in the figuring of the New World as an indolent female. During the period under examination in this chapter, the rise of the absolute state and mercantile capitalism, religious wars, colonisation of the so-called New World, and repeated and ongoing incidents of the plague, with a clear spike just prior to the possession incident in Loudun, all converge in the ritual of possession-exorcism to speak of and ameliorate anxiety regarding social instability in early modern France.

Extensive social change is generally accompanied by anxiety and anxiety can produce shocking effects demonstrable in the late twentieth and early twenty-first centuries with the blatant use of torture on the racialised bodies of men and women by a country that at one time prided itself on its human rights record. Social anxiety has produced military conflict, increased use of internal force on citizens by the state, attacks on neighbouring countries, penalisation of often marginalised segments of the social body, and so on. I am not, however, attempting to excuse such actions, rather I am attempting to think about them and how gender/sex acts as a primary site by which to express such anxiety. Gender/sex is clearly an unstable category showing marked social and historical shifts, and, being unstable, requires constant shoring up. Myth, ritual, and sign-symbol are particularly efficacious for shoring up unstable categories and so it should be of no surprise that they are central to the attempt to secure and fix the category of gender/sex, and so symbolically stabilise an unstable social body.

Ritual operates on the level of the body, in the domain of the biological and subsequently there is a perceived marked concreteness about it. In the rite of possession-exorcism there are three marked stages, following van Gennep's model: obsession by the demon (separation), possession and exorcism (liminality), and expulsion of the demons, often accompanied with the punishment of an accused person sometimes designated as sorceress or sorcerer (reintegration). In the rite of possession-exorcism there is a ritual play wherein opposition and tension exist between the female-feminine and the male-masculine. Women on one side who represented the female-feminine (for the most part) were penetrated by the demon and in need of rescuing and disciplining. These fallen women brought shame on the community and it was necessary that the men who were the "protectors" (and tormentors) of these women reclaim them since they were "their" women.

The male-masculine exorcists brought their arsenal to the agonistic struggle between deity and the devil. The female had been captured and it was necessary through all means possible to take her back, even if this should mean her death. The agon was between the proper men of god and the hyper-masculine demon with the prize being control over the body of the female. Common to both the hyper-masculine demon and the masculine exorcist was a perception of the female body as abject and inert. In the end the winner will claim the entirety of the social body for in the ritual play the female body acts as a metonymy for the social body at large.

Ritual is performed,[40] and typically performed publicly, particularly when identity is at stake. When, in ritual performance, gender/sex is narrated, enacted and embodied it is given existence in a very concrete and real fashion. The male-masculine exorcists performed a proper masculinity and demonstrated that this kind of masculinity was far superior than that of the hyper-masculine demon and sorcerer. True, the questionable masculinity of Surin made a dent in this armour, but as always the exception proves the rule. Surin as melancholic, a melancholia that brought him to attempt suicide, was penetrated since he was not properly dry and sealed, and therefore not properly masculine. Anges, along with her possessed sisters, performed a proper femininity and demonstrated their bodies to be properly feminine, albeit their spiritual strength was weak, and hence the penetration of their bodies by demons. If they had not been tempted by the devil, represented by the handsome face of Grandier, of whom we are told that a number of the nuns were scandalously enamoured,[41] their faith would have provided the necessary boundary. Like early modern France in the religious wars, their bodies were a field of battle between deity and devil; like early modern France their boundaries were not sealed and so the plague, demonic instead of bubonic, struck; and like early modern France it was necessary that they come under the boot of a master.

But what of women in this ritual play? Were they mere passive vessels for the demon and simple canvases for the art of the exorcist? I would argue against this conceptualisation for the female in her possession spoke with a masculine tongue; the enlarged blackened tongue that cursed both priests and their deity.[42] Possessed she held court, critiqued the current political and social state of affairs, and dazzled princes and cardinals alike. Certeau notes that:

> Face to face with the man. But also face to face with the priest. The possessed do not have, before the exorcists, the reverential docility of the witches of bygone years. They insult them, deride them, strike them, without sparing the bishop....The minutes of one such proceeding speaks of the prioress 'who, being agitated, soon after, she or the Devil through her, gave a slap to said Father Gault. Because of which Father Lanctance, an exorcist, to chastise the devil, delivered five or six hard slaps to the face of said Sister des Anges, who laughed.' (Certeau 1996, 104–105)

It may have been the devil's tongue, but the possessed women used it well against their exorcist tormentors.

Notes

1. The number of those put to death as witches continues to be a point of contention. Recently it has been argued that the number should be in the tens of thousands and not hundreds of thousands. See, for example, Christopher Mackay's introduction to the *Malleus Maleficarum* (2006b, 1) and Jonathan Pearl's introduction to Bodin's *Demon-Mania* (2001).This last text proposes, following Brian Levack (2006), a figure of 4000 executed in France between 1450 and 1700 with the bulk taking place between 1550 and 1650, and a total figure of 60,000 executed across Europe (Bodin 2001, 20). William Monter argues that Levack's numbers are still too high and proposes 40,000 executions. In the instance of France, Monter suggests reducing the total by half, arguing that "the vast majority of these 'French' trials and executions need to be moved inside the western boundary of the pre-1648 Holy Roman Empire..." (2002, 13–14). One

might also note that Barstow's feminist study is not cited in all but one (Pearl) of the above texts. It is as if feminist historians have not weighed in on this subject.

2. Levack's text was originally published in 1987.

3. These two Dominican monks are popularly known as Heinrich Kramer and Jacob or James Sprenger. However, I shall, following current scholarship, adopt the Latinised names of the authors of the *Malleus*.

4. Discursive formation here refers to theological, legal, medical, philosophical writings and artwork concerning demons, demonology, transcripts of possessions and witchcraft trials.

5. Silverman's argument is derived from a close reading of trial transcripts that require the accused to be put to the question (or tortured). She notes that when torture is indicated in the sentencing variant forms of "'pour de sa bouche savoir la vérité' (to know the truth from his mouth)" are used. (2001, 80). She notes that it is the mouth that is signified and further comments that the truth was understood to be drawn from the recesses of the human body and therefore conceptualised as having a marked physical location in the body (2001, 81).

6. The mark of the devil was a little contested proof of witchcraft. Typically marks on the body were tested to see if they would bleed or were devoid of feeling by the insertion of a needle. For example, see Remy 1970, 8–11; . 2006b, 501–507; del Rio 2000, 75; de Lancre 2006, 126–127.

7. Interestingly, the possession of the nuns of Loudun and the death by fire of Grandier would demonstrate a similar pattern of crisis and lull.

8. As Lawrence Brockless and Colin Jones comment, acts of penitence "in Bourg-en-Bress in 1504 were… as many as fourteen daily" while "every head of family in Toulon in 1664 was instructed to kneel outside his front door three times daily and beg God's forgiveness" (1997, 68). The aetiology of the plague was not discovered until 1894 by Alexandre Yersin for whom the bubonic plague bacillus was named (*Yersinia pestis*) (Brockless, *et al.* 1997, 41).

9. Typically customary law was combined with Roman law, but the difficulty was that customary law varied across France and showed a marked divide between Northern and Southern France. The customary law of Provence in the twelfth century contained Roman elements and by 1130 there was a law school founded in the diocese of Die in the Rhône valley. It would not be until the late seventeenth century with the work of Jean Baptiste Colbert, chancellor of King Louis XIV, that the codification of law understood as Royal Ordinances was effected. The Royal Ordinances, however, did not seriously impact core civil law or customary law, although the latter's limits were defined (Stein 1999, 56, 105–106).

10. A *retentum* consisted of additional written instructions regarding the sentencing of the accused. It was generally kept a secret from the accused and the public, who would hear the sentencing, but did not hear these additional instructions (Silverman, L. 2001, 13). Silverman comments that the *question préalable* often had attached *retentums*, while this was less the case for the *question préparatoire*. She argues that this may have been the case in light of the evidentiary nature of the *question préparatoire* (Silverman, L. 2001, 76).

11. See Afua Cooper who describes the *brodequins* and its application in Montreal, Canada (1734) to Marie-Joseph Angélique, an enslaved Portuguese born black woman,

accused of arson. Angélique denied her guilt, but confessed with the application of the *question ordinaire* and *extraordinaire* (2006, 14–19).

12. Lancre was a sixteenth and seventeenth century French magistrate of Bordeaux who was sent by Henry IV to deal with the so-called witchcraft plague of Pays de Labourd (a Basque speaking region in south-west France). Here Lancre tried numerous people for witchcraft, eight priests among them, and burned approximately seventy people, three of these being priests who were executed in Paris. This number is low compared to his estimate that at least one-third of the Basques were witches and should be punished. In 1612 Lancre's *Tableau de l'inconstance des mauvais anges et demons*, which related his activities in Labourd, was published.

13. See also Bruce Lincoln (1989, 142–159) on the subject of inversionary festivals and ritual.

14. Lyndal Roper has argued that the gender/sex ideology that Laqueur proposes in his text tended to be primarily found in medical texts, and not necessarily the means by which early moderns understood their bodies (Roper 1994, 16). Certainly I quite agree that there is much variance in conceptualisations of gender/sex in this period, since at this juncture in time concepts such as the self (individualism), the body, the soul, sexuality, existence, the universe, Christian social formation and deity were shifting and demonstrating a marked instability. But in fairness to Thomas Laqueur part of the intention of his book *Making Sex* is to point to the instability of the category of gender/sex, to historicise it and demonstrate how medical texts in particular registered this instability and the historical shifts. As he comments: "Thus the old model, in which men and women were arrayed according to their degree of metaphysical perfection, their vital heat, along an axis whose telos was male, gave way by the late eighteenth century to a new model of radical dimorphism." (1992, 6) In my reading of Laqueur, I would suggest he is presenting as a primary thread a number of dominant discourses that contributed to the discursive formation of gender/sex in the early modern period. Furthermore, Laqueur does not read these medical texts in isolation. As he argues, "social and political changes are not, in themselves, explanations for the reinterpretation of bodies. The rise of evangelical religion, Enlightenment political theory, the development of new sorts of public spaces in the eighteenth century…the birth of classes single or in combination—none of these things *caused* the making of a new sexed body. Instead, the remaking of the body is itself intrinsic to each of these developments." (1992, 11, emphasis original)

15. As Mary Lindemann comments: "The term [melancholy] relates to black bile; melancholiacs were thought to suffer from an excess of that humor….The most famous work on melancholy, Robert Burton's *Anatomy of Melancholy* published in 1621, displays on the title page of the fourth edition the many visages of the affliction: 'Jealousye', 'Solitarinesse', 'Inamorato', 'Hypochondriacus', 'Superstitious', and 'Maniacus'." (1999, 32) She further comments that although the records regarding women and melancholy and/or madness are woefully incomplete, nonetheless from the material on hand women appear to be in the majority as sufferers of melancholy (1999, 33–35).

16. Weyer goes on to explain that this young woman, or any possessed person for that matter, could not possibly disgorge such objects from her stomach as such large and/or sharp objects could not pass through the oesophagus. Therefore, he contends, as he

does through his entire text, that it is the devil who covertly hides these objects in the mouth of the possessed deceiving the eyes of the spectators (1991, 297).

17. According to P.G. Maxwell-Stuart, there was a magical tradition that employed virginal young boys and male youths as mediums. Members of this group were felt to have the ability to identify witches simply by looking into their eyes (2003, 99).

18. Surin was a Jesuit priest sent to assist in the exorcisms of the nuns. He arrived in Loudun December 1634 after the execution of Grandier. Surin, already oriented toward the mystical and sympathetic to the "weaker" sex, was withdrawn from the proceedings of the exorcism in October 1636, due to his obsession and possible possession by the demons afflicting Jeanne des Anges. In 1637 he returned to the Jesuit infirmary in Bordeaux after exorcising Jeanne des Anges' last demon, at the demon's request, and then met up with her for the last leg of her six month grand tour of France in 1638 which ended at the tomb of Saint François de Salles. Still ill, in 1644 Surin was confined to an asylum for melancholics and would suffer from "madness" for another fifteen years (Goldsmith 2001, 49, 43; Certeau 1996, 201, 212; 1992, 223).

19. Pierre de Lancre comments that: "This makes me believe that after the devotion and good instruction of so many devout religious figures chased the demons and the evil angels from the Indies, Japan, and other places, they were unleashed on Christendom in large numbers. And having found that both the people and the terrain [Pays de Labourd, see note 12] here are well disposed, they have made it their principal abode." (2006, 59)

20. Institoris and Sprenger comment that "…it is not possible for the Devil to inhabit the soul because God alone glides into the mind…" (2006, 296).

21 Demonic obsession is the beginning of possession in narratives of this type and consisted of trembling, sleeplessness, and hallucinations. At this juncture the demon "plagues" his victim without yet possessing him or her.

22. It would appear that the nuns opened themselves to possession through usury and/or, as the nuns claimed, having had commerce with the old woman whom they subsequently took to be a witch. This unfortunate woman was put to the *question* and died as a result. She did not, however, confess to being a witch (Weyer 1991, 305).

23. Martín del Rio speaks of such signs and claims that although the devil does not require such signs to do harm, they signal the presence of devil and malfeasance (2000, 248–253).

24. See Weyer (1991, 286–290, 295–296) who contends that the ejecting of objects from the body is an illusion of the devil, while Institoris and Sprenger (2006b, 70–71) argue that indeed the devil has placed such objects in the body as a sign of a pact.

25. Jean Mignon was the convent's new chaplain and the ordinary confessor of the nuns. He was among the first exorcists of the nuns, and, Aubin contends, was an "intriguer, malicious, and ambitious". Aubin indicates that Mignon knew the haunting was a hoax perpetrated by the younger nuns who were trying to frighten the older nuns as well as the convent students. According to Aubin, Mignon allowed it to continue and indeed helped it along in order to elevate himself (1705, 5).

26. According to Carla Mazzio, an explicit association between the tongue and the penis developed in the sixteenth and seventeenth centuries. She comments that: "As associations between the tongue and the penis became more explicit in the 16th and

17th centuries, so too did the imagined relationship between rhetorical and sexual performance." (1997, 59)

27. Nicolas Remy (1530–1612) comments that the ringing of church bells is "odious and baleful to Demons" (1970, 76).

28. F.D. Salles refers to François de Salles who was a French saint and a supporter of female spirituality.

29. Surin's method of preaching to women was officially condemned in 1639, although this did not stop him from continuing to develop personal and experiential piety over and above doctrinal piety (Goldsmith 2001, 60, 66 n. 18).

30. Throughout Europe the possession-exorcism ritual was predominantly Catholic Christian. Protestant groups did not have an arsenal such as the host, holy water, crucifix, or relics for exorcism, and typically communities would simply pray over the body of the possessed in order to effect an exorcism.

31. There are of course a few female demons, or male-female demons, and certainly the succubus who sexually seduced men. In the case of the latter the assumption was that the demon took a female form, whereas in the case of the former female demons as such were seen to be in the minority. In the Munich handbook of necromancy, for example, eleven demons are listed with only one apparently female, although one male demon was said to have a female face (Kieckhefer 1998, 165–167).

32. The inhalation of large amounts of sulphur dioxide can cause swelling of the lungs and difficulty breathing, aside from a very sore throat and eye irritations. Inhaling pine pitch will cause dizziness and nausea. It is no surprise, then, that during the years of exorcism, prior to Surin's arrival, Anges suffered from a number of respiratory illnesses.

33. Grandier was said to have been involved with some of the young women of Loudun, one of whom had a child. In this characterisation, he fits the figure of the lustful cleric of early modern France, a figure seen in popular plays and stories, and representative of anticlericalism in popular culture. See Peter Burke's *Popular culture in early modern Europe* (1994, 155–156) for a discussion of this figure.

34. Martín del Rio was equally dismayed by the *maleficum* attributed to the male witch called a *sagittarius*. The *sagittarius* was the archer sorcerer from the Institoris and Sprenger text who shot his evil from afar. Rio comments that: "They stick pins in them [images], or melt them in the fire, or break them in pieces, and this makes sure that those people represented by the images waste away or suffer some other kind of death." (2000, 126)

35. Certainly the belief in this kind of sorcerer could explain the large number of blacksmiths accused of witchcraft in Northern France. They were the third largest group of men after shepherds and clerics (Monter 2002, 42).

36. A typical practice of witch accusations and trials was to have the sorceress/sorcerer attempt to remove the spell or demon from the victim.

37. Juan Marin argues that Surin's melancholia was dismissed by his contemporaries as "feminine disturbances" (2007, 65) suggesting that his melancholia, obsession, and possession, close association with women such as Anges, and interest in Teresa of Avila marked him as questionably masculine.

38. As mentioned previously, Lancre comments that the priest who becomes a magician is a succubus, or a female demon who assaults the bodies of men (2006, 475).

39. Nicolas Remy comments that "all female witches maintain that the so-called genital organs of their Demons are so huge and so excessively rigid they cannot be admitted without the greatest of pain. Alexée Drigie ... reported that her Demon's penis, even when only half in erection, was as long as some kitchen utensils which she pointed to as she spoke; and that there were neither testicles nor scrotum attached to it." (1970, 14) The demon, then, is here conceptualised as hyper-masculine since he is both ithyphallic (an exaggerated erect penis) and castrated.

40. I am following Stanley Tambiah (1985) with regard to ritual performance.

41. We read from Anges' autobiography: "At that time the priest [Grandier] I spoke of used demons to excite love in me for him. They would give me desires to see him and to speak with him. Several of our sisters had these same feelings without communicating them to us. On the contrary, we would hide ourselves from one another as much as we could." (Anges in Certeau 1996, 104)

42. Mazzio quotes from Jacques Guillemeau's *Child-Birth* (1612) "the navel must be tyed longer, or shorter, according to the difference of the sexe, allowing more measure to the males: because this length doth make their tongue, and privie members the longer: whereby they may both speake the plainer, and be more serviceable to Ladies...the Gossips commonly say merrily to the Midwife; if it be a boy. *Make him good measure*; but if it be a wench, *Tye it short*" (1997, 59–60)

5 Spectacles of Gender
Performing Masculinities in Ancient Rome and Modern Cinema

...history as used in film is a useful device to speak of the present time while also being a discourse about the past.

Pierre Sorlin in Wyke 1997, 13

Introduction[1]

In this chapter I am interested in thinking about the body as a sign-symbol used to speak about gender/sex. Sign-symbols are useful devices to speak about power, politics, gender/sex, race, or social organisation. The body, as I have hopefully made apparent in the previous chapter, is the pre-eminent sign-symbol by which to speak the codes, rules, values, and organisation of a social body. However, the bodies that typically signify in such a fashion are the bodies of those who operate on the boundaries of the social body either as the *infamia* of the ancient Roman world, the female in a majority of social formations, the racialised body in a racist society, the ethnic body in xenophobic societies or the peasant/worker body in a class-structured social formation. Typically it is the marked body, for example, female, black, peasant, etc., that is most useful as a synecdoche to speak about boundaries, centres and margins, power, and proper and improper social relations. In this chapter, then, my interest circles around the body of the *infamia* of ancient Rome, particularly the figure of gladiator, in order to think about proper and improper Roman masculinity. Having discerned this, I then examine ancient Rome and the simulacrum of the gladiator figure in modern cinema in order to ask how they are deployed to extend and/or counter the discursive formation of masculinity in United States.

The phenomenon of cinema intersects with our culture in interesting and analysable ways. If we approach cinema as a contemporaneous historical representation of both the microcosm (in the sense of regulatory mechanisms of Eurowestern social borders) and the macrocosm (in the sense of symbolic discourse with regard to their imaginary mechanisms), the necessity to understand ritualistic, mythic, and symbolic systems immediately confronts the academic feminist in search of the linguistic structural underpinnings of gender/sex ideology; in other words, the signing of gender/sex.

In this chapter I first examine the phenomenon of the gladiatorial spectacle in ancient Rome, particularly its later manifestation in the several centuries prior to the Christianisation of the Roman state apparatus under Constantine (325 CE). In this examination, I discuss the production of a maleness-masculinity that was symbolised and signalled in these combats making some preliminary comments as to the structural aspects of gender/sex that are encoded in these activities. From here, I then shift to think about the signing of maleness-masculinity in film and the use of historical notions of Rome and Roman to do this. Central to this analysis is the film *Gladiator*, produced in 2000 and directed by Ridley Scott. My intention is to use this film as an exemplar of the signing of maleness-masculinity with regard to its ritualistic (combative), mythic (prowess), and symbolic (the sword as phallus) enunciations. Lastly, in this chapter, I theorise about historicity and the link between the ancient and modern in the Eurowest, and argue that ancient Rome is frequently called to the task of providing a mythic foundation that can fix maleness, masculinity, and men as eternal and immutable. My interest is to better understand how gender/sex is coded in the modern world, and how particular discourses such as history, evolutionary biology, primatology, medicine, and popular culture in the novel, film, and art are central to the discursive formation of gender/sex. This discursive formation, I have argued and continue to argue, is then deployed through myth, ritual, and symbol providing gender/sex with a concreteness and reality that is, as any good Marxist would contend, mystified.

Coding gender/sex in ancient Rome: Masculinity and combat

Typically when examining the ancient Roman amphitheatre one feels compelled to distance oneself from the subject matter by commenting on the appalling activity enacted therein. If indeed I felt that the Eurowest had reached a point of non-barbarity I might feel compelled to express my disgust with the blood, faeces, tragedy, slaughter, and death that took place as part of the spectacle that provided entertainment for the Roman people. However, the moral high ground is not available to me as part of Eurowestern social formations in light of such spectacles as the Gulf War that was bought to us live on television, the invasion of Iraq or the faces of little children from third world[2] locations brought to our television screens for purposes of charity work, but which also make us spectators of the abject pathos of the "other" all the while that we of the first world are secure in our knowledge that all is right and well in our world. And although militarism and world hunger organisations have markedly different intentions, both emerge from and are defined by Eurowestern racial and capitalistic ideologies; hence my locating both in the same sentence. Therefore, I would agree that the ancient Roman world was barbaric, but so too is our world.

The Roman world of the first centuries CE was shifting from the self-identity of a republic to that of an empire, or this is how Rome's history is figured in the current economy of the popular historicising, what I would call mythologising, of ancient Rome. In this play, the figure of Cicero can be juxtaposed with Julius Caesar, the first symbolically representing the republic and the second the Empire. The first is a philosopher and statesman, the second a warrior and tyrant. Further, although there is a certain amount of sympathy for Cicero, at least in the presentation of Roman history, his longing for the past and the time of the Republic is often depicted as a refusal to understand the necessity of progress, which the rise of the Roman Empire is understood to mark. Therefore it is Julius Caesar who commands respect and attention in our histories and stories and not Cicero. The Ides of March that mark the murder of Caesar, immortalised by Shakespeare's "Et tu, Brute", is common knowledge, but Cicero's murder is largely unknown and lacks the same kind of symbolic value. Cicero, then, although known remains unknown; Caesar is an integral part of Eurowestern culture.

In this play between Cicero and Caesar, something else should be apparent. The figure[3] of Cicero is that of a long-robed philosopher and statesman, but one who lacked a sword or breastplate and therefore potentially feminine, and certainly feminised when juxtaposed with Caesar. Cicero was known to "whine", a voice symbolically association with women and children, he was ruled by his "viper-tongued" wife, and doted on his daughter. The figure of Caesar, however, although equally long-robed, was properly masculine being imaged with sword and breastplate. Caesar figures as a general and military man, and therefore carries the masculine. Also notable is the gender/sex play in the figuring of the Empire as masculine since it dominated, ruled and was a military might, whereas the left behind Republic is implicitly feminised in its association with the old, the senile, the feeble and a time past, regardless of its military history.

Now the Roman Empire did not always figure this way in popular imagination of the Eurowest. The Roman Empire at one point, up until the mid-1980s, figured as decadent, demonstrating a downward spiral in its movement from the time of the Republic, which was figured as just, staid, dependable (if a little boring), and in the prime of masculinity with iron-grey bearded men in stately robes, while the Empire and its emperors figured as despotic, hysterical, irrational, self-indulgent, and effeminate, particularly represented by such figures as Nero, Caligula, and, of course, Commodus, characterised in Scott's film. One emperor seen to stand apart from this is Augustus, who as mediator between the Republican past and the Empire of the future embodies both and therefore escapes being marked as despotic.[4]

As the Roman Empire was seen to progress in popular imagination, it climbed to its zenith of power, and along the way emperors are either individually marked as despotic (e.g. Nero, Caligula, Commodus), as tyrannical (e.g. Tiberius, Domitian), stern but just (e.g. Vespasian, Titus, Hadrian) or essentially good (e.g. Augustus, Marcus Aurelius, Constantine). Throughout the years Rome as empire is seen to maintain the smooth operations of its bureaucratic infrastructure, to lesser or greater degrees, until its final death throes in the fifth century CE.

The power that was Rome continues to fascinate both academic and popular imaginations. But in the recent past its figuring has altered. The Roman Republic is no longer romanticised and instead it is the concept of "empire" as a world power that has caught the current postmodern imagination. In the postmodern world, with the demise of the Soviet Union and the domination of the globe by the United States (or equally American multinational corporations), the United States has become *the* power that overshadows all others. Those of us outside it are both fascinated with and yet horrified by its hegemonic power. This power dances before our eyes mesmerising us as we stand transfixed waiting for it to strike: we are enraptured. The similarities between Rome and U.S. hegemony are marked and the current *enrapture* with the Roman Empire is explicable. Roman hegemony in the ancient Mediterranean world operated as a process of civilising (civilisation in the form of taxes, roads and armies—the *pax Romana*) while the civilising of the postmodern world under the deft hand of Eurowestern capitalism (lead by the United States) has taken the form of gross national debt, satellite systems, and automated arsenals— the *pax Americana*. The dialectical play between peace and oppression that one sees in both historical locations can explain the symbolical convergence of the Roman Empire and the American empire—a

convergence that is both consciously cultivated and unconsciously operative in the film *Gladiator* directed by Ridley Scott (who also directed *1492:
Conquest of Paradise* (1992) and *Blade Runner* (1982)) and produced by
Dreamworks⁵ (founded by Steven Spielberg, Jeffrey Katzenberg and David
Geffen). Explicitly, the symbolic convergence between hegemonic powers acts as a deconstructive device with regard to U.S. governance and
politics, but implicitly this symbolic convergence relies on a particular
conceptualisation of masculinity (the romantic hero) and the family
(nuclear) in order to deconstruct U.S. political hegemony. What remains
assumed and uncontested are the hegemonic implications with regard to
the gender/sex ideology and heterosexism deployed in the film. The play
in the film between the contestation of oppression and the enforcement
of oppression is manifested in the sign-symbol of the ancient Roman
arena: a sign-symbol of both power and decadence.

Social world of men in the Roman Empire

The Roman Empire was without a doubt a patriarchal world, patriarchal in
the sense of the power of the *paterfamilias* or the father as ruler of the
family (aspects of this kind of masculine figuring of power are also evinced
in the relations between master/slave, ruler/ruled, and patron/client).
Although some women certainly involved themselves in politics, Livia
Drusilla (58 BCE–29 CE) the spouse of Augustus for example, women
and their sexuality remained under the control of the men of their families. A marked example of this is Augustus' daughter Julia (39 BCE–14 CE)
whom he married off three times, each time in order to cement either a
political or family alliance. After she had provided several male offspring
in line for the title Imperator, all of whom Augustus outlived, he banished
his daughter from Rome for improper sexual behaviour and left her to die
on an island (Hanson 1999, 43). (Julia's mother Scribonia, Augustus' second wife, accompanied her daughter and shared her exile.) Although
connected to the first family of Rome and thereby positioned to access
some power, Julia did not have power over her own life and remained
under the power of her father.⁶

   How was the respectable man figured in the first centuries of the
Roman Empire, and how do gladiators figure as a possible negative or
positive figure that intersects with the dominant masculinity? To get at
these questions it is necessary to investigate the social world of ancient
Rome and the dominant gender/sex ideology that marked women as
female and feminine and men as male and masculine. The production of

femininity and masculinity, and femaleness and maleness is always generated on the level of the social, and then subsequently translated to the
socially defined domains of the biological (femaleness/maleness) and the
metaphysical (femininity/masculinity). This play is part of the semiotics of
gender/sex as outlined in chapter one.

The social world of ancient Rome was hierarchically stratified in terms
of economics, for example, the poor and the wealthy or those who did
not own land and those who did; status, for example, senatorial/eques-
trian/plebeian classes, freeborn/freed-person/slave, non-citizen/citizen,
client/patron, gladiators/soldiers, or actors/writers; and geopolitical location, for example, some peoples of the known world were seen as more
"natural" to subjugation and slavery such as those from Judea or Asia
Minor (Horsley 1998, 36). The stratifications of the Roman social body
operated in accordance with a valuation of humans constructed on the
basis of landownership, status, occupation, social and familial affiliations,
location, and, of course, gender/sex: "Everyone raises a son even if he is
poor, but exposes a daughter even if he is rich." (Posidippus,
11E=Stobaeus, *Flor*.77.7, in Horsley 1998, 36) However, the valuation
of human beings was not simply a one-way process of negating or
marginalising a certain group; instead it operated within a binary system
that hierarchically organised all aspects of the social body through signification, with myth, ritual, and symbol acting as the primary vehicles for
this signification. Therefore the binaries of slave/freeborn, non-citizen/
citizen, or woman/man were social categories that, when played out in
binary logic, explicitly marked value, (–) or (+), providing social and cultural meaning through myth (for example, the rape of the Sabine women),
in ritual (for example, the inversionary aspect of the private Saturnalia
wherein slaves wined and dined, served by their masters), and in sign-
symbol (for example, the *imagines* (ancestor masks) of elite Roman men).

The social world of ancient Rome was vertically structured and complex. However, one begins to see the outline of what was construed as
the elite, and therefore ideal, model of masculinity with the rise of the
Roman Empire, and in the figure of the emperor as the pinnacle power—
seen in his deification, being construed as the saviour and father of his
people, the man who oversaw the military, financial, political, and social
operations of the vast empire, and the one who brought the *pax Romana*.
Linked to, and symbolic of, the power of the Roman Empire and its emperor was the Roman amphitheatre. In the amphitheatre Rome's power
over other peoples and life itself was clearly and clamorously demonstrated.[7] The emperor as the saviour of his people lorded (in reality and
figuratively) over the arena and the lives of the *noxii*, otherwise known as
the walking dead, who entered it. His power, derived from the empire,

manifested itself in the rejection or admission of a plea for clemency, *missio*, made by those condemned to the arena. This power is symbolised in the modern understanding of ancient Roman power with a gesture of thumbs up or thumbs down. However, this gesture of power may not have been a signifier of *missio* or *sine missione* (without clemency) in the ancient arena. In archaeological remains the gladiator is shown holding up the index finger in order to request *missio* (the end of the fight) while in another depiction of defeat, wherein the gladiator exposes his neck for the death blow, two fingers, the index and middle finger (what has since become the sign of Christian blessing) are extended in order to signify *missio*.[8] The gesture has in literature and cinema been altered to one wherein the thumb is either up or down to signify life or death in the representations of the Roman world. Peter Potter argues that the understanding of *sine missione* is unclear, while *missio* was the technical term used for the end of the games. Another term, *stantes missi*, was used to signify "standing release". Ultimately, however, the *munerarius*, the person who offered the combat to the public and who set the rules for the combat and the choice of weapons, was the authority of whom the gladiator requested *missio* (Potter 1999, 307). However, although the *munerarius* was looked to, sitting in the amphitheatre in his box elevated above all others was at times the emperor, the first man of Rome, and it was he who held ultimate power by virtue of this role.

In the amphitheatre the discourse between the emperor (and his elite) and the plebeian masses, in the gesture of *missio*, was a discourse between those who held power and those who were held down by that power. In the arena, challenging the emperor's power, requests for the reduction of taxes and the booing or cheering of leading Roman citizens (both experienced by Cicero) were all forms of political commentary enacted by those who had little or no real power. Equally, the emperor demonstrated his power by acting as *editor* (the individual who funds the *munera*), by granting life or death in the arena, or, as with Caligula, by having spectators thrown into the arena thereby changing their role from one of spectator to one of spectacle. The social and political tension that enveloped the amphitheatre could even spill outside its walls as was witnessed at Pompeii in 59 CE when a riot broke out between the local inhabitants and those from Nunceria who were considered rivals of Pompeii. Although the violence that erupted in Pompeii does not appear to be a rupture between classes of people, plebs and patricians, nonetheless the social tensions experienced in the body-politic were certainly expressed in the violence that ensued. Subsequently, gladiatorial spectacles were banned in Pompeii for ten years. Status was normatively evinced in the arena through violence.

The seating of amphitheatre was hierarchically arranged by class and gender/sex with the "best" seats reserved for the male elite and then tiered according to status location in the social body. Vestal Virgins also had preferred seating, while women in general were to sit in the back rows. Equally the *damnati* of the amphitheatre were tiered with gladiators on the top (while gladiators themselves were classed into hierarchically arranged groups based on experience and expertise[9]); the *bestiarii* or those who fought the beasts next; and then those unfortunates, the *noxii*, who were either exposed to the beasts (often tied to a stake)—the *damnati ad bestias*—or executed during the midday games. Criminals, Donald Kyle relates (1998, 53–54), were brought into the arena either roped or chained around the neck wearing little or no clothing. Their crime and sentencing was proclaimed for the spectators (see discussion further on in this chapter with regard to ideological state apparatuses) whereupon they were either tied to posts or went unarmed to face their deaths. More often than not death by beasts was a common penalty for slaves, foreign enemies or those Romans convicted of some heinous crime (as deemed by Roman law so that, for example, sacrilege to the deities was a heinous crime).

The kinds of death faced were affected by class and gender/sex. Slaves and lower social groups were often thrown to wild animals or simply slaughtered, while captured soldiers faced the sword, either without weapon or with an ineffectual weapon such as a wooden sword. As to the gender/sexing of death, female animals were set upon female *noxii* or sexual punishment such as rape by a bull (a re-enactment of the myth of Pasiphae) was the death designed for the female. These dramatic executions, or as K. M. Coleman (1990) calls them "fatal charades", tended toward the eroticisation of torture and death suggesting that gender/sex ideology was central to the form the spectacle would take (see also Wiedemann 1992, 84–89; Kyle 1998, 54–55).

Although there is always complexity in any social body and ideals are not necessarily what people enact in their day-to-day lives, the ideals of elite identity are often the means by which the majority measure themselves. In the Graeco-Roman world spanning the first three centuries of the Common Era, Roman ideology regarding the ideal human and ideal masculinity or femininity, among other important identity markers, was made manifest in a multitude of ways, but myth, ritual, and sign-symbol were central to the deployment of such ideals. The Roman amphitheatre was an icon of Roman power. Within it was deployed a discourse of power that engaged the binaries of death/life, slave/free, barbarian/citizen, animal/human, and female/male, while the ritual play therein enfleshed these abstractions so that they appeared in concrete form. The amphitheatre was an ideal setting for the discourse of power and a perfect stage on which to symbolically act out the drama of Roman hegemony.

In the vertical construction of Roman power slavery was a normative institution that economically and socially supported and shaped both the Republic and the Empire. Although women's social power ebbed and flowed during these periods, women throughout embodied the perceived natural category of the female and represented the metaphysical category of the feminine. Much feminist work has been done analysing women's power in ancient Rome; work that examines how women operated in socio-religious and philosophical movements,[10] and how the categories of female and feminine were denigrated either as "other" (examples seen in the work of Galen—working within the Hippocratic frame) or the misbegotten male (as found in the natural histories of Aristotle). The potent power of the female (signified by the uterus) and the feminine (signified by the breast) in the Graeco-Roman manifestation of patriarchal relations was placed under the power of the male and the masculine in order to subdue, control, and sign it anew in terms of phallic creation and nurturance. Equally, that which was female/feminine, and not bound and controlled by properly male/masculine men who represented phallic power, signified as wanton, wasteful, excessive, debilitating, childish/petty, emotional, chaotic, and ultimately destructive, whether it was embodied by men, women, slaves, gladiators or emperors. Commodus, an emperor of second century CE Rome (r. 180–192 CE), was depicted in ancient texts, and contemporarily in the film *Gladiator*, as effeminate and thereby marked as a failed man, and inevitably because of this a failed emperor. Dio Cassius Cocceianus, who lived during the reign of Commodus and wrote his *Roman History* during the reign of Severus (r. 193–211 CE), comments that:

> This man [Commodus] was not naturally wicked, but, on the contrary, as guileless as any man that ever lived. His great simplicity, however, together with his cowardice, made him the slave of his companions, and it was through them that he at first, out of ignorance, missed the better life and then was led on into lustful and cruel habits, which soon became second nature. ...[Rather than defeat the Marcomani] he made terms with them; for he hated all exertion and was eager for the comforts of the city. (Dio 1961, 73)

The ideal man in this socio-historical location was fully male and properly masculine; in other words, virile, intelligent, and forceful. He was also from a good family, held political office, embodied a natural authority, was militarily adept, owned and worked his land, and was patron to many and a client to none. All of these characteristics signified the upstanding and proper elite Roman male citizen. As Harriet Flower comments, the *imagines,* or Roman ancestral masks, "defined honour and glory in precise terms, namely the holding of political office coupled with the successful exercise of military command" (1996, 12). According to Dio's commentary on Commodus, then, although Commodus managed to hold public office, he was after all the emperor, he did not manage to successfully exercise military command and therefore was not properly masculine. As Dio comments, Commodus was a coward, weak of character, and avoided military duty, albeit he was enamoured of the figure of the gladiator and sought to emulate it. However, the figure of the gladiator, although conceptually linked to the figure of the soldier, nonetheless evinced a problematic masculinity since he was socially outside the norm, considered a part of the underclass, potentially or figuratively a slave and one who could never consider himself (or herself in the case of a gladiatrix[11]) part of "good" society. As Ian Morris contends, citing Erich Gruen (1990), "posturing and symbolic activity" were more important to the organisation of civic life than is acknowledged (Morris 1992, 53), while Flower argues, following a number of historians, that shame and honour were central to social organisation (1996, 13–14).[12] The gladiator, although esteemed for his fighting prowess, nonetheless was a socially marginalised figure. As Alison Futrell comments, gladiators were considered *infames,* "a category of shame that also included actors, prostitutes, pimps, and *lanistae,*[13] all occupations that involved the submission of the body to the pleasure of others" (2006, 130).

The gladiator was a liminal figure of Roman society, neither really inside nor fully outside.[14] He is a paradoxical figure in that he shifts between the status of slave and free. For example, upon entering a gladiatorial school, gladiators took an oath that consisted of agreeing "to be burned by fire, bound in chains, to be beaten, to die by the sword" (Kyle 1998, 87). (See also chapter three.) The gladiator, regardless of his social status (there were elite, free, and freed persons who took the oath and fought in the arena as gladiators), was ritually bound to the *lanista.* This binding was enacted through an oath and initiation wherein the initiate was struck with a rod, the act of which signified a willingness to submit to the rules of combat (Ville 1981, 246–249 in Potter 1999, 312; Kyle 1998, 87). This ritual binding produced a class of men who were marked as having little to no autonomy much like slaves and the majority of women.[15]

The majority of those who became gladiators in ancient Rome were enslaved prior to entering the arena having already been condemned to it or sold to a gladiatorial school (Kyle 1998, 79–90; Potter 1999, 311–312). Typically slaves were treated as outside or external to social relations and society in general, but clearly slavery, in a slave society, is a central aspect of social organisation. Slavery establishes the structure of the social body, that is, its form and boundaries—constituting the heights and the depths of the society—and its content, that is, citizen, non-citizen, patron and client, free person, freed-person, and slave. In Rome, then, slaves were not simply outside of the social body, but occupied a place both inside and outside of it: inside as the property of those with power and outside as those who did not belong to themselves. Their legal status was one of essential slavery as they did not own their bodies and their bodies were subject to the violence and whim of the arena (Futrell 2006, 131).

The gladiator was enslaved to the arena, but he was able to reclaim his lost self through combat in the arena. If the gladiator could survive five years in the arena, the typical length of time to achieve freedom (Kyle 1998, 105 n. 23), then he was freed. The risk of death to regain control of one's body makes apparent the duality of the gladiator's status—for while in the arena, although he was a slave, there was also the possibility of securing freedom. The gladiator was a marginal figure and although marginalised this marginality shifted to include liminality once the arena was introduced. While in the arena, then, the gladiator was a liminal figure: a slave but potentially free and alive, but also potentially dead. Unlike a typical slave, the gladiator was in a position that allowed him to circumvent the rules of society as long as he submitted to the rules of life and death in the arena.

Masculinity and power

I previously introduced the term *noxii* and defined it as the walking dead. More specifically, this term refers to convicted criminals of the Roman Empire. Another term used for those unlucky persons who participated in the arena, willingly or not, the latter being most often the case, was *damnati* meaning those condemned to the arena. This larger category incorporated not only those who would certainly die in the arena, but those who might also survive (Kyle 1998; Futrell 1997).[16] To be named as either *noxii* or *damnati* was to take on a new identity; an identity removed from that of the human. Like the beasts of the arena, those renamed as *damnati* had no use-value other than to provide entertainment by facing death in the arena. There was no sympathy for these unfortunate persons because, according to the rules of Roman society, they had forfeited it either by acting in a criminal fashion or by resisting the rule of Rome. Furthermore, through the act of having been renamed, these persons were marked as "other" and therefore were regarded as a threat to Rome. In order to maintain and ensure the continuation of the Roman Empire, those who represented a threat were publicly disciplined. This disciplining was ritually performed in order to demarcate and define the boundary between those who adhered to the system and those who challenged it. The arena, as Erik Gunderson argues, functioned as a stage where normative social relations were performed:

> The arena plays an important role in the moralisation and maintenance of Roman social roles and hierarchical relations. Juvenal and Tacitus insist that there is something vital at stake in the arena. ... The arena can thus be taken as an apparatus which not only looks in upon a spectacle, but on which in its organisation and structure reproduces the relations subsisting between observer and observed. The arena thus becomes a mapping of a technology of power whose consequences are felt beyond the arena as a mere festive institution. I would then propose that there is no radical "outside" to the arena and that when a Roman takes up a position in the sand, in the seats, or outside the building à la Juvenal or Tacitus' Messala, the apparatus of the arena serves to structure the truths of these positions. (1996, 115)

Gunderson correctly argues that the arena functioned as an Institutional State Apparatus,[17] but equally because of its punitive nature the arena also functioned as a Repressive State Apparatus; in other words it was a tool used to police and discipline members of the social body and its enemies. Futrell in her text, *Blood in the Arena: the Spectacle of Roman Power* (1997), argues that the arena was directly connected to the imperial power of Rome via its affiliation with the Roman army (1997, 90, 150–151). She points out that:

1. There was a style of amphitheatre that was particular to the military in that it tended to be smaller and less ornamental.
2. Amphitheatres were, in many instances, constructed in close proximity to Roman military camps throughout the Roman provinces.
3. The gladiator was often a martial model for the soldier with regard to armed expertise, bravery and loyalty—even unto death (in particular crises gladiators were recruited into the Roman army).
4. The arena was incorporated into the imperial government as "standard operating equipment of the Roman military from the early years of the Principate, the time when we first see clear Imperial manipulation of the amphitheatrical institution" (1997, 150).

Furthermore, as Futrell notes, in the scenes engraved upon Trajan's column depicting his military triumphs, the amphitheatre looms large in the background symbolically pointing to Roman authority, discipline, and power (see note 7). With the military might of Roman conquest the proper socialisation of the barbaric hordes under the paternalistic hand of the

ultimate *paterfamilias*, the emperor,[18] was possible, while those who re-
sisted the guiding hand of the "father" ended up the *damnati* of the
arena. Power clearly resided in the sign-symbol of the amphitheatre.

The emperor, although all powerful, was also ultimately a liminal figure, much like the gladiator.[19] In this shared liminality each is located on
opposite sides of a power grid. The figure of the emperor, holding
principatus as commander-in-chief, was fully masculine, masculine as
defined by Roman ideals of proper upper-class masculinity: *gravitas/
auctoritas* (seriousness, order, authority), *existimatio* (moral reputation),
and *dignitas* (Coleman 1990, 46, n. 22). These characteristics were central to elite masculinity and required that upper class men at least give the
appearance of engendering them. High born men, nobles, were understood to embody the ideal of masculinity and therefore this masculinity
must be above reproach. Noble honour, founded on such principles as
existimatio, auctoritas, and *dignitas*, must be both physically and socially
impenetrable. Nobility of birth and character typically acted as a shield
that protected the high born, but equally it could come under attack by
one's enemies. The poet Gaius Valerius Catullus of the first century BCE,
for example, opened his infamous "hate" poem that lampoons his enemies Aurelius and Furius with the threat of sodomy and forced fellatio, a
threat that was meant to shame them (in Clarke 2003, 120). As John R.
Clarke comments in his text *Roman Sex 100 BC—AD 250*, the proper
Roman man found "sexual pleasure by inserting his penis into the vagina,
anus, or mouth of a beautiful sex object" but certainly was never himself
penetrated (2003, 87). Jonathan Walters concurs concerning such ideals
of masculinity and argues that men claiming to be properly virile (*virilis*)
were penetrators and never penetrated:

> Roman sexual protocol that defined men as impenetrable penetrators can most
> usefully be seen in the context of a wider conceptual pattern that characterised
> those of high social status as being able to defend the boundaries of their body
> from invasive assaults of all kinds (an exception to this general pattern is the case
> of the Roman soldier). ... A Roman social protocol that employed a rhetoric of
> gender thus appears to be part of a wider cultural pattern whereby social status
> was characterised on the basis of perceived bodily integrity and freedom, or the
> lack of it, from invasion from the outside. (1997, 30)

As the epitome of *virilis*, the emperor was located on the high end of the
power grid, while the figure of the gladiator resided on the low end of the
power grid. The gladiator, branded by slavery and/or criminality, and envisioned as a potential threat to the order associated with the empire (*pax
Romana*) and the emperor (*pater patriae*, father of the fatherland), embodied a deviant masculinity; deviant in that it was an uncontrolled masculinity. His male sexuality was marked by alienness, barbarity, excess,

and wildness. The gladiator was a sign-symbol of chaotic male sexuality or a sexuality that was unguided by reason and therefore akin to female sexuality in its wantonness. Akin to female sexuality in its chaotic nature, gladiatorial masculinity was a hyper-masculinity.

To further complicate the issue of Roman ideal masculinity and the figure of the gladiator was the soldier. The soldier in the ancient Roman world was both a threat and a benefit to the empire. The army, properly controlled, loyal and unified, protected, maintained and extended the Roman Empire. The *pax Romana* was built and enforced by its armies. It was the military might of Rome that made it an empire. The soldier of Rome was to be loyal and brave. He was to endure with fortitude physical hardship, prefer the company of men, and die rather than allow himself to be captured. Prisoners of war who sought to be ransomed were refused, as those who were captured rather than die in battle were seen as deserving of their newly acquired slave status. Livy relates a story that speaks to the Roman military ideal: "you have forfeited your status, lost your civic rights, been made slaves of the Carthaginians. Do you think to return for ransom, to that condition which you forfeited by cowardice and turpitude." (Livy 22.60.14–15 in Kyle 1998, 48) As for soldiers who deserted the army, they were either killed on the spot when apprehended or enslaved to find their death in the mines (*damnati in metallum*) or were put to death in a public forum (in the amphitheatre once it was institutionalised in the early Empire). For example, in 146 BCE Scipio Africanus Minor crucified and beheaded Roman and Latin deserters, while non-Roman deserters and runaway slaves became *damnati ad bestias*. In other instances, such as in 214 BCE, it is recounted that 370 deserters were captured, publicly scourged and then thrown from the Tarpeian Rock (Kyle 1998, 48–49).

Disobedience in soldiers equally resulted in severe discipline. According to Polybius, if a unit of soldiers was considered disobedient, then lots were drawn and one of every ten men marked by lot ('black pebble') was bludgeoned to death by the other "luckier" members of his unit. This process was called *decimatio*. Those who were not killed, but struck the killing blows, were then put on rations of barley, rather than wheat, and forced to encamp outside the safety of the camp wall (Polybius, *Histories* 6.38 in Hopkins 1983, 1). The soldier could be fined, flogged, beaten with a cudgel or killed depending on his infraction. For example, apparently masturbation was an infraction worthy of a beating, while seeking to escape a beating brought further disgrace on oneself and one's family (Polybius, *Histories* 6.19–42 abridged in Lewis and Reinhold 1966, 437–438). The soldier, although a citizen, was one who of necessity was required to act as if his body (and life), like the gladiator, slave or woman, belonged to another: his unit, unit leader (centurion), lieutenant (tribune), general (praetor), emperor and, ulitmately, Rome. Although the soldier was a free man, his oath put him in a similar position to that of a slave during his time of service. Walters comments that: "Viewed from this perspective, the Roman soldier [whose duration of commitment to the army consisted of 20–25 years], symbol of all that is manly in Roman society, is dangerously like the slave, that ever-present unmanly inferior and outsider." (1997, 40) But, unlike the slave, the soldier was understood to be sexually impenetrable even if a sword cleaved his flesh. The wounds of a soldier were honourable, and not a mark of weakness or penetrability.

The gladiator incorporated the masculinity of the soldier, as he too was a warrior, but he had been sold or condemned to the arena. Soldiers, although sworn to give their lives over to Rome, were not marked by *infamia* (lacking in reputation) as was the gladiator.[20] The necessity of soldiers for the continued existence of the Empire and their role as its protectors ensured that their status carried social respect. But the warrior who resided outside of the legitimating institution of the army was a threat to the social order. The (in)famous gladiator Spartacus, said to be a Thracian by birth, and who Appian suggested had been a soldier in an auxiliary unit of the Roman army, is a cogent example of the threat the slave of the arena, the gladiator, represented. The warrior, female or male, who acted on behalf of her/himself or on behalf of another, other than the state, is the "other" that on one hand secures the status of the "same" but equally demonstrates the precariousness of the category of the "same". The gladiator as "other", or the warrior exterior to the institution of the army, threatened the stability of Roman society in a number of ways: he marked the unstable space between the spectators and victims as he was *damnatio* but with a chance of emerging a free man from the hell of the arena; he could penetrate or be penetrated by the sword and therefore was both predator and prey; he was enslaved but could walk away free; he was an unruly masculinity in that he lacked *existimatio*, *auctoritas* and *dignitas*, but equally he was an unruly masculinity momentarily contained by the agonistic ritual enacted in the arena. The gladiator, then, was both hero and defamed in a single breath.

The semiotics of gender and Ancient Rome

The gladiator of the ancient world was a liminal figure on the level of civil-political status, but equally so with regard to gender/sex. He evinced a hyper-masculine sexuality: he was completely and only sexual. In the semiotics of gender I have formulated, there are three linguistic designators: first, "the masculine" which operates in the domain of the metaphysical and is correlated with sign-symbol; second, "men" which operates in the domain of the social and is correlated with myth; and third, "the male" which operates in the domain of the biological and is correlated with ritual (this equally relates to "the feminine", "women", and "the female"). These three linguistic designators are dialectically related so that social relations, which are themselves mythically encoded, for example, Romulus, Remus and the founding of Rome or the rape of the Sabine women, are supported and manifested on the level of the symbolic (metaphysical), for example, masculine as the active principle, feminine as passive principle, and the ritualistic (biological), for example, male as strong, hard, and impenetrable, female as weak, suppliant, and penetrable.

In Roman gender/sex ideology the figure of the gladiator signifies negatively within the social and the metaphysical, two domains of the semiotics of gender. With regard to the metaphysical domain and sign-symbol, the gladiator signifies negatively in terms of the ideal masculine in that he did not display dignity, authority, and morality. As to social domain and myth, the gladiator was as a public performer, one who sold his body, and therefore was considered one of the *infamia*. As Catherine Edwards (1997, 69) points out, "[a]n *infamis* had, as a consequence of moral turpitude, lost the status of a full citizen", if indeed they had the status in the first place.

But this only scratches the surface. The lack of moral turpitude is not simply a mark that resides on the surface. Rather, it emerges from within to manifest itself in the actions of those found to be criminals, who fell prey to or were born into slavery, who were deserters, who acted on stage, or who sold their bodies (or had their bodies sold) for sex. Cicero comments that in general *infamia* can arise from condemnation for an offence, but "true" *infamia* arises from having committed the offence regardless of whether punitive sanctions follow the act (*Leg.* 1.90.50–51 in Edwards 1997, 69). For people such as prostitutes, gladiators, and actors, all of whom were socially stigmatised as aberrant and morbid, to flaunt their bodies, their licentiousness and their moral turpitude in public performance made apparent their inherent *infamia*. Rather than hide their shame, they revelled in their *infamia*, and, like the monstrous, the carnivalesque and the exotic, they were fascinatingly repulsive.

In ancient Rome, most particularly, it was the figure of the gladiator that signified the "sublimely obscene" in his (her) violently raw and savage sexuality. This savage sexuality evoked voyeuristic repulsion for the figure of the gladiator. The gladiator was, to use Julia Kristeva's term, an abjection (1997, 229–247). The gladiator mesmerised the spectators and we can speculate, then, that the gladiator was a fetish—the raging phallus—that mediated power between the mob and the emperor, the abject and the elite, and the dead and the living. As a fetish, the gladiator was a synecdoche that partially represented ideal masculinity directly through its absence.[21] The phallus as a sign-symbol of masculine power must be bound within patriarchal structures. Patriarchal structures ensured rule by elite older men. However, these men must of necessity work within these same rules so that the rules they create equally bind them. Morality is not a free-floating category, but rather is a firmly founded code that ensures the proper maintenance and functioning of the system of ruling relations. This code is one rooted in mythemes, such as the rule of a supreme deity as father, wise leader, stern judge, and firm commander (for example, Jupiter, who combines "politics and law, power and justice" (Dumézil 1996, 179)); in ritual, for example honouring the ancestors, the Manes, or formally opening the season of war (*Equirria*, *Quinquatrus* and *Tubilustrium*[22]); and in sign-symbol, for example the lance, the amphitheatre, the arch topped by a *quadrigae* (four horses abreast pulling a chariot). Within the ruling patriarchal relations of Rome, the gladiator as the untamed warrior, uncontrolled by the centurion or military leader, outside the institution of the army and only under the control of the *lanistae* (managers)—who were equally morally suspect and marked by *infamia*—signalled an aggressive and sexual maleness that operated on the very boundaries of the Roman patriarchal code of masculinity and further threatened to exceed these boundaries (for example, the case of Spartacus).

It is only on the level of the biological (ritual) that the figure of gladiator properly operated within the gender/sex ideology of ancient Rome. The gladiator's emphatic sexuality, his excessive aggressiveness, his licentiousness, and his lewd and threatening display of phallic power was legitimated when it was ritually contained by the instruments of the Empire. This excessive male sexuality, although problematic when performed outside of the amphitheatre, when performed in the arena acted as ritual display of the potential power of masculinity.[23] This power was legitimated when it was harnessed and controlled within the ritual space of the arena where it was performed as spectacle. It was a spectacle of raw male power, but a power secured within and controlled by the elite men of the Roman Empire. It was only these men who had the resources, and who were required by their elite status, to act as *editors* for the games. The gladiators, the animals, and the *noxii*—all—were the *damnati* of the repressive and ideological state apparatus. Some were to die, few were to survive, but all were marked by the twin signs of sex and death controlled by the ruling elite of the Roman Empire.

American late capitalism and the mirroring the Roman Empire

*We reach here the very principle of myth: it transforms history into nature...mythical speech...is not read as motive but as reason...*Roland Barthes (1972, 128)

Historians should try and understand not whether a particular cinematic account of history is true or disinterested, but what the logic of that account may be, asking why it emphasizes this question, that event, rather than others. Maria Wyke (1997, 13)

Having examined how the gladiator figured in the ancient world, his excessive and uncontrolled male sexuality, the question might be: why this figure as the heroic protagonist and namesake of the film *Gladiator* directed by Ridley Scott and produced by Douglas Wick (executive producer Walter Parkes, co-head of Dreamworks)? In order to understand the "why" in terms of the use of the figure of the gladiator, it is necessary to grasp how myth functions. Roland Barthes' work on myth and its symbolic discourse assists in this endeavour.

Drawing upon the work of Ferdinand de Saussure (1966), Barthes argues that myth is a second order semiotic system. Myth draws upon an already established linguistic sign in order to signify its meaning. Myth, Barthes explains, will take a sign such as the black pebble and resignify it. A black pebble is simply that on a linguistic level: a small round smooth object of a particular hue. The already linguistic black pebble comes to myth as a fully composed sign, but at this juncture, in the second order semiotic system, it acts as the signifier (arbitrarily chosen and not for any inherent meaning in "black pebble") whereupon it is joined up with a new signified that is a current socio-historical concept, in this instance the act of judgment, which allows it to sign anew. In the socio-historical frame of ancient Rome the black pebble signalled death (*decimatio*) (Barthes 1972; 1988). Because myth and sign-symbol operate a-historically, in other words, their historicity operates abstractly and has been deracinated, they can be used to signify also in the current socio-historical field. For a smooth transition between socio-historical fields to occur, and for the engagement of the powerful operative of historicity, the signified of the sign-symbol, or its socio-historical concept, needs to be both underscored—it is historical—and also discarded—the actual historical conditions (the conditions of its meaning having emerged in a particular socio-historical period of human activity) are repressed and replaced with a mythic history. This allows myth and sign-symbol to draw signification from the past, but a past that has been reconceptualised, thereby allowing the myth and sign-symbol to signify meaningfully in the present. Therefore, its structural elements are retained (its metaphysical history rather than the history of the social) and brought into the present, while its socio-historical aspects are left to moulder in the past.

From Gore Vidal's *Roman Scandals* released in 1933, to *The Robe* (1953), *Ben-Hur* (1959), *Cleopatra* (1963), and *Spartacus* (1960) to name but a few, the ancient Roman Empire has operated as a potent signifier in the modern Eurowestern imagination and is, in this, both a powerful myth and sign-symbol. Ridley Scott's film *Gladiator* draws upon the power of ancient Rome and some of its figures, the gladiator, the emperor and the soldier in particular, to develop its story. From the first sweeping panoptic view of ancient Rome as a mighty power, at the centre of which is the arena, the power and might of Rome are emphasised. The first mythic concept provided in the film is that of the Roman Empire as definitive of empire (and emperor therein) while the second mythic concept is the figure of the gladiator. In the first mythic concept, Rome as empire, the viewer is presented with a double exposure that encapsulates two images; the first is vivid, the Roman Empire, while the second is osbscured, a faint shadow but still discernable, the American empire. The myth of Rome becomes a vehicle to speak about the myth of the United States. Therefore, the concepts of autocracy, militarism, democracy, power, Rome, and its emperor are all proposed in the film, but in order to challenge them. Emphasised in the film is a history of Rome as a tyrannical power gone wrong during the first centuries of the Common Era represented by the emperor, but equally emphasised is its so-called democratic past otherwise known as the Republic and represented by the Roman Senate.

Marcus Aurelius (r. 161–180), the film's emperor (played by Richard Harris), supposedly because of his desire to re-empower the Roman Senate, is killed by his power hungry and effeminate son Commodus (played by Joaquin Phoenix). The story the audience is presented with is, from the outset, a fictionally constructed history of Rome. For example, Aurelius died in Vindolona (modern Vienna) from the plague in 180 CE and not at the hands of his son as the film presents. But this is beside the point since Rome and its "history" are but ways to think about "empire" as it currently operates in the twentieth century of the Eurowest. In ancient and modern histories, Marcus Aurelius is typically seen to mark the end of the age of "good" emperors (notwithstanding Tiberius, Caligula, or Nero), although it is not with his death but instead at the end of Commodus' reign, that the downward spiral of the power of the Roman Empire is understood to have begun.[24] Certainly the typical historical narrative of the origins, development, and death of Rome in the Eurowest has always been problematic since it is largely shaped by and within a romantic narrative so that a moment of origin, a rise to power, and a fall from grace frame the history of Rome.[25] It is precisely this kind of framing, however, that allows for Rome, its emperors, soldiers and gladiators to be used in twentieth century film to speak about nationalism, American empire, and masculinity.

As I have suggested above, through the act of conceptual double exposure, the image of the United States as empire is faintly seen behind the image of the Roman Empire in the film. Simultaneously, in this play, the figure of the president resides behind the figure of the emperor in order to critique not American power *per se*, but the office of president in our contemporary period. In this use of Rome as mythic foundation of (and critical engagement with) U.S. power, one notes an adherence to the historical structure of the past at the same moment that there is an emptying out of the past's actual content. This is effected by locating the political and juridical origins of the United States (and in this the United States is equally functioning as emblematic of the Eurowest) in ancient Rome, and its institution of "benevolent empire" (positively valued in relation to roads, aqueducts, bureaucratic government, food distribution, law, and so forth), but what is called into question at the same time is the misuse of power by individual emperors (therefore the office of emperor is called into question while leaving the political formation of empire itself intact). For example, in the film the arena is not presented as problematic in and of itself. Rather, the arena only becomes a problem when it is used to seek status, power, and wealth. Therefore, the *lanista*, Proximo (played by Oliver Reed), is presented to the audience as a sympathetic figure while his enslavement of human beings, the *damnati* of the arena,[26] is not critically engaged. The arena, as a site for the enslavement and slaughter of people, and therefore a social and political tool as well as signifying the concept of empire (RSA and ISA), is not the subject of critique in the film. In this first of the mythic narratives of Rome, the signifier, Roman Empire (behind which is the U.S. empire), is linked to the signified, the concept of order as demonstrated by roads, government, food distribution, and protection (army), the combination of which produces the sign of proper rule (implied to be good in and of itself). Therefore what is positively signed in the film is the natural and divine design of absolute rule in order that civilisation continue and progress. The rule of patriarchal hegemony, then, is an aspect of both progress and civilisation since it is the natural order of things. And it is this positive signification of rule that allows the film to negatively signify power in the figure of the emperor, or a single ruler (behind which is American presidential power).

The figures of both emperors in the text of the film, one good (Marcus Aurelius) the other evil (Commodus), and the sub-plot in the story about

the reassertion of oligarchic senatorial power—senatorial power that is in
the film misrepresented as democracy—call into question and critique
the concept of ruler. Commodus in the film, although somewhat masculine in that he can in combative play demonstrate himself to be a good
fighter, is not a soldier. He is presented as having arrived at the front lines
at the end of the conflict with the Germanic tribes in a covered and
armoured wagon. In the wagon he is depicted lying on silken cushions
while speaking with his sister Lucilla (played by Connie Nielsen). Although
armoured in this scene, he is suspect, depicted as he is in decadent
(might I say feminine?) surroundings. In this scene his armour can only
signify his flamboyant play with soldiering and mark him as either a child
or a transvestite since he travels to the war in a covered wagon as a
woman might. In his meeting with Maximus (played by Russell Crowe),
the general who would become the enslaved gladiator, Commodus' jeal-
ousy is visible as he vies with Maximus (who makes no effort) for his
father's approval. Marcus Aurelius is not fooled by his son, and plans on
adopting and bequeathing the Empire to Maximus in order that Maximus
can return power to the Senate and return Rome to its past glory as a
Republic ruled by the Senate. Commodus, learning of this, kills his father,
and then attempts to kill Maximus (who is also aware of Aurelius' plans)
with Maximus' own officers. Maximus does manage to escape, but is
unable to prevent the murder of his wife and son, who are living on his
estate in Spain. Found on the road unconscious, Maximus is enslaved and
becomes a gladiator under the direction of Proximo and is befriended and
healed by the black gladiator, Juba (played by Djimon Jounsou). Maximus, a soldier, is unwilling to fight in the arena, but when his life and the
lives of his men, the group of gladiators for whom he has become leader,
are threatened Maximus fights, and fights well. His ability takes him to
Rome for a final confrontation with Commodus, who is depicted as de-
lighted to take up the role of the gladiator.

Throughout the text of the film, Commodus is constructed as effeminate, sexually perverted, morally corrupt, vain, and vicious.[27] Commodus'
lack of proper masculinity is mirrored by Maximus' fullness of proper
masculinity. Maximus is presented as a disciplined warrior and associated
with a senator, Gracchus (played by Derek Jocobi), who is portrayed as a
true Roman patriarch (*paterfamilias*) intent upon restoring the Republic.
Commodus' sexual deviancy, marked by excess, further proof of his lack
of proper masculinity, is signified by his incestuous desire for his sister, his
questionable fondling of his nephew, and his effeminacy.

The character of Commodus is used in the film to call into question
the office of the emperor since the power of this office can be seen to
corrupt leaders who succumb to furthering their own ambitions. It is not

Roman power or its manifestation that needs challenging, but its corruption by and of individuals. The Roman Empire and its systemic oppression, enslavement, slaughter, and patriarchal and hierarchical systems of governance are presented as inherently and potentially good if properly managed by a group of men, senators, who, in the film, are used to signify democratic rule. Always lurking behind the figure of the emperor is that of the U.S. president, who, through the character of Commodus, is equally called into question.

So who was the Commodus of history? As I have indicated, the actual emperor Commodus was considered to have been a despotic ruler. But his despotism was located not in his lust for his sister or young nephew. Indeed, he had his sister and her daughter banished and then executed for plotting against him. Nevertheless, the Commodus of Roman histories was also depicted as problematic. Dio Cassius condemned him because of his explicit association with gladiators and his fighting in the arena as a paid gladiator or *bestiarius* (a gladiator-like person who fought the beasts of the arena), his supposed use of poison as a means to dispatch his enemies, the many persons he had killed, his egotism, and because he preferred the comforts of the city to the discomforts of campaigning (Dio, 73–121). When, in 193 CE he was strangled to death in his bed, and Pertinax named briefly as emperor thereafter, few grieved the passing of Commodus. Dio Cassius relates:

> In this way was Pertinax declared emperor and Commodus a public enemy, after both the Senate and the populace had joined in shouting many bitter words against the latter. They wanted to drag off his body and tear it limb from limb, as they did do, in fact, with his statues. … For no one called him Commodus or emperor; instead they referred to him as an accursed wretch, and a tyrant, adding in jest such terms as "the gladiator," "the charioteer," "the left-handed,"[28] "the ruptured". (125)

It would seem that Commodus was a questionable enough emperor without having to develop his character toward sexual deviancy. However, for the audience of the film this kind of development clearly signals him as debauched by drawing upon current signing systems that speak of sexual deviancy. And, since the hero Maximus was characterised as a gladiator, the figure that at the time of the Roman Empire signified as sexually and morally questionable, one believed to evince an uncontrolled and problematic male sexuality, and who lacked reputation, morality, authority, and dignity, such signification had to be cut off from the figure of the gladiator and instead was, in the film, impugned to Commodus. This shifting of negative signification was achieved through the contemporary signifiers of sexual deviancy, in this instance implied homosexuality (the viewer is never sure about Commodus' desire with regard to Maximus), pederasty (his sexual interest in his nephew), and incest (his sister). Such sexual predilections, of course, would not necessarily signify as problematic in ancient Rome since sexual relations between men did not come under the same kind of censorship as it does in the modern United States (Williams 1999, 7), and incest was defined by a different set of rules.[29]

How then do we shift to the challenging of the office of emperor through the character of Commodus in the film *Gladiator*? Commodus' lack of masculine virtue, as evinced by his despotic character, [30] suggests to the viewer that the office of emperor was what made the Roman Empire vulnerable. The signifier, the office of emperor, joined with the signified of absolute power located in one person, signified corruption. Transferred to the modern period, the sign of corruption in the figure of the emperor can be used to call into question the hegemonic power of not the United States *per se*, but the figure of the president. Presidents, like the past emperors of Rome, have been signified in such a way that who they were as president is characterised by a word or phrase, for example as weak (e.g. Johnson and Carter), morally deficient (e.g. Nixon), sexually promiscuous (e.g. Clinton), power mongering (e.g. Bush and Bush Jr.), and sometimes not very bright (e.g. Regan and Bush Jr.). The perceived rare good emperor (e.g. Marcus Aurelius) or president (e.g. Kennedy) cannot redeem the office itself.

Transcoding the phallus from sceptre to sword: the reclamation of "real" masculinity

Having looked at how the film *Gladiator* develops a commentary on the current socio-political history of the U.S. government, and its development of masculinity and political power, I now want to think about how an essential masculinity is established, redeemed, and recouped in this film, particularly in light of feminist critiques of masculinism in the late twentieth and early twenty-first centuries.

The figure of Maximus, the hero of the story, is a man's man. He is a "natural" leader of men, a leader who is not invested in power over others, and instead seeks to ensure justice, peace (although he is a soldier) and a fair distribution of wealth. Maximus' estates are in Spain and therefore far from the centre of political corruption (Rome). He is presented as a family man who rushes to his family after the attempt on his life in order to see to their safety but, of course, finds them dead. Throughout the film, the images of his wife and son (who are unnamed) beckoning him to the green lands of Spain emerge at his most trying times, and they are there to greet him upon his death. The death scene emerged in tandem with Maximus having saved the Roman Empire from Commodus, whom he killed in the arena, and thus ensured that it was restored to the Senate. Of course historically this did not occur: Pertinax was named emperor by the army and Senate after Commodus, but was then himself murdered by soldiers eighty-seven days later.

Clearly the film shifts from the "actual" history of Rome with its reassertion of senatorial power, but nonetheless the film uses the historicity of an imaginatively evoked Rome in order to signify an essential, eternal, and real masculinity (male power) that has been currently seen, since 1960 and second wave feminism, to be under attack. This masculinity is founded in the figure of Maximus as soldier, leader of men, as dignified, pious, truthful, uninterested in monetary gain, and the head of a family. All these characteristics are masculinised in that they are developed in relation to his identity as a man in a social context. Therefore, the viewer is presented with a military man whose sense of justice and honesty are delineated in light of his role as a "good" general. He eschews politics as undignified for a soldier, and is presented as an honest and unpretentious man. Maximus rejects the initial flirtatious advances of Lucilla, his old flame and sister to Commodus, in light of his loyalty to his wife. He is a leader of men, but one who is also loyal to his commander, the emperor, and he is brave in that he faces death alongside his men. Even his faithful horse and dog willingly go into battle with him. The Germanic peoples, attacked by him under the orders of his emperor, are never presented as an oppressed and conquered people, soldiering is not presented to the viewer as a questionable occupation, and nor is Maximus' unquestioning obedience to the Roman Empire ever seen as problematic. Justice, honesty, loyalty, and bravery are delineated as free-floating signifiers that have no social context. They are mystified and represent a gender/sex ideology of an idealised patriarchy projected back onto Rome as if masculinity in ancient Rome was the origin of true and real masculinity that has been lost and must be re-found and signified anew in order to restore the natural order of the rule of benevolent men.

In the further development of Maximus as the authentic masculine, mapped out in the romantic narrative, he must be challenged in order to be purified of any possibly taint of fallen masculinity (most particularly any desire for personal political power). The romantic narrative requires that the hero falls from grace, that is, a place of power (or equally emerges from a location outside of grace), that he struggles in his fallen state with tests of strength and intelligence, and in this struggle is then purified of any potential characteristic that might taint his rise to the masculine heroic. The hero, phoenix-like, rises from the ashes and surmounts the insurmountable in his reclamation of good power, which in the film is masculine power developed in relation to the figures of the father, general, and homeless and enslaved gladiator. By having moved away from the centre of power to the margins of society as a gladiator, Maximus is able to represent any or all men who are properly masculine. In *Gladiator*, the hero's journey is a movement from a proper and privileged citizenship to the liminal role of gladiator, where his old identity of Roman general is excised (in one scene Maximus cuts the soldier's tattoo from his arm) in order that he be initiated into his new status, the gladiator. From here the hero is able to challenge the misuse of power and at the same time demonstrate its proper use.

The myth and sign-symbol of the gladiator signify anew in the film *Gladiator*. As mentioned earlier, the history of the myth and sign-symbol of the gladiator (and equally Rome) are retained in the same moment they are jettisoned. Therefore in the signifier the historical aspects of the Roman gladiator are marginalised and played down, while a purified "masculine" (its hyper-masculinity repressed) is retained. In the text of the film the signified linked to the signifier of "gladiator" is "masculinity", under threat in the current socio-historical location, and what is signified in the joining of the figure of the gladiator with threatened masculinity is a real and heroic masculinity; one that will restore the proper order of things (just as Maximus does when he kills Commodus and abolishes the office of emperor) and that will save the world. In other words, what is signified is the establishment of patriarchal American democratic global power that will save the world.

By locating real masculinity in the figure of Maximus and a failed masculinity in that of Commodus, one notes a subtext in the film: the phallus as proper power is true and real masculinity when signified by the sword (warrior) and not the sceptre (king). The role of the warrior is glorified, while the role of the king (president) is rejected, and it is through kingship (presidency and its associated power as a corrupting power) that proper masculinity is transformed into failed masculinity.[31] This, then, is projected from the microcosm (individual) to the macrocosm (society) to reflect power on the level of nation. In the film, if Rome is to reclaim its proper masculinity, then it must eschew the office of emperor, since it had through its corruption introduced the uncontrollable feminine into the mechanisms of the state apparatus. Therefore, read as a statement with regard to the current period related to U.S. power (mid twentieth to early twenty-first centuries), for the "American empire" to reclaim its proper power, it must reclaim and reassert the myth of good and benevolent masculinity located in the sign of the sword properly controlled by "democratic" (oligarchic) rule. The office of the president has weakened the masculine power of the nation by allowing weak and corrupt—feminised—persons to control the office. It must be reclaimed by the "warrior" president, one willing to kill in order to secure the power of the state, as signified more blatantly in such films as *Independence Day* and by such presidents as George W. Bush who landed on *USS Abraham Lincoln* in May 2003 for his "photo op" decked out in a flyer's suit with a large banner behind him declaring "Mission Accomplished".[32]

Dancing with Rome: myth and masculinity

When we draw from the ancient world a ground for the current world we are engaged in the act of mystification. Since Rome is one of the mythic foundations for the Eurowest, it is the ideal setting to establish a (new) ground for a myth of masculinity. The play with the ancient world in modern cinema, although quite fascinating and enjoyable, at times evidences and disseminates ideals held in general by those who make and those who consume the films. Currently there has been a crisis with regard to masculinity and maleness. Under fire from feminisms and called into question by queer theory (maleness), Eurowestern elite (white) masculinity, once the epitome of humanity, runs the risk of becoming what the rest of those "others" are: social, ephemeral, unstable, and relative. In order to rescue and guarantee a fixed, immutable, enduring, and stable masculinity (projected as universal and therefore not impeded by class, race or geography), the ancient world becomes a primary site by which to locate the origins of masculinity as a singular and universal category. But this masculinity is of a particular kind. It is not one polluted by the feminine (Commodus), as the feminine is established, since around 1800 in the Eurowest, as a distinct and separate category—one that is properly distant from it and subordinate (subordinate being benignly signified as "protected"). This masculinity is properly impenetrable and it claims authority, but the authority posited is neither belligerent nor oppressive (Maximus). Instead the authority suggested by the figure of Maximus, is one of *gravitas, auctoritas, existimatio* and *dignitas* all aspects of proper masculinity that operated within the gender/sex code of ancient Rome, but which, in the film, are transformed into "a" or "the" truth of masculinity (heroic), and as such projected as universal transcending both time and space.[33]

Notes

1. This chapter is an altered version of Spectacles of Gender: Enacting the Masculine in Ancient Rome and Modern Cinema. *Religious Studies and Theology*, Special Volume: Materializing Roman Religion. Guest Editor Lisa Hughes, 24 (1) 2005: 75–110.

2. I use "third world" as a phrase that recognises the post WWII cold war politics wherein the so-called democratic first world struggled with the so-called communist second world over countries and lands both wish to pull into their camp called the third world. No hierarchic structure is implied.

3. I use the term figure to denote representation within a semiotic frame. Therefore, for example, the historical Cicero and Caesar are unavailable to us today and all we have are traces of their historical existence. So figure, then, refers to something which is a likeness of and a standing in for, but always removed by several degrees.

4. I intentionally use the term despot in order to underscore the gendering of terms. While a despot is seen as feminine and hysterical in his misuse of power, a tyrant is seen as masculine and coldly rational in his misuse of power. The representation of Commodus in the film *Gladiator* is an excellent example of the figuring of the despot as feminine.

5. Dreamworks has produced such movies as *Deep Impact* in 1998 (saving the father-daughter relationship), *American Beauty* in 1999 (the emasculating and unfaithful wife), *The Legend of Bagger Vance* in 2000 (male bonding across a racial divide demonstrating that masculinity is an essence that transcends race and class), and *Almost Famous* in 2000 (young man coming to responsible—read patriarchal—manhood), all of which are films deeply invested in recouping masculinity within the ideological frame of conservative and nostalgic family values, or a family value that rejects feminist discourses.

6. There were two kinds of marriage *cum manu* and *sine manu*. In the former, marriage with hand, refers to a contract wherein a woman came under the legal authority of her husband, while *sine manu*, without hand, refers to a marriage wherein the woman remained under the authority of her father. In the former she could inherit, or share equally in the inheritance with surviving children, the estate of her husband should he predecease her, while in the latter she remained under the authority of her father and inheriting from his estate. By the first century BCE *sine manu* was the most common form of marriage arrangement. See D'Ambra 2007, 46–91 for a discussion of marriage and the family in Republican and Imperial Rome.

7. Alison Futrell (1997, 73–96) makes an excellent argument for the interrelationship of the imperial cult and the *munera* or gladiatorial games. She notes how amphitheatres throughout the Empire are found in association with military outposts, and how the amphitheatre figures prominently in imperial imagery. For example, Futrell notes that Trajan's column has the amphitheatre as a backdrop to Roman conquest and the maintenance of its frontiers. Furthermore, when Trajan wished to celebrate his Dacian victory in 110 CE, he did so by holding games wherein "ten thousand combatants, many of them Dacian prisoners, faced death" (1997, 91).

8. For examples of these gestures see Wiedemann 1992, 101, figures 12 and 13; and for interpretation of *missio* and *missione sine* see Potter 1999, 306–307.

9. According to Potter (1999, 317–318) by the late first century CE an official ranking of gladiators was developed in order to prevent uneven matches between

them. The lowest rank was that of novice (*novicus*, new arrival at the *ludi*), a recruit (*tiro*, one ready to engage in his/her first combat in the arena), and a veteran (*veteranus*, one who had emerged alive from a first combat). The last category, the veteran, consisted of those who were members of a *palus* which were graded according to four categories of expertise. Aside from ensuring that gladiators were well-matched, which related mostly to putting on a good show rather than compassion for those fighting in the arena, class and grade represented economic value in relation to cost of the games.

10. See for example Blok and Mason 1987; Cameron and Kuhrt 1983; DuBois 1988; Hallett and Skinner 1997; Kraemer 1992; Lefkowitz and Fant 1982; Pomeroy 1975; Rabinowitz and Richlin 1993; Richlin 1992.

11. In this chapter I do not examine the gladiatrix, although I hope to examine this interesting figure at some point in the future. She evinced a problematic femininity in that she was a public figure, something proper women never were, and she was employed in a masculine occupation.

12. Flower comments that the idea of Rome as a shame culture has been challenged by scholars, but she argues that this conceptualisation can be used if honour is given pre-eminence. Rome, then, should be understood as a society where honour is central and linked to this is shame (1996, 13–14, n. 69 & 70).

13. The *Lanistae* were the managers of a troupe of gladiators while the *Lenones* were the keepers of brothels. Both kinds of roles and the people who occupied them were considered morally bankrupt. As Catherine Edwards notes: "Seneca refers to the panderer and the trainer of gladiators as 'the most despised of men'." (Seneca *Ep*, 87.15 in Edwards 1997, 82)

14. Futrell indicates that there were three main sources for those who performed in the arena: slaves, criminals, and free volunteers. Slaves generally came from the Roman wars of conquest in the Republic and early Empire, but in time slaves, who had been born into slavery, began to be trained in the gladiatorial schools. Criminals were condemned to death in the arena or to a gladiatorial school, a lesser punishment, while some Roman elite, such as Commodus, entered the arena of their own accord (2006, 120).

15. The otherfication produced in this ritual binding may well have had a lesser impact on upper class (equestrian or senatorial) men who wished to engage in gladiatorial combat. Those who wished to fight as gladiators made their intention known to a magistrate, whereupon they negotiated a contract in terms of the fee. But they also took the gladiators' oath and engaged in the initiation wherein they agreed to submit to the rules of combat. Always, when boundaries of status or sex are transgressed, one risks social discipline such as death, imprisonment, ostracism, and/or shunning from one's immediate and larger social group. The only time this kind of transgression is tolerated is when it is encapsulated by ritual. Therefore the presence and use of ritual was possibly the reason why elite young men were allowed to perform as gladiators.

16. Kyle's interesting study of death as spectacle in ancient Rome also investigates what happened to the thousands of bodies of animal and human victims of the arena. Kyle suggests that the animals were eaten and the human victims were thrown into the Tiber and provides a good argument for his position (1998, 213–241). However, I am still not convinced. The exotic nature of many of the animals such as elephants, giraffes, leopards, ostrich, lions, rhinoceroses, and so forth suggests to me that their consumption

should have left some sort of record, such as sales of these meats, free banquets that included these exotic foods, or recipes for cooking exotic beasts such as the rhinoceros. Furthermore, the disposal of the arena's human victims in the Tiber is understandable in light of its ritual significance, but it strikes me that in order for this rite of disposal and disrespect to maintain its symbolic potency it could not have been enacted on every victim of the arena—who were slaves to the penalty—but only a select few who were deemed important. There were, of course, potters fields and mass graves for the dumping of the bodies of the poor and possibly the condemned, but considering the large number of human victims of the arena, produced over a relatively short period of time, archaeological remains such as burial or cremation pits should be in evidence and yet none have been found. I suspect there were multiple means for the disposal of the remains, and cremating the remains and then disposing of them in the Tiber may have been one method, but another equally viable method may have been to simply feed the dead to carnivorous animals housed during the period of the games (anything from several weeks to several months). The games did not merely have political and social value, but had economic value. The games were an industry wherein profit was a consideration and therefore feeding living animals with the dead of the arena, human and animal, would keep maintenance costs down.

17. The Institutional State Apparatus (ISA) and Repressive State Apparatus (RSA) are concepts developed by Louis Althusser (1995) following Antonio Gramsci (1971) (see Introduction).

18. The emperor as a social and cultural figure was the commander-in-chief and therefore positioned as the ideal military man; the first citizen and therefore positioned as the ideal statesman; and the *paterfamilias* and therefore positioned as the ideal father (see also Futrell 1997, 147).

19. For a discussion of the association of liminality with kingship see Bruce Lincoln 1991.

20. For a discussion on the social category of *infamia* in ancient Rome see Edwards 1997, 66–95.

21. I would to thank Ken MacKendrick for his assistance toward the development of the gladiator as fetish in his helpful comments on the first draft of this chapter.

22. These were the spring festivals that opened the warlike season related to the Roman agrarian/war deity Mars. The *Equirria* took place February 27th and March 14th and consisted of races on the Campus Martius; the *Quinquatrus* was on March 19th and consisted of the lustration of arms; and the *Tubilustrium,* on March 23rd and May 23rd, consisted of the festival of trumpets. For a discussion of the ritual related to these festivals see Georges Dumézil 1996, 205–245.

23. See also Clarke (2003) for a discussion of ithyphallic representations in Roman art.

24. The Severan dynasty from 193 until 235 CE is seen as the period of time of the weakening of the Roman armies, while 235–284 CE is known as the period of military anarchy wherein the troops acclaimed twenty emperors, there were thirty "pretenders" to the throne, and only one emperor died from natural causes.

25. See Hayden White 1987; 1973 for a discussion of narrative frames wherein historical data are given meaning through the kind of narrative frame employed.

26. In the film Marcus Aurelius is the "good emperor", who frowned upon the *munera* suggesting, of course, a critique of the arena. However, in the film, rather than it proposing a critique of the arena as an institutional state apparatus, what is critiqued is the hedonism that the filmmakers suggest should be attributed to those who attended the games. Such people, it is suggested, lacked gravity and authority. Commodus, then, who in the film is depicted as spending his time viewing and participating in the games, lacks proper masculinity and instead is a feminised (vain) and despotic emperor. Although certainly how one allotted one's time between work and leisure signified in particular ways in ancient Rome, the games in the arena were in fact typically associated with festivals and triumphs and therefore did not signify in the same way that other "idle" pastimes such as the board game *alea* did. See Nicholas Purcell (2004) for a discussion of gaming and dicing in ancient Rome.

27. However, his sister, who is potentially perverted largely through her association with Commodus, is redeemed through her role as protective mother of her son.

28. According to ancient historians, Commodus fought as a left-handed gladiator.

29. There was no *connubium* between children of whole or half blood and therefore any such relationship was one of criminal fornication or *stuprum* (McGinn 1998, 140–143).

30. Although called a tyrant by ancient historians, Commodus' masculinity was represented as problematic in his association with gladiators and his lack of military zeal, which is translated in the text of the film as potential homosexuality especially in relation to Maximus whom Commodus is depicted as desiring.

31. The film *Independence Day* (1996) also uses this masculine myth so that the president in the film is depicted as a warrior first, rational ruler second, caring father third, and understanding husband fourth.

32. Certainly with the recent turn of events in the United States and the election of Barack Obama, Bush Jr. no longer signifies as the "warrior president". Indeed, five years later his "Mission Accomplished" debacle signifies as the president's childish play wherein he pretended not only to win the war, but that he was a true warrior.

33. Dare I say Barack H. Obama?

6 Sign-symbol and Icon
Deconstructing the Eliadean Paradigm

Introduction

This chapter[1] is a departure from the semiotics of gender since the intention here is to think about theorising symbol and icon. Therefore, gender/sex recedes to the background for the time being, and instead this chapter is devoted to thinking about a theory of symbols and icons. Too often in the discipline of religious studies, among others such as anthropology or literary criticism, sign-symbols and icons are presented and analysed as if they are supernatural (outside of human intention) or natural phenomena (belonging to the realm of nature) requiring a distinct and unique theory, one that assumes from the outset the viability of a supernatural or natural origin. There is an expectation that any object marked off as "sacred" is somehow inherently powerful and dangerous.[2] Jonathan Z. Smith, reading Colin Turnbull's text *The Forest People* (1961), comments that such an approach, and one taken by Turnbull with regard to his expectation concerning the Congolese Mbuti's most "sacred object" the *molimo*, "plays the role of the 'superstitious', 'primitive' European who has apparently read too many books in the religious studies field and thinks of sacrality as something inherent, as something fraught with ambivalent danger" (2004, 112).

One of the intentions of this chapter, then, is to deconstruct this dominant theory of symbol found in the work of Mircea Eliade (and popularised by Joseph Campbell).[3] This deconstruction reflects a desire on my part to theorise sign-symbols and should not be read as simply one more critique of Mircea Eliade. However, since it was Eliade who primarily established and legitimised a conceptualisation of religion as a divide and movement between the sacred and profane, and symbols as necessarily operating within this kind of frame, he has shaped how symbol and icon are theorised in the study of religion, as well as in other disciplinary fields. This chapter seeks to demonstrate several problems with his methodology, and to subsequently present and argue for a semiotic theory of symbol[4] or what I have called the sign-symbol throughout this text. Jumping off from there, the chapter then moves on to theorise about the icon, which is a rather interesting variation of the symbol. Ultimately, I argue that it is a third order semiotic and use Gaṇeśa as a case study of icons.

There have been numerous treatises that engage or theorise symbol. Some of the better-known twentieth century scholars have been Susanne Langer (1942), Ernst Cassirer (1957), Mircea Eliade (1961), Paul Ricoeur (1969), Victor Turner (1967), Mary Douglas (1970), Clifford Geertz (1973), and Jacques Waardenburg (1980). Shifting to a semiotic reading of the symbol, Roman Jakobson (1962), Ferdinand de Saussure (1966), Claude Lévi-Strauss (1967), Roland Barthes (1968; 1972), Umberto Eco (1984), and A. J. Greimas (1987) are examples of the more noted twentieth century scholars emerging from the French school of semiotics, with a touch of the American school under the influence of Charles Sanders Peirce.[5]

Both groups engage symbol differently. The first group, of which Eliade is a member, tends to see two kinds of symbols, natural and linguistic, and identify, more often than not, religious symbols as natural symbols.[6] This group engages the symbol via hermeneutics, which seeks to plumb the depths of a symbol to find its "truth". In this kind of development a supposed deep content (meaning) is sought while form (the container) is simply understood as a vehicle for that content (much like the body is for the soul in much of monotheistic theology). For example, one of Eliade's central concepts is the *axis mundi* or "the centre of the world system". In his text *The Sacred and the Profane* he comments that: "The cry of the Kwakiutl neophyte, 'I am at the Centre of the World!' at once reveals one of the deepest meanings of sacred space." (Eliade 1967, 36) Rather than engage space as socially, politically, or ideologically determined, or symbol as coding said space in such a manner (e.g. a national flag), or reading symbol as contextually and linguistically determined, Eliade denotes the space in relation to the symbol (e.g. tree, pillar, stone, etc.) as "sacred". Arriving and stopping at the "sacred" as part of analysis forecloses, as I will discuss below, any possibility of explanation.

The second group of theorists, who operate in the field of semiotics, do not create such a division and engage symbol as a sign (Greek *sêma* or *sêmeion*). Influenced by Ferdinand de Saussure's theory of linguistics, symbols are linguistic signs that emerge from social systems and signify, shape, model, and communicate these systems. Semiotics does not rely on hermeneutics although certainly semantics are of interest. Meaning is significant, but getting at the meaning requires that one understands the efficacy of a sign-symbol:

...semiotics is the study of words felt as words, not simple substitutes for the objects named. Language is perceived in itself, not as a transparent, transitive mediator of a different thing. A semiotics of poetry pursues the transformation of *verbal* material, it finds the *phonic* sources of semantic features. Semiotics in general is the study of signs as signifiers (not content, not signifieds). The semiotic mind asks not what signs mean but how they mean. Semiotics is a forced march into the form of meaning, a form felt to constrain one perhaps totally. (Blonsky 1985, xxvii)

In the first section of this chapter, then, I focus on symbols conceived of as natural and then linked by Eliade to the logic of a sacred/profane divide understood via a hermeneutic methodology in order to demonstrate the problems of the continued use of Eliade's theory of symbol. In the final section I offer a brief exposé of the reading of sign-symbols within a semiotic frame in order to provide an alternate method for engaging the symbol. Although a semiotic analysis of symbols is certainly more difficult, complex, and at times seemingly convoluted, an analysis of how symbols are constructed and deployed within social bodies need not be forestalled and foreclosed by something called the sacred.

Mircea Eliade and symbolism

Jonathan Z. Smith, who, like Eliade, is engaged in the comparative study of religions, critiques Eliade's work on a number of levels. Two of these critiques are central to my current engagement with Eliade's theory of symbol. At the outset the environmental field that contains the symbol in Eliade's work is the oppositional pair that together allow for a notion of the "natural symbol" to operate, the sacred and the profane. Smith argues that Eliade invests the sacred with ontology, or a being beyond the word itself. In this kind of formulation, the sacred, and the symbol therein, is dealt with as something *in* and a *part of* existence. In his framing then, the sacred, as being in existence, acts as the locus of original and authentic creation. It is this locus of authenticity, Eliade argues, that humanity seeks to make visible with its various myths, symbols, and ritual. Smith has concurred with this reading of Eliade, commenting that "Eliade appears to suggest that the Sacred is the Real, understood as Being, power, creativity, as opposed to the profane, which is unreal, 'absolute non-Being', or chaotic" (Smith 1978, 91). In Eliade's logic, the sacred is understood to manifest itself (itself having being in existence)—which of course suggests that it is either a conscious power that seeks to enter into human social and historical activity (much as the deity of the *Tanakh*), or that there is some guiding force behind this thing called the sacred (much as the central deity in Christianity). The implication is the removal of the symbol from social activity, be that activity historical, cultural, economic, or political. It would seem that symbols—true symbols—are not of human devising. Rather, true symbols, in other words religious symbols otherwise known as natural symbols, speak of, and point toward, a reality that sometimes can be glimpsed, but always remains outside of human activity since it is from that otherworldly place. Following Smith then:

> Eliade revalues these categories [space and time] by relating them to the manifestation of and participation in transhuman Reality. Both space and time are, for Eliade, modes of irruption and repetition. … Both space and time are experienced by religious man as "non-homogeneous". Hence both reflect the experience of a breakthrough of the normal ontological levels, and this break allows the possibility of participation in Reality—of reifying or sacralizing the profane. (1978, 94)

In his discussion of symbol Eliade establishes a natural division between two modes of existence or two kinds of environment, the sacred and the profane. It is the former which includes what he has termed sacred and/or religious symbols:

> The abyss that divides the two modalities of experience—sacred and profane—will be apparent when we come to describe sacred space, and the ritual building of the human habitation, or the varieties of the religious experience of time, or the relations of religious man to nature and the world of tools, or the consecration of the human life, the sacrality with which man's vital functions (food, sex, work, and so on) can be charged. … [The] sacred and profane are two modes of being in the world, two existential situations assumed by man in the course of his history. (Eliade 1967, 14, emphasis original)

In Eliade's work, then, the symbol is not first and foremost a semiotic device that is linked to language. Instead, symbols are entities (living and non-living) in and of themselves, natural or human-made objects (e.g. a stone or a cross), or concepts, and infused with an otherworldly or transcendental power. These objects then become the means by which the sacred enters the profane (as "modes of being"). These objects are then treated by Eliade as devices that allow for an interchange between his two theorised domains, the sacred and the profane. Symbols are not semiotic devices that model, shape, and allow people to express their systems of belief and practice. Rather, they are objects that make apparent the universal and *sui generis* (McCutcheon 1997) nature of "religion", otherwise known as the sacred. In Eliade's theory it is the sacred and profane divide that allows the manifestation of "religion", and symbols therein, rather than religious systems that propose in their representation of existence a sacred and profane divide. According to Eliade, then:

Man becomes aware of the sacred because it manifests itself, shows itself, as something wholly different from the profane. To designate the *act of manifesta-tion* of the sacred, we have proposed the term *hierophany*. It is a fitting term, because it does not imply anything further; it expresses no more than is implicit in its etymological content, that is that *something sacred shows itself to us*. ... In each case we are confronted by the same mysterious act—e.g. the manifestation of something of a wholly different order, a reality that does not belong to our world, in objects that are an integral part of our natural "profane" world. (1967, 11, emphasis original)

In Eliade's work the symbol—be it a centre, world tree, knot, shell, fire, water, word, or stone—always is explained as the sacred, although the adjectives used to describe its sacredness can and do vary. The sacred stone or tree is a natural object, to which an unnatural power has affixed itself. This power radiates through the object pointing toward, and in that moment proving the reality of, the sacred realm. It is at the door of the sacred that the meaning of the symbol stops. For instance, Eliade, provid-ing examples from a variety of social and historical locations (China, India, the Middle East, Australia, and Africa), suggests that it is the symbolism of "the centre" that is manifested in the cosmic mountain, cosmic tree, and the pole that would be a tree. This symbolism of the centre he first associates with the division of space between that which is ordered and that which is chaotic. Within the ordered space, at its centre, is a space that is defined or marked as sacred. He argues that:

It is there, in that Center, that the sacred manifests itself in its totality, either in the form of elementary hierophanies—as it does among the 'primitives' (in totemic centers, for example, the caves where the *tchuringas* are buried, etc.)—or else in the more evolved form of the direct epiphanies of the gods, as in the tradi-tional civilizations. (Eliade 1961, 39)

Here deity and human, or at least the spaces they occupy, are thought to meet marking this central meeting space as sacred. It is its sacredness that marks this space as the centre, and it is the centredness of the space that marks it as sacred. Here the analysis of the symbol ends. There certainly is some delineation of the evolution of the symbolism of the centre from ancient to so-called primitive to traditional to modern societ-ies, developed in terms of progress and linearity, but in large measure the symbolism of the centre can never be read beyond its signing as sacred.[7] This is the final and ultimate significance of the symbol.

One notes, then, that Eliade's logic of the sacred/profane divide limits and determines the meaning and function of symbols in systems of belief and practice. They are not semiotic devices that shape and express meaning. Rather, they are windows that provide either a shining through of the sacred (symbol) or are things in which the sacred manifests itself (icon).

For Eliade, symbols may well be words, like *logos* or "sacred" for example, but as words they are expressing a deeper reality, one that requires a hermeneutical sounding in order to get at the "otherworldly" referent of the symbol. The linguistic properties and logic of the symbol are an encumbrance that one must break through:

> Symbolic thinking is not the exclusive privilege of the child, of the poet or of the unbalanced mind: it is consubstantial with human existence; *it comes before language and discursive reason*. The symbol reveals certain aspects of reality— *the deepest aspects*—which defy any other means of knowledge. Images, symbols and myths are not irresponsible creations of the psyche; they respond to a need and fulfil a function, that of bringing to light the *most hidden* modalities of being. Consequently, the study of them enables us to reach a better understanding of man—of man "as he is", before he has come to terms with the conditions of History. (Eliade 1961, 12, my emphasis)

In terms of methodological problems, Smith argues that Eliade's mode or style of comparison is morphological. This mode of comparison operates within "a fixed order of permanent structures" (Smith, 1978, 256) so that, although there may be many manifestations, these manifestations all reflect a limited number of archetypes that remain fixed and permanent. Furthermore, these manifestations are defined by Eliade on a continuum from the simple to the complex, simple being assigned to "primitive" systems of belief and practice (e.g. Australian Aboriginal), and complex to more advanced systems of belief and practice (e.g. Christianity). Aside from the ethnocentric and colonialist implications here, the problem with operating in terms of a closed system is, as Smith argues, that it ignores both social and historical vagaries and differences. Thus, for example, a temple in ancient Uruk and a mosque in modern Cairo are conceived in exactly the same way, as sacred space. The social, cultural, and historical differences that separate these two are seen as irrelevant for analysing the phenomena of the temple and the mosque. Equally, the social differences marked by time, culture, and geography are also seen to be irrelevant. These differences, as Smith has pointed out, are neutralised in Eliade's comparative examination of religious phenomena by treating them as superficial differences that operate on the level of shifting kinds of manifestation that all point to a limited and fixed number of archetypes. Only the archetypes point toward the truth that resides beneath them:

> Comparison, while global in scope, nevertheless remains strictly limited in procedure. One may compare within the system or between the pattern and a particular manifestation. Comparisons within the [morphological] system do not take time or history into account; comparisons between the pattern and manifes-

tation are comparisons as to the degree of manifestation and its intelligibility and do not take historical, linear development into account. (Smith, 1978, 259)

Smith's even-handed critique of Eliade makes apparent some of the more salient problems when thinking about symbols within an Eliadean paradigm. Eliade's project—to return modern humanity to its proper place in creation through authentic religious experience—shapes his history and comparison of religions, and religious phenomena.

In Eliade's methodological treatment of the symbol, the intention is to ferret out the deep meaning of the symbol. In order to theorise the sacred and those phenomena affiliated with it from the place of the profane, hermeneutics becomes the quintessential method of choice. He states:

> As we were saying, he [the historian of religion] too often forgets that he is concerned with archaic and integral human behavior, and that his business ought not therefore to be reduced to *recording the historical manifestations of that behavior*; he ought also to be trying to gain deeper insight into its *meaning* and its articulation. (Eliade 1961, 33, emphasis original)

The process of reading the deep meaning of the symbol requires a hermeneutical reading of the symbol. The hermeneutical endeavour seeks to *reveal* the truth. It is "[t]he art or science of interpretation, esp. of Scripture, commonly distinguished from *exegesis* or practice exposition" (Oxford English Dictionary). The hermeneut goes into the symbol seeking to find its mysterious otherness in an effort to capture the mystery. In terms of Eliade's hermeneutical endeavour, the truth of the symbol is seen to have originated exterior to the social and historical conditions of human societies, but subsequently manifests itself within these societies via the symbol. The game, then, is to ascertain what that truth is, and as this truth is *the* truth it is temporally and spatially universal. Matei Calinescu (1988) remarks:

> Eliade's fantastic of interpretation persuades the reader to look at images, symbols, metaphors, stories, or inventions as possible bearers of epiphanies or remembrances. By means of these devices the imagination breaks out of the amnesia in which modernity has trapped it to recall and revive lost worlds of meaning. The larger message of Eliade's fantastic prose is, in brief, that interpretation remains our best hope for an anamnesis of mythic truth. (quoted in Allen 2001, 215)

What Eliade seeks is the originary and archaic truth of the symbol that is subsequently altered by human sociality and history. This is precisely why the symbolism of the centre can be a cosmic tree, a pole that would be a tree, a mountain, or a temple. Each of these is seen to link with the heavens above, as the place of transcendent deity, and/or the ground beneath it, as the place of the immanent deity. It is this (gendered) otherness, the numinous, that is the truth which is sought. Eliade opens *The Sacred and the Profane* with reference to Rudolf Otto's *The Idea of the Holy* and, following him, states that "[t]he numinous presents itself as something 'wholly other' (*ganz andere*), something basically and totally different" (Eliade 1967, 9–10). It is this that Eliade seeks to reveal in the symbol via the hermeneutical method. The truth of the symbol does not reside in the social and historical character of the symbol for this is simply the human creature's action, thought, or word seeking to express the truth. Since the human creature is social and historical the appearance of the truth is concealed beneath the mundane (read profane). But the truth can be found, suggests Eliade, by comparing different manifestations of a symbol in order to arrive at its originary and pure moment or its initial movement out from the "numinous" or "sacred" that is the centre. For this truth to be realised, then, the social and historical accretions of the symbol must be scraped away.

In Eliade's hermeneutics the centre is the most significant and intentional place where the sacred can break through. But why is it specifically the centre that brings one closer to the numinous or the sacred? He states:

> It [the centre] calls attention to something in the human condition that we may call the *nostalgia for Paradise*. By this we mean the desire to *find oneself always and without effort* in the Center of the World, at the heart of reality; and by a short-cut and in a natural manner to transcend the human condition, and to recover the divine condition—as a Christian would say, the condition before the Fall. (Eliade 1961, 55, emphasis original)

For Eliade, symbols are not semiotic devices, for that would make them completely profane. The symbol shares in both the sacred and the profane: it is profane in that it initially belongs to the profane world (a tree, a rock, a mountain), but when the symbol signifies, as a centre for example, it shows its sacredness. The play between the form and the content that Eliade conjectures upon is not about emptiness and presence, nor is it about the polysemy of words (see further below). Rather, form and content mirror the profane and sacred divide, and are thus used to assert the truth of this divide. The form is profane, the content is sacred, or the form is the social and historical manifestation, while the content is the archetype.

In Eliade's work there is no clear intention to analyse the symbol. The intention, as I see it, is to demonstrate the truth of the logic of the sacred and profane divide, and hermeneutically to plumb the depths of human expression to find traces of the divine (see Douglas Allen 2001, 211 for a similar understanding of Eliade). In his development of the symbol, then, Eliade leaves us at the door of the sacred with little or no understanding of how symbols sign, or even clearly what they sign other than sacredness. It would appear that in Eliade's work, the logic of the sacred and profane divide is already a code that seeks to establish a model of existence, rather than a theory of how systems of belief and practice use symbols to code and decode existence. Furthermore, the sacred, which stands as the central explanatory category of his theory of symbols, is used to gather up and contain all symbols even though it too is a symbol. Therefore what we see in Eliade's theory is the use of one symbol to explain all symbols. Logically this is like using an apple to explain the category of fruit. An apple is an example of fruit but in no way can it be used to explain the category or even exemplify all other fruit in that category such as a blueberry, a banana or even a pineapple. The sacred, like the apple, belongs to a category, that is, symbols and fruit respectively, and does not explain it. His hermeneutic approach, then, operating within this logic, is little more than belief put forward as explanation.

The sign-symbol

If, unlike Eliade, one approaches the symbol as a semiotic device, the potential for a thorough-going analysis increases. Working within semiotics, signs are understood to shape, signify, and communicate human existence, an existence that is social and one that is historically contextualised. Operating thusly one is able to explicate how the sign-symbol functions, how its meanings shift, and how it operates within human social systems. The semiotic engagement with symbols brings symbols within the human realm of activity. Symbol, then, is a linguistic device by which humans model, signify, and communicate existence. As Thomas Sebeok, an American semiotician, states: "I have also argued that the derivation of language out of any animal communication system is an exercise in total futility, because language did not evolve to subserve humanity's communicative exigencies. It evolved … as an exceedingly sophisticated modelling device … in *Homo habilis*." (1994, 114) The significant idea here is that language (the verbal signs of semiotics as differentiated from the non-verbal signs) is a modelling device or a way by which humans corporately and individually code and decode existence. Language, and symbols therein, is understood first and foremost to model human perception of existence.

Within a semiotic frame, the sign-symbol is a figure, a shape, an image, an object, a sound, a word, a phrase, or a gesture that models, shapes, and communicates meaning. However, a sign-symbol is more than a word. Sign-symbols communicate beyond the primary order of meaning that words operate within. Following Roland Barthes[8] (1972, 109–159), sign-symbols operate as a second order semiological system so that sign-symbols begin as fully fledged signs (words) in order to sign secondarily as sign-symbols. Barthes, drawing upon Saussure's tripartite typology of the sign (signifier, signified, sign), theorises a second order semiotic wherein the fully fledged sign—for example a (red) rose—is the signifier of the sign-symbol. The signifier is linked with a new signified (concept) that produces a newly formed sign, love. Furthermore, the components of the sign-symbol, the signifier and signified, are not read as sequentially moving from left to right. Rather, it is a simultaneous process where both the signifier and signified together produce the sign. This kind of engagement with sign-symbol seen in Figure 6.1 below makes apparent how the sign-symbol is brought into existence in and through language.

One comes in contact with sign-symbols in every aspect of life and within the interpretive frame of systems of belief and practice. Sign-symbols, similar to other figures of speech such as metaphor, metonymy, and synecdoche, speak beyond their primary signing. For example, a cross within a Christian frame is the signifier and points one toward not just a cross as a cross, but to a signified (the concept) that carries the idea of a crucified deity. Within the meaning frame of crucified deity the concept of deity dying for the sins of humanity is evoked, and deity dying for the sins of humanity points to the salvation of humanity— or does so to those who choose to believe. The signifier (the cross), and linked with it the signified (the crucified deity), produce the sign (redemption for humanity). A cross within the Christian frame, then, can be a sign-symbol of social power (e.g. Constantine), of perceived metaphysical power (triumph of the Christian deity), and of Christianity itself—in which case

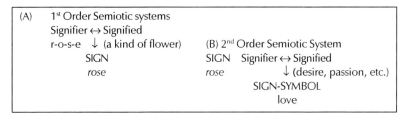

Figure 6.1 Sign-symbol

it is a sign-symbol that represents a whole and therefore acts like a synecdoche.

The cross became the sign-symbol upon which Christianity elaborated its understanding of the past, present, and future, its worldview and the world's end. But this sign-symbol, like any other, is never fixed or static. Because it is produced or augmented and made meaningful within a particular social and historical context, the sign-symbol does change. For example, in the mediaeval period the cross was seen to represent the journey of Christ, his movement from the world in-between to the world below, and to the world above. The cross, the signifier, was linked to the concept of this mystical journey, the signified, and signed the journey Jesus/Christ was thought to have taken—a journey all Christians take upon death. Yet, in the ancient world of the early Christianities this kind of signification was absent since the cross was a Roman tool of shame and punishment, and those who suffered were criminals or the oppressed. Here the cross affiliated with Jesus signified oppressed humanity and a promise of its vindication, however that was manifested.[9] Although this discussion does not do full justice to the sign of the cross throughout Christian histories, it does make apparent how sign-symbols change to reflect even the same system of belief and practice as it develops over time.

Sign-symbols, then, can change over time so that meaning can be added or meaning can be taken away. In another example, the swastika demonstrates the historicity of sign-symbols. The swastika is a geometric sign found in the ancient world (primarily India, but also Greece and around the Mediterranean) and was used for the decoration of pottery, and may have included in its semantic intentions the notion of the four intersecting corners of the world (for multiple significations of the Swastika see Aigner 2002; Srivastava 1998; Quinn 1994; Wilson 1986). At the end of the nineteenth century it was adopted by Rudyard Kipling, then working as a journalist in India, for its connotations of good luck and auspicious beginnings. In the twentieth century this figure was picked up and used by the Nazi regime, which drew upon the ancientness of this geometric figure in order to signify the continuity of this regime with the ancient (Aryan) world. The ancientness of the sign was linked to the German *Volk*, now collected under the sign-symbol of the swastika, to connote something new: the enduring roots of the German people. The perceived archaic root of the swastika was used in order to signify the continuity from the ancient world to the modern world of Nazi Germany. This continuity from the ancient to the modern was called upon to further signify racial purity. The locating of roots in the ancient world was the founding of an originary moment and, as first and undiluted, this moment signifies purity. Furthermore, continuity suggested a continuous *unbroken* line from this originary moment to the present of the German *Volk* and unbroken again brings within its signification purity—the Germans were a racially pure people like the originary ancient people. One notes that in 1935 Kipling, in reaction to its use by the Nazis, removed his trademark swastika from his book bindings saying that it had been "defiled beyond redemption" (quoted in Gilmour, 2003, 304) and after WWII the swastika, linked to Nazism, signified evil, while its appropriation by neo-Nazi groups is used to signify their link to, and belief in, Nazi ideology. Indeed all links of the swastika to the ancient Aryan world and good fortune have been subsumed, at least in the Eurowest, by this indelible association with Nazism and all its connotations.[10] Nevertheless, if one considers the movement and the multiple meanings encountered in the sign-symbol of the swastika and then asks how it signifies, rather than what it means, one finds some interesting answers.

I have briefly argued that symbolism is a second order semiotic and that language is the ground upon which the house of sign-symbol is built. I have referred to the signifier and indicated that in a simultaneous movement the signifier and signified are linked in order to produce the sign-symbol. As mentioned, this kind of logic brings the investigator to language rather than the closed door of the sacred. From here, one can ask how the sign-symbol develops such an extensive repertoire so that the swastika as sign-symbol uses surplus of meaning (excess semantic content) to signify while simultaneously it is both form and content and therefore is multi-dimensional. In the most general sense, the sign-symbol has a surplus of signification in that there is always more meaning than first encountered. The cross is not just two pieces of wood affixed to each other. This is called the polysemy of the sign-symbol that allows for the multiplicity of meanings associated with it: each meaning evokes a subsequent meaning that can then lead to another meaning. This is precisely why sign-symbols are such useful ideological devices, as, for example, the swastika was just such a valuable ideological device for the Nazi regime.

Added and closely linked to the multiplicity of meaning is the form and content of the signifier of the sign-symbol (see Figure 6.1). In Roland Barthes' theoretical frame, the signifier of the sign-symbol, as a fully formed linguistic sign, is both form (structure) and content (meaning). The signifier is at the outset in the sign-symbol a fully formed sign (see Figure 6.1). This fully formed sign (for example the word "rose") is emptied of its particular meaning or content (a rose, this rose, the rose) and instead an abstraction is generated: *rose* as such. The rose as signifier is then linked to a new signified (for example, desire, passion, romance, longing) and produces the sign-symbol, love (see Figure 6.1). The process is this: the word rose is a fully formed sign that carries a meaning or has content. This meaning, however, is pushed to the periphery or background and obfuscated by a new signified that is linked to the sign-symbol. This then allows the sign-symbol to carry both the "new" and "old" meaning simultaneously. The play of form and content is one that denotes both presence and absence, and emptiness and fullness. This logic of the sign-symbol is described by Barthes (1972, 123–124) by means of an analogy. It is, as he states, like the process of seeing simultaneously a window and the world beyond it. We can see the window at the same moment we see through the window to the world outside. The form, the window (the word rose), is present (has presence), we can see it, but is absent in that we see through it and are not looking at it as a window *per se*. The content, the landscape beyond the window, is distant from our immediate experience (empty), and yet full, full of the world beyond. Thus when one sees the sign-symbol (e.g. a rose, a cross, or a swastika), its form is present and absent: we can see the rose, cross, or swastika but its particular meaning as such is pushed into the background and obscured (empty), and subsequently filled up with new meaning (full). In other words, the literal meaning is pushed into the background so that the sign can act as a form for the signifier to link with a new signified in the second-order semiotic to produce the sign-symbol (see Figure 6.1). This then allows the sign-symbol to mean anew: love (rose), sin, suffering and salvation (cross), or ancient and pure (swastika). According to Barthes:

> In a simple system like language, the signified cannot distort anything at all because the signifier, being empty, arbitrary,[11] offers no resistance to it. But here, everything is different [Barthes is referring to the second order semiological systems or sign-symbols]: the signifier has, so to speak, two aspects: one full, which is the meaning … one empty, which is the form … What the concept distorts is of course what is full, the meaning: … [sign-symbols] are deprived of their history, changed into gestures. (1972, 122)

It is this perception of fullness, of a content that runs deep into the substratum that provokes some to believe that the real can be accessed, and it is this that has bedazzled and seduced theorists of "religion". The symbol within such a paradigm of understanding is not a mere semiotic device; rather, it is something much more, and something that is seen to link the believer with the believed, the subject with the referent, or the human with the sacred. This understanding of symbol, one that many followers of Eliade use, is misleading—misleading because the sign-symbol is seen to represent a truth of some underlying and eternal reality rather than the current social and historical system of belief and practice wherein it was developed. Within the system of belief and practice, of course, it may be understood to represent some eternal truth, but this is a *belief* about the symbol and does not speak to its process. And it is this belief that an Eliadean theory of the symbol circles around and uses to explain the symbol (e.g. the sacred), rather than investigating just how it is that the sign has been reformulated as a sign-symbol and made to signify in a particular fashion. The researcher who follows the Eliadean theory of symbol is simply restating the beliefs of the religious or cultural system under examination rather than analysing the sign-symbol. For example, the swastika did not represent the truth of the unbroken link of the German *Volk* to some eternal and pure moment, but was used to signify this *belief* engendered by the Nazi regime.

Secondarily, the Eliadean who also assumes a sacred/profane divide (for example, who assumes that word and symbol are inherently different), and then calls on hermeneutics to plumb the depths of the sign-symbol, ends up simply asserting his or her own beliefs, beliefs engendered by the Eliadean paradigm which assumes a numinosity, a sacredness, or an archetypal quality, as central to the sign-symbol. In the Eliadean formulation, then, how the sign-symbol operates and provides meaning, how it shapes and is shaped by shifting social and historical contingencies, how sign-symbols carry ideological imperatives, or even how sign-symbols are linked to and developed within systems of belief and practice to re-present these systems, are neglected.

I have argued that sign-symbols must be understood and analysed within a linguistic frame. Sign-symbols are material even if they are no more than words. There is a materiality to language and to the signifier. In the semiotic understanding of sign-symbols, sign-symbols are at their core linguistic signs even if they appear as abstractions. Beginning with Saussure's theory of linguistics and with an assist from Barthes' theory of myth (with some adaptations, see note 8), sign-symbols are amenable to analysis insofar as they are first and foremost thought of as a part of language. Secondly, as linguistic (and therefore a product of human sociality) sign-symbols act as models for and of existence. These models are derived from and produced within socio-cultural domains that are historically and socially contingent. And, as previously argued, the emergence of language as an adaptive feature of human evolution should not be solely or initially linked to communication but rather to cognition and in this, then, to modelling. Humans develop models by which to comprehend and encode existence. Models allow us to make sense and shape the world(s) in which we live. But they are never neutral as they are models through which humans, collectively and individually, represent existence; they are both prescriptive and descriptive and have extraordinary power. A variant of the sign-symbol making apparent this extraordinary power is the very interesting and rather odd phenomenon, the icon, to which this chapter turns next.

Icons

Unlike Charles Sanders Peirce's understanding of icon,[12] in my theory and practice the icon is often differentiated from the sign-symbol; or rather the sign-symbol is differentiated from the icon. This flip in my reference reflects a tendency to treat icons as symbols, but not symbols as icons. What is the difference? Are icons those natural symbols that Mary Douglas (1970), among others, assumed were different from linguistic symbols? Is there something about their very concreteness that establishes a category difference between the two? How do icons and sign-symbols differ from each other if at all?

Simply put, an icon is seen to share in the thing to which it points. In other words, the icon images *and contains* that to which it points, while a symbol points to the thing, is representative of the thing, but does not necessarily image or contain the thing. According to the Oxford English Dictionary, the term "icon" comes to us today through Latin but is derived from the Greek εἰκών referring to "likeness, image, portrait, semblance, similitude, and simile".[13] However it is a significant further development of this concept. For example, the cross does not resemble the Christian Church or deity although certainly the cross is a synecdoche affixed to many Christian churches. The cross is also understood to resemble the object to which Jesus was affixed in the New Testament. Further, a cross is presumed to intimidate and control demons suggesting an "iconicity", but in these instances the cross remains a sign-symbol in that it is precisely the social implications of the cross as a Christian sign-symbol of power that cows the "Christian" demon. The cross, then, in instances of, for example, demon (or popularly the vampire) cowing, operates as a sign-symbol insofar as it is understood to figure the power of deity, rather than contain some significant aspect of deity. The sign-symbol such as a cross does not contain a supernatural something; rather it simply points to it and in doing so (re)presents the power of deity. An icon, however, is conceptualised by believers as containing something supernatural and therefore it has an inherent power. So, for example, concrete Marian and Christ images found in a number of Christian-oriented social locations are understood to have power that can be dispensed to, or tapped by, the believer. This power is often perceived as healing power or a power of well-being (physical, spiritual, economic, emotional or social), although certainly the power is also seen to manifest negatively, injuring those who handle it improperly, ignore it or are disrespectful. A basic understanding of the icon, then, is that residing within is a supernatural power that can be tapped. Therefore, the icon, unlike the sign-symbol, is seen to contain and discharge power and this effect is possible because of its materiality. The power, itself, however, is understood to have been emplaced in the object by a supernatural entity either through happenstance or ritual efficacy.

The idea that the icon contains and manifests the power to which it points is an aspect of the icon that appears to be shared by a number of socio-cultural formations even if conceptualisation of the image and the kind of power it is understood to hold vary.[14] For example, in twentieth century folk Catholic Christianity in Mexico and folk Orthodox Christianity in rural Greece the conceptualisations of an icon's power differ. In the Mexican context the power in an icon is not seen to be infinite but requires intermittent charging. This can be done by returning the icon to a natural site associated with it or by putting it in close approximation to another powerful icon. In their four pilgrimages the ritual dancers of the Tojolabal and Tzeltale of Mexico transport the icons of their respective communities to pilgrimage sites for the icons to visit each other and/or so that they can be recharged (Poole 1991).[15] However, in rural northern Greece icons do not need recharging as their source of power is seen to be infinite and indeed these icons are able to "reproduce" (Danforth 1989, 70–71). In the Anastenaria, as the festival of firewalking is known, the icons associated with Saints Constantine and Helen are used in the local annual procession and firewalking ritual. The Anastenaria is understood to bring well-being to the community of the Kostilides, healing to those who need it, and psychological and physical well-being to the Anastenarides, or the firewalkers.[16] So, while conceptualisation of the amount and sustainability of the power of an icon differs, what is similar is how they are understood to actually imbue some sort of power; a power that is materialised in the concrete object and subsequently available to ritual participants and/or local folk.

In terms of the icon as artefact, its reproduction and shaping also take different forms so that, in rural Greece for example, when an old icon is repaired discarded pieces from the refurbished icon are used to initiate a new icon (Danforth 1989, 73). Loring Danforth comments that

> The oldest icon of Saints Constantine and Helen, known as "the old one from Kosti" (*Yerokotsianos*), which was brought from eastern Thrace ... is often referred to as the "father" of all the other icons. ... The other icons of the Anastenarides are called "children" of this icon.... "All the icons of Saints Constantine and Helen came from one, just as all men are descended from

> Adam. Icons have children and multiply just like men." According to most
> Kostilides, certain icons of particular saints have more power than others, and
> the older an icon is the more powerful. When a new icon is made, it acquires
> power because some material substance from its "father" is incorporated into it.
> (1989, 170)

As icons have fathers and even grandfathers (referred to in the plural as
"papoudes" or "fathers, grandfathers, and old men"), they also have a
genealogy (Danforth 1989, 169) and clearly the genealogical trajectory is
based on patriarchal relations much like the kinship organisation of the
Kostilides. However, this kind of conceptualisation is not the case in the
Mexican, Latin and South American contexts or other locations in rural
Greece (or in the Indian context more of which I will consider shortly). In
these locations icons are generally "discovered" through the supernatural
intervention of the deity or saint associated with the icon.[17] And, although icons in Latin and South America can and do share power, they
are not understood to do so within a patriarchal genealogical narrative.
Icons in this context tend toward the notion of originary, or a one-of-a-
kindness. However, although icons are seen as unique, nonetheless unique
icons can and do share deities. Indeed there are numerous icons but
these are associated with only a limited number of deities or saints.[18]

In India the icon has had a long history of development. According to
Richard Davis, artefacts associated with deities that may have had ritual
significance are found as early as the Indus Valley or Harappan civilisation
(c. 3300–1700 BCE). However, the ritual instructions for the enervation
or awakening of artefacts, anthropomorphic and non-anthropomorphic
and fashioned and *svayambhū* ("self existent"),[19] first appear in appendi-
ces of Vedic texts in the fifth century CE. However, the practice of the
establishment of the deity in the artefact, called the ritual of enervation,
does not appear to be fully developed until the Vaiśṇava saṃhitās and
Úaiva āgamas texts in the seventh and eighth centuries CE (Davis
1997, 26). Most scholars believe that the ritual of enervation emerged in
the mediaeval period of India and therefore associate it with the Bhakti
movement (Eck 1998, 45).

The long history of the icon in India, almost fifteen hundred years,
means that the concept of the icon and the ritual of enervation have
changed over time reflecting as they will social and historical contexts.
However, the basic understanding of the icon, as an existent object that
contains and manifests the power of the associated deity, remains consis-
tent. The icon is perceived as a material object, for example, a rock,
stone, carved wood, moulded clay, shaped bronze, and so forth, that has
been enervated by a deity through the ritual action of the Brahmin priest.
Enervation, in the instance of artefacts made by people, is an extensive

ritual process that establishes (*pratiṣṭhā*) the deity in the artefact. In the instances of found artefacts, viewed as natural icons, the ritual is minimised and generally seems used to ensure proper enervation by deity. Ritual, then, is quite consciously central to the creation of an icon in this context.

In the mediaeval period of India, Davis notes that there were five phases of establishment (*pratiṣṭhā*). The first phase consisted of choosing the raw material and ensuring that it was proper to the deity, for example, if wood then the proper tree was found and those entities possibly inhabiting the tree were ritually invited to depart. The second phase was concerned with the physical construction of the image itself, in other words the actual shaping of the raw product to resemble the deity, while the third phase consisted of the initial awakening of the image, central to which was the eye-opening wherein various substances such as honey, are smeared on the eyes and then removed by the Brahmin priest with a gold pin. The fourth phase consisted of a rite of purification that entailed immersing the artefact in water for a number of days, and the fifth and final phase called "affusion" was the performance of rites that provided the artefact with powers and capacities. This last phase of the ritual consisted of pouring substances (e.g. "water infused with plaksa-fig, holy fig, acacia, and banyan trees, with plants deemed auspicious and with sacrificial grass" (*Bṛhatsaṃhitā* 60.8–10 in Davis 1997, 34–36)) and/or reciting mantras over the artefact (Davis 1997, 34–36).

However, self-existent or self-manifesting (*svayambhū*) icons are found artefacts, and the majority of Gaṇeśa's significant shrines have this kind of an icon.[20] These do not require the full five phase ritual (Courtright 1985, 207): instead the ritual process (called *jirṇoddhāra*, meaning "a rescuing of what is worn out") consisted of only the last three phrases, but it also included a pacification ritual meant to ensure that any forces that may have entered the object "while its guard was down" were expiated (Davis 1997, 252–254).[21]

In the three locations I have referred to above, the context does indeed demonstrate differing understandings of the icon. In the temples and homes of India humans are central to the ritual of establishment, while in folk Greek Orthodox Christianity and folk Catholicism in Mexico, although humans are central to the care and worship of icons, they do not ritually enervate the icon as the icon is understood to be self-motivated in terms of power. In rural modern Greece, humans do "discover"[22] icons, but they also create new icons through the incorporation of a part of an old icon. In modern Mexico, like much of South and Latin America, icons are typically "discovered", although different systems of belief and practice, such as Condomblé or Umbanda, understand icons to be infused with aspects of both Catholic and African (e.g. Yoruban or Dahomean) origin. Furthermore, the icons operative in these Christianities tend to be manufactured artefacts such as statues, rather than natural objects such as rocks, stones or pieces of wood as found in India. For example, the image of the saint/orisha La Caridad del Cobre/Oshun was said to have floated into the Bay of Nipe near the mining province of Cobre in Cuba. Some fishers rescued the originally manufactured object from the ocean and subsequently a number of miracles occurred that were attributed to it (Brandon 1997, 51). In this location, then, an icon is an artefact that has been fashioned by humans, but one that has been subsequently chosen by a supernatural being, for example, a Catholic saint or deity, or, as in the Santerìan example, a Catholic-Yoruban saint/orisha who is understood to manifest her/his power in the chosen artefact.

Having briefly compared the conceptual understanding of the icon in three different contexts, the logical parameters are made visible. The icon is, like the sign and sign-symbol, a linguistic device. But the icon is material in the most literal of senses and is approached as something that is self-animated. Can or should icons be analysed as sign-symbols, or is there a step or aspect that needs to be introduced in order to deal with its materiality and sense of animation? In the following section I propose that icons could be analysed via a recourse to semiotics but to do this I suggest a third order semiotic since it would, I believe, do justice to the materiality of the icon. What I think one has in the icon is an embedding of the first and second order semiotic (sign and sign-symbol) that then allows it to sign anew as an icon. Such a process might be seen as operating in line with Claude Lévi-Strauss' structured sets, as related to *bricolage* and myth, wherein "the characteristic feature of mythical thought, as of *'bricolage'* on the practical plane, is that it builds up structured sets, not directly with other structured sets but by using the remains and debris..." (Lévi-Strauss 1966, 22). I would venture, then, that the sign and sign-symbol are incorporated within the icon to produce a third order semiotic.[23]

Semiotic reading of an icon: Gaṇeśa

In order to lay out a semiotic reading of an icon, I will draw upon the ethnographic work of Paul Courtright on Gaṇeśa and his presentation of icon as it functions in the context of rural southern India. In terms of structure and how the icon signs, I argue that the icon is a linguistic device regardless that it is an artefact. Although conceptualisation of an artefact does not often entail understanding it as a linguistic device, following J.T. Mitchell, as well as Roland Barthes, I argue otherwise and maintain images signify or mean through their linguisticality (cf. Hall, 1997). In other words, it is the artefact linked to the structured sets of language and the sign-symbol that allows it to signify as it does. Mitchell argues that:

> the relationship between words and images reflects, within the realm of representation, signification, and communication, the relations we posit between symbols and the world, signs and their meanings. We imagine the gulf between words and images to be as wide as the one between words and things, between (in the largest sense) culture and nature. The image is the sign that pretends not to be a sign, masquerading as (or, for the believer, actually achieving) natural immediacy and presence. (Mitchell 1986, 43)

Mitchell argues that there is an ideological imperative operating in the dichotomy between image and word. The ideological imperative embedded in this opposition privileges one over the other locating text/word with the mind and image with the body. However, as Mitchell convincingly argues, both image and word belong to the genus language, although they represent different species. If language is understood at the outset as an "exceedingly sophisticated modelling device" wherein "representation, signification, and communication" are characteristics that determine it, one notes, then, that both image and text share these characteristics and therefore can be theorised as having a common ancestor, language. How they differ, and therefore represent two different species of the genus of language, can be related to how they model: the image is a showing that can and does evoke text, while the text is a telling that can and does evoke image. But in terms of modelling, what is different is where the emphasis is laid: the image's emphasis is on a showing wherein text augments the showing, while the text's emphasis is placed on a telling wherein image augments the telling. As Mitchell comments:

> The recognition that pictorial images are inevitably conventional and contaminated by language need not cast us into an abyss of infinitely regressive signifiers. What it does imply for the study of art is simply that something like the Renaissance notion of *ut pictura poesis* and the sisterhood of the arts is always with us. The dialectic of word and image seems to be a constant in the fabric of signs that a culture weaves around itself. (1986, 42–43)

Having established, in my mind at least if not the reader's, that images are equally linguistic, the proposal that icons belong to a third order semiotic system gains some credence. In Figure 6.2, then, is a schematic of the semiotic system with the first order being the sign, the second order the sign-symbol,[24] and the third order the icon. The icon in the Saussurean-Barthean frame functions as a third order semiotic.

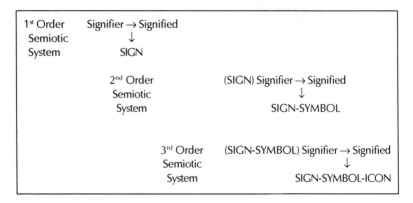

Figure 6.2 Third order semiotic

The above schematic provides one with a sense of the layers and the movement accrued in how the icon models, signifies, and communicates. In order to better understand the above schematic I will use it to develop a reading of the icon of Gaṇeśa.

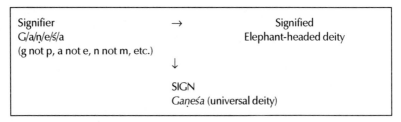

Figure 6.3 Gaṇeśa as linguistic sign (first order semiotic)

In the first order semiotic system, Figure 6.3, wherein a sign is developed, we have a group of letters gathered together that in this instance name the deity as Gaṇeśa. The choice of letters is unmotivated so that the only reason 'g' is in place is because it is not 'p', 't' or 's'. In other words, there is nothing inherent in the letters of the signifier G/a/ṇ/e/ś/a that link them to the signified. Connected to this unmotivated gathering of letters is the signified, or the concept, which in this instance is elephant-headed deity. The two, signifier and signified, read simultaneously produce the sign Gaṇeśa or the elephant-headed deity found in India.

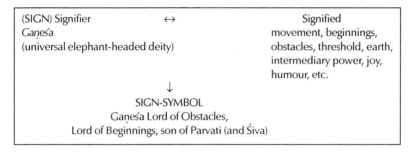

Figure 6.4 Gaṇeśa as sign-symbol (second order semiotic)

In Figure 6.4 above, the second order semiotic picks up the sign from the first order (or structured set in Lévi-Straussian terms) and at this point it has content. However, as Barthes argues, the content is distanced from— it is a ghostly presence—and becomes the form of the signifier of the sign-symbol. This is what Barthes means when he indicates that the signifier is both full and empty: the content is the fullness that is distanced from and subsequently made absent. It becomes form in order to act as the signifier in the second order semiotic system. In this operation the sign produced in the first order is emptied of its history. In this instance, then, the sign "Gaṇeśa" is emptied of any specificity related to geographical origins, and social group, and linked with a broad spectrum of concepts that allow Gaṇeśa to act as a universal deity. The sign, which is now the signifier, is gathered up in the second order semiotic system and linked to a new signified (the concept) to create the sign-symbol. The new signified consists of such ideas as movement, beginnings, obstacles, threshold, earth, intermediary power, rain, prosperity, humour, and joy, and is linked to the signifier Gaṇeśa allowing the sign-symbol Gaṇeśa, now laden with meaning, to emerge. The various notions found in the signified are polysemic with related and antithetical terms working in concert with, and supported by, the vast mythological corpus that has grown around the deity over a long period of time (Courtright 1985). The signifier Gaṇeśa (a fully developed sign in the first order semiotic system) is linked to a plethora of ideas embedded in the signified to produce the sign-symbol Gaṇeśa. Gaṇeśa, then, becomes lord of obstacles, lord of beginnings, an intermediary between humans and other deities, the son of Parvati, and adopted son (or unnatural son depending on the myth) of Śiva.

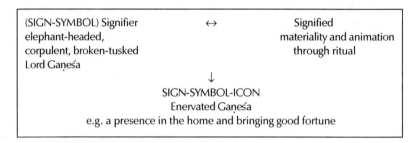

Figure 6.5 Gaṇeśa as sign-symbol-icon (third order semiotic system)

The third order semiotic, as seen in Figure 6.5, builds upon the first and second order semiotics to arrive at signification as an icon. Drawing upon the fully developed linguistic sign and the fully developed sign-symbol, the new signifier embeds both at this level of signification. In the third order semiotic the fully-fledged sign-symbol acts as the signifier, and again the content, or its meaning, is distanced from and recedes into the background. The sign-symbol has become form in order to be filled with a new signified that includes materiality and animation, exemplified in the south Indian context by the ritual of establishment. The signifier and signified are joined to present something new, the sign-symbol-icon of a material and animated Gaṇeśa. Again, in this development that which is distanced from is not lost. It must be retained, but at a distance in order that the icon take full form. As Barthes has argued with regard to the emergence of the form in the signifier of the second order semiotic system:

> But the essential point in all this is that the form does not suppress the meaning, it only impoverishes it, it puts it at a distance, it holds it at one's disposal. … The meaning will be for the form like an instantaneous reserve of history, a tamed richness, which is possible to call and dismiss in a sort of rapid alternation: the form must constantly be able to be rooted again in the meaning and to get there what nature it needs for its nutriment; above all, it must be able to hide there. (1972, 118)

This would appear to be equally necessary in the third order semiotic system. Set at a distance are the particulars of the sign and sign-symbol Gaṇeśa. The history of the sign (a specific people and geographical place) and sign-symbol (polysemy of concepts and layers of mythology) recede into the background and are there in order that the form may take shape. This form is the image of Gaṇeśa, a verbal image with its history removed at a distance. The collage that is Gaṇeśa is invisible and instead a whole but empty image of Gaṇeśa acts as the form of the signifier in the third order semiotic. Inherent in the first order and second order semiotic is a verbal image of Gaṇeśa that allows for a concrete imaging of this figure: the signified in the first order is "elephant-headed" while the signified in the second order incorporates such concepts as prosperity, which, in this location, is signed by corpulence. As Davis comments, "Gaṇeśa's insatiable appetite for this food [*modaka*—sweet wheat or rice balls], and the obesity resulting from it, symbolises the abundance of his life-giving power as the remover of obstacles" (1997, 111).[25] The sign and the sign-symbol are joined and provide a verbal pictorial map by which to construct or properly identify the image that will be Gaṇeśa.

In the third order semiotic the signifier is the sign-symbol fully formed wherein the image of Gaṇeśa, his elephant-headedness, his corpulent body, his broken tusk, his effeminate masculinity along with a plethora of signifying accoutrements that mark him recede but retain a presence in order that form becomes image. The signifier is joined with a new signified, materiality and animation exemplified in this location by the five (or three) phase ritual of establishment: choice of material, fabrication of deity from the material, initial wakening, purification and affusion in order to bring the sign-symbol-icon into existence. The signified, then, consists of concreteness, animation, and power related to that animation, all of which produce what I will call the sign-symbol-icon or the fully enervated Gaṇeśa.

The icon fully formed, then, is multi-layered. The icon is understood to be a literal and living representation of deity (or saint) and has powers that can be called on and dispensed.[26] It is multi-layered in that embedded within it is both the sign and the sign-symbol. The inclusion of these two linguistic devices indicates that it shares traits with the sign and the sign-symbol, but the icon has diverged and has two new attributes: it is material and animated and no longer abstract and static. Because of this divergence, and the icon's reliance on two structured sets or the sign and the sign-symbol, the icon belongs to a third order semiotic within the semiotic system.

The sign-symbol, as related earlier, includes in its play not only a superfluity of meaning, form and concept that brings to the symbol a presence but also an absence (the sign-symbol is both full and empty): the form of the "pure" linguistic sign is held to, but the concept, its signified (in the first order semiotic), is distanced from and held in abeyance in order that the signified (concept) in the second order semiotic be emplaced. These aspects, as noted by Barthes, allow for the multi-dimensionality of the sign-symbol. In a third order semiotic, the signifier consists of the visual attributes that act to encode the figure/artefact of Gaṇeśa. Distanced, but spectrally present, is the collage that is the deity. This signifier is linked to a new signified, materiality and animation, both engendered in this location through ritual. In the end the materiality and animation (in Gaṇeśa vis-à-vis the ritual of enervation) fills the emptied form to become its content and an icon emerges.

The icon is very sign-symbol like, and indeed one might ask why differentiate an icon from a sign-symbol? The symbolism of the sign-symbol is, as I have argued, embedded in the icon, much as the sign is and therefore it is equally a sign and a sign-symbol. But the icon is conceptualised as more than this. In all locations discussed in this chapter, as well as in most other social and historical locations, central to the idea of the icon is materiality and linked to this materiality is the secondary idea of animation, which is derived from the sign and sign-symbol. Although certainly sign and sign-symbol have a materiality in that a sign can be spoken or depicted and a sign-symbol painted or carved, the materiality of an icon is conceptually linked to animation (signified) and it is this conceptualisation that marks the icon as different from the sign-symbol. Therefore, what the sign and the sign-symbol are conceptually understood to lack is a quality of animation: the cross suggests power and therefore animation, but the source of that power and animation is located elsewhere so that the cross is simply a vector for that power. With the icon the power is seen to reside in the material substance of the artefact which animates it. The icon, unlike the sign or sign-symbol, is approached as if it is a living thing. The sign-symbol is qualitatively different from the sign and therefore requires further thought as to its linguistic and epistemological functions. This is precisely what Barthes, among others, sets out to do. Equally, I would argue, the icon is qualitatively different from the sign-symbol and requires further thought as to its linguistic and epistemological functions.

Notes

1. This chapter is a significantly extended version of Deconstructing the Eliadean Paradigm: Symbol. In Willi Braun and Russell T. McCutcheon, eds. *Introducing Religion: Essays in Honor of Jonathan Z. Smith*. London: Equinox, 2008.

2. For a discussion on the concept of the sacred and its multiple understandings, as well as how it might be understood within a cognitive frame, see Anttonen 2000.

3. Recently a friend and colleague, Willi Braun, directed me toward another work that shares my critique of Eliade's theory of symbolism. See Dubuisson 2006, 267–276.

4. An interesting and enlightening example of a Peircean semiotic reading of a symbol can be found in Westerfelhaus and Singhal 2001.

5. There are a number of semiotic schools or circles, such as the Copenhagen circle with Louis Hjelmslev's work at its centre and the American school founded on the work of Charles Sanders Peirce, to name but two. For a discussion on the history of semiotics and the various theoretical developments since the period of the ancient Greeks beginning with Hippocrates see Martin and Ringham 2000; Sebeok 1994; Clarke 1987; Blonsky 1985; and Eco 1984.

6. This division is not as clear-cut as I present it. Mary Douglas and Victor Turner do engage symbols structurally, while Clifford Geertz and Turner read symbols in terms of language, themselves having been influenced by the "linguistic turn". But none of the three engage symbols as pure linguistic devices and they tend to make a distinction between natural or religious symbols and pure linguistic symbols. See, for example Clifford Geertz 1973;1974; Mary Douglas 1966; 1970, and Victor Turner 1967.

7. One notes in Eliade an evolutionary schema that acts as a backdrop for his theorising of the symbol, the sacred, or religions in general. Hence "primitive" and ancient coupled together and in opposition to traditional and modern is his general view of the social organisation (profane) that overlays the metaphysical organisation (sacred).

8. In Roland Barthes' significant article "Mythologies Today" (1972) he names myth as a second order semiotic system, but then proceeds to develop his analysis examining symbol rather than myth , e.g. the image of a black Algerian saluting the French flag. In light of this, then, I use this work in order to understand sign-symbols. In Barthes' theorising, I would argue, he calls the second order semiotic "myth" because of the signified (concept), which is typically a mytheme or even a fully fledged myth. However, it is the sign and sign-symbol which are the final product in the interplay between signifier and signified, as Barthes also argues.

9. Keith Hopkins comments: "The image of the cross, a symbol of punishment for slaves and bandits, reminds us of early Christianity's appeal to the oppressed, and its promotion of a heaven which would be a world upside down: the poor would be privileged and the rich would be refused entrance." (2004, 217 n.25)

10. I would like to thank my copy editor Tamsin Bacchus for sharing with me this information concerning Kipling and his use of the swastika.

11. The issue of arbitrary relates to the signifier as unmotivated. In the word "rose", for example, there is nothing intrinsic to the word that links it to its signifier. Saussure states: "The idea of 'sister' is not linked by any inner relationship to the succession of sounds s-ö-r which serves as its signifier in French; that it could be represented equally by just any other sequence is proven by differences among languages and by the very existence of different languages: the signified 'ox' has as its signifier b-ö-f on one side of the border and O-k-s (Ochs) on the other." (Saussure 1966, 67–68)

12. Icon as I am referring to it is not the concept of icon that appears in C. S. Peirce. Peirce theorises that: "A sign is an icon, an index, or a symbol. An icon is a sign which would possess the character which renders it significant, even though its object had no existence; such as a lead-pencil streak as representing a geometrical line. An index is a sign which would, at once, lose the character which makes it a sign if its object were removed, but would not lose that character if there were no interpretant. Such, for instance, is a piece of mould with a bullet-hole in it as sign of a shot; for without the shot there would have been no hole; but there is a hole there, whether anybody has the

sense to attribute it to a shot or not. A symbol is a sign which would lose the character which renders it a sign if there were no interpretant. Such is any utterance of speech which signifies what it does only by virtue of its being understood to have that signification." (in Innis 1985, 9–10) Although I would suggest that Peirce's development of resemblance with regard to icon, as he understands it, brings his definition of the sign as icon close to the notion of icon that I develop in this chapter.

13. According to the OED etymological chart, icon as image appears in English usage in the sixteenth century.

14. The perceived power and the particular image, or form taken, are two aspects of icons that serve as examples of cultural variation.

15. In her ethnographic study of these dancers Deborah Poole notes that there are three primary functions that dancers perform. They transport the *lámina* or icons to the pilgrimage sanctuary and back, they appease the power of the sanctuary (be it Christ or the Virgin) on behalf of their communities and so hopefully earn for their communities spiritual benefits represented materially, for example an abundant crop, while they also fulfil the passing of "cargo" or fiesta sponsorship. The cargo (literally burden) is often shared by several members of the community or an individual, all of whom gain status in the community by taking up the socio-economic burden of the fiesta (Poole 1991, 310).

16. The Anastenarides are those people who are said to follow the path of the saints, a path that often includes participation in the firewalking ritual. Often those who become Anastenarides have been afflicted by Saints Constantine or Helen and they are only healed when they actively begin to serve the saints (see Danforth 1989, 75–83).

17. This can also be the case in rural Greece particularly in relation to shrines and pilgrimage sites. See for example Dubisch 1995.

18. This does not mean that icons in Latin and South America do not have relations with each other, they do. Icons will often be taken to visit each other. However, although icons are recharged they are not apparently related in terms of one icon parenting another icon.

19. Self-extent icons are "natural" objects, such as a stone or rock, that either symbolically represents the deity, for example, the *linga* with regard to Śiva, or an officially recognised aspect of the deity is perceived to be present in the natural artifact. Paul Courtright in his work on Gaṇeśa indicates that: "Most of the images in both the *aútavināyakas* and other shrines in Maharashtra are called *svayambhū* ('self-existent'). That is, they are not carved by image makers and installed by priests. Instead they are rocks that bear a striking resemblance, in the eyes of the faithful, to the head of an elephant. Like the *úālagrāma* stones of Vaiśṇavism and the *bāṇalinga* of Śaivism, *svayambhū* images appear without human agency as embodiments of Gaṇeśa's sacred presence in the world and require no rites of sacralization [*prāṇapratiṣṭhā*] for their sacredness to be apparent to his devotees." (Courtright 1985, 207)

20. The self-manifested icons of Gaṇeśa tend to be stones or some other natural substance the shape of which brings to mind the elephant-headedness of Gaṇeśa.

21. Davis also mentions such rites for the reconsecration of defaced or deteriorated icons, as long as the image of the associated deity is still discernible (1997, 252–254).

22. By "discover" I mean that the icon communicates with a person, usually through dreams, so that it can be found and then properly instituted in the material system of

worship, for example, a chapel or shrine and worshipped. This kind of discovery is a phenomenon that works in both the Roman Catholic and Greek Orthodox Christian systems of belief and practice, and, although linked to the formal institutional practices, there can be strong "folk" currents underscoring the worship of the icon. One finds the notion of "discovery" in India as well, but here dreams are not a factor. Instead one stumbles over an old statue or representative of the deity, and subsequently it is presented to priests who determine if it is indeed an icon. If it is determined to be an icon, ritual is used to purify and re-enervate it, whereupon it is re-established in a temple or shrine (see Davis 1997, 113–142).

23. In Peircean semiotics the icon is a sign the ground of which involves formal resemblance and therefore it belongs to the first degree of reality. Peirce argues that there are three degrees of reality and calls them firstness, secondness, and thirdness. Icons as first "cannot have any degree of internal complexity, they cannot be indices (secondness) or symbols (thirdness)" (Parmentier 1994, 17). This is in some measure the reverse of what I am arguing in this chapter.

24. As indicated in footnote 8, Roland Barthes' significant article "Mythologies Today" names myth as a second order semiotic system, but then proceeds to theorise a symbol rather than myth *per se*. I, like others, use his theorising of myth toward understanding the linguistic nature of what I then call the sign-symbol.

25. This corpulence as a sign of prosperity is also commented upon by Courtright: "Gaṇeśa resembles Kubera in functions. Kubera is the lord of wealth and king over the *yakṣas*; his retinue includes a host of auspicious beings, such as *guhyakas, kinnaras, gandharvas*, and *apsarases*. Kubera has a fat, dwarfish body similar to that of Gaṇeśa as well as an almost tusk-like moustache ..." (1985, 130–131)

26. How this is achieved varies according to social and historical context.

Conclusion

Gender Ideology, Systems of Belief and Practice, and Epistemology

"Religion" is a categorical formation developed in and by those who operate inside social formations and cultural paradigms and by those who operate outside and seek to analyse and comprehend them. A social formation is, following Stuart Hall, a society with "a definite structure and well-defined set of social relations" (1996, 9), while a paradigm, in my usage, refers to an operative model of existence. Paradigm is, according to the OED, "a conceptual or methodological model underlying the theories and practices of a science or discipline at a particular time; [hence] a generally accepted worldview". Social formations and paradigms are in constant flux and are, therefore, dynamic.[1]

Aspects of social formations and paradigms are broken down and defined so that some are called political, others social, some economic, some private, some public, some cultural, while others are designated religious. In all instances, what is apparent is that the development of categories by which to construct and know that "worldview" is central to human activity. Therefore, as I see it, in our human efforts to name and determine existence we create categories that are products of, and therefore fit into and legitimise, our social formations and models of existence.

One particular Eurowestern category that came into significant play during the period of European colonisation, operating within a dominant Christian paradigm, was "religion". Religion, which of course has had a number of meanings in the history of the Eurowest,[2] was, and continues to be in some measure, a categorical term used to demarcate a "true" belief, for example Christianity, from an untrue belief, for example "Hindoos", "Mohammedans" or so-called heathens,[3] or to mark others as having no belief, for example Australian aboriginals and the concept of Dreamtime or so-called savages.[4] This understanding of religion dates from the mid sixteenth century and included the notion that religion was a necessary attribute for proper social formation and paradigm. Although certainly this meaning of religion had much to do with the European Reformation, it was also very useful when it came to legitimising aggressive global activity across the Atlantic in the following decades. It is semantic baggage like this operating in relation to the category of religion that makes it a problematic category. Too narrow and ideologically bound, religion as a definitive taxon is not useful for my purposes. Therefore, when I endeavour to think about myth, ritual, and sign-symbol and their intersection with social formations and paradigms, I instead use the phrase "system of belief and practice".

Myth, ritual, and sign-symbol are three significant categories that function to shape and define a paradigm and/or social formation. These three categories, central to systems of belief and practice, are often approached as if they are windows to the "real" world; a real world understood to reside beneath, behind, or beside the social worlds of humanity. Frequently, myth, ritual, and sign-symbol are treated as somehow containing kernels of truth that have suffered from historical and social accretion. For some, mythic narrative is the historical ground from which deity(ies) arises, for example, most Christianities, for others ritual is the primary site where deity(ies) breaks through to the social and historical realm, for example, Judaism or Santoría, and for still others sign-symbols and icons are the unconscious abstractions or materialisations that deity(ies) shines through, for example, icons used in pilgrimage. And although many recognise that myth, ritual, and sign-symbol are used in hegemonic practices as a means of legitimation, nonetheless the categories of myth, ritual, and sign-symbol are often treated as external to ideology. Ultimately, then, in the study of systems of belief and practice myth, ritual and sign-symbol are sometimes engaged as an instantiation of the divine rather than as social and historical categories that describe and prescribe human social systems. In framing myth, ritual, and sign-symbol as instantiations of the divine, their content may be analysed, but that which holds the content, the form, is left intact and unanalysed. The logic, function, and construction of myth, ritual, and sign-symbol remain unexamined and instead they are dealt with as natural categories, or categories produced in nature, which, due to their naturalness, are capable of containing the divine, much like the notion of the icon.

Like myth, ritual, and sign-symbol, gender too is often treated as a natural category. And even if many have come to recognise the social and historical nature of the category of gender, there are still many who hold to the view that sex is the natural category on which gender is constructed. Sex is located in the realm of nature and the natural so that maleness and femaleness operate definitively with regard to species, genera, and even to the level of class. However, as I have argued at the outset of this text, when theorising gender I follow Delphy, Butler, Foucault, and Sedgwick, among others, and treat sex also as a social and historically determined category. Furthermore, I would argue that gender precedes sex and is the social category on which sex is constructed.

Equally, I also believe that the categories of race, class, ethnicity, sexual orientation, kinship, and other identity markers are interrelated with gender/sex in order to augment gender, as in the case of the representation of non-white female sexuality in white racist hegemonies as hypersexual, for example, Saartjie Baartman (1789–1815) the Khokhoi woman exhibited in sideshows as the "Hottentot Venus" (McClintock 1995, 40–42) or as asexual, as in the "mammy" figure in the United States. In terms of the intersection of gender/sex, class, and sometimes race, there is the figure of the hypersexual "welfare mom" who is perceived both as a pariah and a parasite on society. Gender/sex likewise intersects with race in order to augment race as in the white hyper-feminine used to draw lines between women who are marked by race and those who are not. All these categories interplay toward establishing proper ways of being within social formations. In this text, then, my intention has been to heuristically hive off the category of gender because it is, I believe, the category most frequently employed across time and space to shape and delimit social formations and paradigms, and because it is given form and legitimation most powerfully through myth, ritual, and sign-symbol.

In the semiotics of gender, my first intention was to show the significance of the category of gender/sex and the necessity of examining gender coding to better understand systems of belief and practice. Within systems of belief and practice there is a conceptualisation of what it means to be a human in the world, and this conceptualisation is typically, but not always, shaped by gender/sex (cf. Ortner, 1996). This is our anthropology. The anthropology envisioned for social formations and paradigms is supported by the biology and metaphysics associated with systems of belief and practice. In other words, nature, deity, and creation, as they are symbolically encoded within systems of belief and practice, are located as the origin and truth of human anthropology. This anthropology is encoded in bodies through such mechanisms as ritual, and given logical coherence in social formations and paradigms through recourse to sign-symbol and myth. Again and again the "worldview" is shaped and aligned through symbolic discourses, be it social formations in ancient or modern worlds or in the so-called old world and new.

In the *Popol Vuh* (Book of Council) of the Quiche Maya (Guatemala) of the post-classic period (1200–1521)[5] deities, creation, and human anthropology are mapped out making visible an ideal schematic that acted as representational of, and legitimation for, the Maya social formation, although the interpretation and ideological use of the myths found in the *Popol Vuh* shift according to different historical periods of the Maya.[6]

In the Quiche Maya myth of creation found in the *Popol Vuh* deities are divided by gender/sex (midwife and matchmaker or Bearer and Begetter) and these gendered beings are presented as working with each other, while Sovereign Plumed Serpent appears at times in the myth to take a dominant position. Existence comes into being through much discussion, debate and worry by the deities. What one notes in the myth is that although male/masculine leadership is assumed in the figure of Sovereign Plumed Serpent, nonetheless, deities gendered female/feminine are not subordinated to deities gendered male/masculine. What is strongly suggested in the myth is a dualist gender/sex ideology wherein creation is brought about through recourse to the masculine (Begetter) who initiates, but necessarily works in tandem with, the feminine (Bearer) who completes creation: feminine and masculine powers are linked and integral to each other in the act of creation. And, although feminine power is placed under masculine leadership,[7] "she" makes her own contributions and participates in the many discussions concerning the form creation will take particularly with regard to that of humans. One reads in the *Popol Vuh*:

> And here is the beginning of the conception of humans, and of the search for the ingredients of the human body. So they spoke, the Bearer, Begetter, then Makers, Modelers named Sovereign Plumed Serpent. … And these were the ingredients for the flesh of the human work, the human design, and the water was for blood. It become human blood, and corn was also used by the Bearer, Begetter. … And then the yellow corn and white corn were ground, and Xmucane [female/feminine] did the grinding nine times. Food was used, along with the water she rinsed her hands with, for the creation of grease; it became human fat when it was worked by the Bearer, Begetter, Sovereign Plumed Serpent, as they are called. (Tedlock 1996, 145–146)

So what can be noted here is that powerful female/feminine figures have access to decision making, although under the tutelage of the male/masculine (*Gukumatz* or Sovereign Plumed Serpent), and that female/feminine power carries a positive value in existence or that at least among the deities female/feminine is coded positive.

The gender/sex ideology presented in this myth suggests gender/sex dualism wherein the male/masculine and female/feminine are separate but equally signify as necessary for creation and its maintenance. It could be argued, then, that the myth speaks to a gender/sex ideology of partial gender equivalence wherein the masculine and feminine are both understood to bring something to the political (e.g. dynasty), economic (e.g. weavers), social (e.g. noble women), and ritual (e.g. Xmucane as Bearer and midwife; Xpiyacoc as Begetter and matchmaker) operations of the Quiche Maya social body. I say partial as the feminine principle of creation, although significant and necessary, remains under the tutelage of the supreme divine masculine, Sovereign Plumed Serpent. What this might suggest, then, is that the female/feminine and male/masculine have their roles to play based on gender/sex, but, at the same time, both roles are necessary for the proper operation of existence.

In the *Popol Vuh*, the creation of humans, or the anthropogonic myth, is a process that takes several efforts on the part of the deities, but in the end the four fathers, called mother-fathers (androgynous patrilineal parents to all Maya), are brought into being. Following their creation, wives are brought into existence and through these wives and descendants the Quiche Maya great houses are said to have been established. In this telling of the tale women, as the female/feminine, are linked to men, as the male/masculine, for the purposes of establishing the great houses; the latter of which were central to the organisation of the Maya social formation. The mother-fathers each had their own power, one that was associated with a particular deity. The houses were hierarchically stratified (externally with reference to each other and internally with reference to the members of each house), but gender/sex, interestingly, did not signify as the primary taxon by which to shape the social body.

The Maya civilisation of the classic period was stratified, oriented toward expansion through colonisation, and functioned, in part, on a basis of slave economy (Coe 1999; Joyce 2000; Fash 2005). The maintenance of the vertical structure with mother-fathers at the top and slaves at the bottom was achieved through other forms of status, although gender was among them. This social organisation on the basis of status was, of course, naturalised and legitimated via reference to the metaphysical and biological domains through myth, ritual, and sign-symbol. By linking social organisation to myth, ritual, and sign-symbol, the group that the arrangements favoured were not seen as instigators and maintainers of their own privilege; rather they simply occupied the social positions narratively established through myth, reinforced through ritual, and given material signification in sign-symbol, the latter visible in statuary, hieroglyphs, and architecture.

In the classic Maya social formation association with a lineage house, either as the dominant lineage house or in relation to it, was a primary means of status. Secondary to this, status was achieved within the lineage house based on primacy (and in all likelihood abilities) with regard to the lineage. Thirdly age signified as important for status, as elders were considered to be more powerful and subsequently in charge of the youth of the house. It was only after these three categories for delimiting the social body that gender came into play in terms of organising the social body of the Quiche Maya (see Tedlock 1996; Coe 1999; Joyce 2000; Andrews and Fash 2005). In this social formation, then, lineage-house status was a primary means by which to organise the social body. Gender/sex was important and certainly figures, for example in marriage arrangements, lineage-house descendants, gendered labour such as masculine warfare and feminine weaving, and most particularly in terms of ritual, but it ranked fourth with regard to status so that women, especially those of the noble lineage-houses, were powerful political, economic, social, and ritual actors in their own right.

In Maya representation the pairing of the female with the male is a frequent motif seen in hieroglyphic inscription, painting and monumental art. During the classic period, the female and male are depicted paired with the female well-clothed (often in layers) and the male partially clothed (e.g. loincloth). Rosemary Joyce has convincingly argued that this depiction of female and male are idealisations that link masculinity with nature and femininity with culture. Further seen in these images, she argues, is a frequency of representation wherein the female is situated at a lower level or is bodily smaller than the male (2000, 54–89). Finally, also noted by Joyce, is the linking of male figures with agonistic ritual (the ball game), tools of battle (spears), and governance (throne), and the linking of female figures with tools of weaving and food production, while both are linked with lineage-houses though ritual representations. The suggestion would be, then, that women and men are seen to work together and to engage in gendered roles, for example, men are warriors, women are weavers. However, because the female is represented as smaller than or, at other times, lower than her male counterpart, the female is most likely subordinate to her paired male, but probably not all males.

But how might this gender/sex ideology work with regard to normative views of human sexuality? In Mayan systems since lineage-house status is the primary category marking social status, behaviour that threatened house status would, one could reasonably argue, come under disciplinary action, for example, if one made a false claim to a lineage-house or status within the lineage-house.[8] Age was the third measure of status, wherein the young are directed by those who are older,[9] while gender/sex was the fourth measure of status, and, as a fourth measure of status, carried less social signification. Linked to this, but not in a causal fashion, may well be the positive coding of both male/masculine and female/feminine as read in the creation myth of the *Popol Vuh*. Both the lesser social valuation of gender/sex as definitive for the social formation, and the positive coding of female/feminine suggest that moving across the boundary of gender/sex via sexuality may well not have signified as threatening.

However, in gender rigid systems, such as the dominant gender/sex ideology of the Eurowest, particularly in North America, over the last two centuries moving across the gender/sex boundary was, and continues to be in many locations, highly problematic, and harsh disciplinary measures were, and are, used to prohibit such venturing (e.g. the madhouse, imprisonment, death, medical experimentation, behaviour modification, etc.). But the gender/sex ideology of the classic and post-classic period of the Maya, status related to lineage-house, lineage within the house, and age were the primary categories by which boundaries were demarcated and maintained. Although gender/sex was important in terms of descent, the cloth produced within the lineage-house, and ritual *cum* political performance, it does not appear to have been a primary means by which to police social boundaries. One also notes that the concept of mother-father (eponymous ancestor), a concept in the *Popol Vuh* that incorporates the creative aspects of both the masculine Xpiyacoc and the feminine Xmucane, represents a blended dual sexuality and this sits at the mythic foundations of both the anthropogonic myth of human creation, and the demogonic myth of the establishment of the twenty-two lineage-houses of the Quiche-Maya. These first four human beings (Jaguar Quitze, Jaguar Night, Not Right Now and Dark Jaguar[10]), although masculine, were named first as feminine, *mother*-father, pointing to a gender dualism wherein the blending of male and female, and masculine and feminine was not unknown. Equally found are classic and post-classic representations wherein female and male representations cross-dress (see Joyce 2000). In gender/sex ideologies where one finds easy movement across gender/sex boundaries; where there is an equitable blending of what is designated male/masculine and female/feminine, the gender/sex ideology is less restrictive. [11]

This very brief discussion of periods of the classic and post-classic Maya systems of belief and practice is to my mind a good example of the importance of the category of gender/sex and how it is deployed through myth, ritual, and sign-symbol. Further, one must always keep in mind that the material conditions of social formations intersect with symbolic systems and together these produce gender/sex ideologies. The relationship is dialectical so that the material conditions of any society shape myth, ritual, sign-symbol, and gender/sex ideologies as much as the social formations of that society are rationalised, justified, legitimated, and made "true" through recourse to those representational narratives of myth, ritual, and sign-symbol, deployed as they are through the domains of the social, biological, and metaphysical and given meaning using the linguistic tools of metaphor, metonymy, and synecdoche.

Notes

1. I follow Thomas Kuhn in my use of paradigm, but add "dynamic" to raise awareness that paradigms, as Kuhn argued, are dynamic structures that are in constant flux (Kuhn 1962, 92–110).

2. For a discussion of the category of religion see Smith 1998 and Masuzawa 2005.

3. According to the OED the standard meaning of heathen appears in common parlance in approximately 971 CE.

4. According to the OED, this meaning of savage appears in common parlance in the late 1500s.

5. The alphabetical *Popol Vuh* is thought to have been written down during the period of Spanish conquest (sixteenth century) by members of the lineages that had once rule the Quiche speaking Maya in Guatemala. Subsequently, at the outset of the eighteenth century, this text was then translated by the friar Francisco Ximénez in Chichicastenango. This text then appeared in the middle of the nineteenth century and was published for the first time 1857. Although Rosemary Joyce locates the *Popol Vuh* as a post-classic text (1200–1521) wherein the Quiche speaking Maya represented a dominant lineage (2000, 77), it has been argued that there is archaeological evidence for figures, symbols, concepts, and reference to rituals found in the *Popol Vuh* as early as the late formative period (400 BCE–250 CE) (Tedlock 1996). Also problematic for arguments concerning the authenticity of *Popol Vuh* is the disappearance of the original document.

6. The traditional time-line of the Maya civilisation is: Archaic 9000–2300 BCE; Early Formative 2300–900 BCE; Middle Formative 900–400 BCE; Late Formative 400 BCE–250 CE; Early Classic 250–400 CE; Middle Classic 400–550 CE; Late Classic 550–850 CE; Terminal Classic 850–1000 CE; Early Post-classic 1000–1200 CE; and Late Post-classic 1200–1521 CE (Joyce 2000, 3; Coe 1999).

7. Rosemary Joyce, among others, comments that during the late formative and into the classic periods in Mayan hieroglyphic and architectural representation women are often depicted clothed in elaborate textiles while men, aside from the elaborate headdress and loincloth, are often partially nude. Interestingly, there are some images of women clearly operating in an authoritative position who are depicted partially nude, for example, Naranjo Stela 24. When women and men are depicted together, frequently she is diminutive to him, or situated at a lower level. In some cases a woman is shown kneeling while a man is shown standing. This is a positioning also used to signify power differentials between men (2000, 54–89).

8. William Fash, in his examination of social history in the Copán Valley, comments that the use of hieroglyphs and pictorial sculptures was one mechanism by which to speak one's status (2005, 98).

9. However, this was not without some contention. The ball-game and ball-court were the centre of aristocratic, masculine agonistic ritual that may well have also pivoted around younger men if the *Popol Vuh* provides us with any evidence, for example, the twin heroes Hunahpu and Xbalanque (their mother was Blood Moon), the celebrated ball-players, who challenge their older twin half-brothers One Monkey and One Artisan (their mother was Egret woman).

10. Following Tedlock 1996.

11. The opposite is not, however, always true.

LIBRARY, UNIVERSITY OF CHESTER

Bibliography

Adam, B. and Allen, S. (eds.) 1995. *Theorizing culture: An interdisciplinary critique after postmodernism*. New York: New York University Press.

Aigner, D. J. 2002. *The swastika symbol in Navajo textiles*. 2nd. Laguna Beach, CA: DAI Press.

Allen, D. 2001. Mircea Eliade's view of the study of religion as the basis for cultural and spiritual renewal. In *Changing religious worlds: The meaning and the end of Mircea Eliade*, ed. B. Rennie, 307–48. New York: State University of New York Press.

Althusser, L. 1995. Ideology and ideological state apparatuses (notes toward an investigation). In *Mapping ideology*, ed. S. Žižek, 100–140. London and New York: Verso.

Amadiume, I. 1987. *Male daughters, female husbands: Gender and sex in African society*. London: Zed Books.

Anderson, P. 1979. *Lineages of the absolutist state*. London: Verso Editions.

Andrews, W. and Fash, W. (eds.) 2005. *Copán: The history of an ancient Maya kingdom*. Sante Fe and Oxford: School of American Research Press and James Currey.

Ankarloo, B. 2002. Witch trials in northern Europe 1450–1700. In *Witchcraft and magic in Europe: The period of the witch trials*, eds. B. Ankarloo and S. Clark, 53–95. Philadelphia: University of Pennsylvania Press.

Anttonen, V. 2000. Sacred. In *Guide to the Study of Religion*, eds. W. Braun and R. McCutcheon, 283–96. London; New York: Continuum Press.

Arnal, W. E. 2000. Definition. In *Guide to the Study of Religion*, eds. W. Braun and R. McCutcheon, 21–34. London; New York: Continuum Press.

Aubin, N. B. 1705. *The history of the devils of Loudun or an account of the possession of the Ursuline nuns. And the condemnation and punishment of Urbain Grandier, a parson of the same town*. London: R. Bassett. Internet Ebook.

Baehr, H. and Gray, A. (eds.) 1996. *Turning it on: A reader in women and media*. New York: St. Martin's Press.

Balsamo, A. 1996. *Technologies of the gendered body: Reading cyborg women*. Durham: Duke University Press.

Banerjee, P. 2003. *Burning women: Widows, witches, and early modern European travelers in India*. New York: Palgrave Macmillan.

Banet-Weiser, S. 1999. *The most beautiful girl in the world: Beauty pageants and national identity*. Berkeley: University of California Press.

Barkow, J. H., Cosmides, L. and Tooby, J. (eds.) 1992. *The adapted mind: Evolutionary psychology and the generation of culture*. New York: Oxford.

Barstow, A. L. 1994. *Witchcraze : A new history of the European witch hunts*. San Francisco: Pandora.

Barthes, R. 1968. *Elements of semiology*. trans. A. Lavers and C. Smith. New York: Farrar, Straus and Giroux, Hill & Wang.

———. 1972. *Mythologies*. trans. A. Lavers. New York: Farrar, Straus and Giroux, Hill & Wang.

———. 1988. *The semiotic challenge*. trans. Richard Howard. New York: Hill & Wang.

Bederman, G. 1995. *Manliness & civilization: A cultural history of gender and race in the United States, 1880–1917*. Chicago: University of Chicago Press.

Bell, C. 1992. *Ritual theory, ritual practice*. Oxford: Oxford University Press.

Bell, D. A. 2007. *The first total war: Napoleon's Europe and the birth of warfare as we know it*. Boston: Houghton Mifflin Co.

Bell, E., Haas, L. and Sells, L. (eds.) 1995. *From mouse to mermaid: The politics of film, gender, and culture*. Bloomington: Indiana University Press.

Benedict, P. 1992. French cities from the sixteenth century to the revolution: An overview. In *Cities and social change in early modern France*, ed. P. Benedict, 7–68. London and New York: Routledge.

Benhabib, S. and Cornell, D. (eds.) 1987. *Feminism as critique: On the politics of gender*. Minneapolis: University of Minnesota Press.

Benjamin, J. 1988. *The bonds of love: Psychoanalysis, feminism, and the problem of domination*. New York: Pantheon Books.

———. 1995. *Like subjects, love objects: Essays on recognition and sexual difference*. New Haven: Yale University Press.

———. 1998. *Shadow of the other: Intersubjectivity and gender in psychoanalysis*. New York: Routledge.

Bhattacharyya, G. 1998. *Tales of dark-skinned women: Race, gender and global culture*. London; Bristol, Pa.: UCL Press.

Black, J. 2007. *European warfare in a global context, 1660–1815*. New York: Routledge.

Blackmore, J. and Hutcheson, G. (eds.) 1999. *Queer Iberia: Sexualities, cultures, and crossings from the Middle Ages to the Renaissance*. Durham, NC: Duke University Press.

Blackwood, E. 2000. *Webs of power: Women, kin, and community in a Sumatran village*. Lanham: Rowman & Littlefield.

Bloch, M. 1977. The past and the present in the present. *Man* **12**:278–92.

———. 1986. *From blessing to violence: History and ideology in circumcision ritual of the Merina of Madagascar*. Cambridge: Cambridge University Press.

———. 1992. *Prey into hunter: The politics of religious experience*. Cambridge: Cambridge University Press.

Blok, J. and Mason, P. (eds.) 1987. *Sexual asymmetry: Studies in ancient society*. Amsterdam: J. C. Gieben.

Blonsky, M. 1985. Introduction: The agony of semiotics. In *On signs: A semiotics reader*, ed. M. Blonsky, xiii–li. Oxford: Basil Blackwell.

Bloom, L. 1999. *With other eyes: Looking at race and gender in visual culture*. Minneapolis: University of Minnesota Press.

Bobo, J. 1995. *Black women as cultural readers*. New York: Columbia University Press.

Bodin, J. 2001. *Jean Bodin on the Demon-Mania of Witches*. trans. R. A. Scott, intro. J. I. Pearl. Toronto: Centre for Reformation and Renaissance Studies, Victoria University in the University of Toronto.

Bourdieu, P. 2001. *Masculine domination*. trans. R. Nice. Stanford, CA: Stanford University Press.

Bowers, M. A. 2004. *Magic(al) realism*. London and New York: Routledge.

Brandon, G. 1997. *Santeria from Africa to the new world: The dead cell memories*. Bloomington and Indianapolis: Indiana University Press.

Bristow, J. and Broughton, T.L. (eds.) 1997. *The infernal desires of Angela Carter: Fiction, femininity, feminism*. New York: Longman.

Brockless, L. and Jones, C. 1997. *The medical world of early modern France*. Oxford: Clarendon Press.

Bultmann, R. 1958. *Jesus Christ and mythology*. New York: Scribner's.

Burke, P. 1994. *Popular culture in early modern Europe*. England: Ashgate.

Burstyn, V. 1999. *The Rites of Men: Manhood, politics and the culture of sport*. Toronto; Buffalo; London: University of Toronto Press.

Butler, J. 1992. Contingent foundations: Feminism and the question of postmodernism. In *Feminists theorize the political*, eds. J. Butler and J. W. Scott, 3–21. New York; London: Routledge.

———. 1999. *Gender trouble: Feminism and the subversion of identity*. New York; London: Routledge.

———. 2004. *Undoing gender*. New York; London: Routledge.

Buxton, R. 1999. Introduction. In *From myth to reason? Studies in the development of Greek thought*, ed. R. Buxton, 1–21. New York: Oxford University Press.

Caciola, N. 2003. *Discerning Spirits: Divine and demonic possession in the Middle Ages*. Ithaca and London: Cornell University Press.

Calinescu, Matei (1988). Introduction: the fantastic and its interpretations in Mircea Eliade's later Novellas. In *Youth without youth and other novellas*, ed. Matei Calinescu and trans Mac Linscott Ricketts. Columbus: Ohio State University Press.

Cameron, A. and Kuhrt, A. (eds.) 1983. *Images of women in ancient antiquity*. Detroit: Wayne State University Press.

Carter, A. 1990 (first published 1979). *The Sadeian Woman: An exercise in cultural history*. London: Virago.

———. 1992. *Wise Children*. London: Vintage.

———. 1993. *The Bloody Chamber*. London: Penguin Books.

———. 1993 (first published 1969). *Heroes and Villains*. New York; London: Penguin.

———. 1994 (first published 1972). *The Infernal Desire Machines of Doctor Hoffman*. New York; London: Penguin.

———. 1994. *Nights at the Circus*. London: Vintage.

Cassirer, E. 1957. *The philosophy of symbolic forms*. Vol. 3. trans. R. Manheim, intro. C. W. Hendel. New Haven: Yale University Press.

de Certeau, M. 1988. *The Writing of History*. trans. Tom Conley. New York: Columbia University Press.

———. 1992. *The mystic fable: Volume 1, the sixteenth and seventeenth centuries*. trans. M. B. Smith. Chicago and London: University of Chicago Press.

———. 1993. *Heterologies: Discourse on the other.* trans. Brian Massumi. Minneapolis; London: University of Minnesota Press.

———. 1996. *The possession at Loudun.* trans. M. B. Smith. Chicago: University of Chicago Press.

Challans, T. L. 2007. *Awakening warrior: Revolution in the ethics of warfare.* New York: SUNY.

Chodorow, N. J. 1978. *The reproduction of mothering: Psychoanalysis and the sociology of gender.* Berkeley: University of California Pres.

———. 1994. *Femininities, masculinities, sexualities: Freud and beyond.* Lexington, KY: University Press of Kentucky.

———. 1999. *The power of feelings: Personal meaning in psychoanalysis, gender, and culture.* New Haven, Conn: Yale University Press.

Clarke, D. J. 1987. *Principles of semiotics.* London: Routledge.

Clarke, J. R. 2003. *Roman sex 100 BC–AD 250.* New York: Harry N. Abrams, Inc., Publishers.

Coe, M. 1999. *The Maya.* 6th. London: Thames and Hudson.

Coleman, K. M. 1990. Fatal charades: Roman executions staged as mythological enactments. *The Journal of Roman Studies* **80**:44–74.

Combs-Schilling, E. 1991. Etching patriarchal rule: Ritual dye, erotic potency, and Moroccan monarchy. In *Readings in ritual studies,* ed. R. Grimes, 104–18. Upper Saddle River, NJ: Prentice Hall.

Connell, R. W. 1987. *Gender and power: Society, the person, and sexual politics.* Stanford, CA: Stanford University Press.

———. 2002. *Gender.* Malden, MA: Polity; Oxford: Blackwell.

Cooper, A. 2006. *The hanging of Angélique.* Toronto: HarperCollins Publishers Ltd.

Courtright, P. 1985. *Gaṇeśa: Lord of Obstacles, Lord of Beginnings.* New York and Oxford: Oxford University Press.

Cowen, D. and Gilbert, E. (eds.) 2007. *War, citizenship, territory.* New York: Routledge.

Csapo, E. 2005. *Theories of mythology.* Oxford: Blackwell.

Cyrino, M. S. 1995. Heroes in d(u)ress: Transvestism and power in the myths of Herakles and Achilles. *Arethusa* **31**:49–51.

D'Ambra, E. 2007. *Roman women.* New York: Cambridge University Press.

Daly, M. 1978. *Gyn/ecology: The metaethics of radical feminism.* Boston: Beacon Press.

Danforth, L. 1989. *Firewalking and religious healing: The Anastenaria of Greece and the American firewalking movement.* Princeton, NJ: Princeton University Press.

Davis, R. H. 1997. *Lives of Indian Images.* Princeton, NJ: Princeton University Press.

Deacon, T. 1997. *The symbolic species: The co-evolution of language and the brain.* New York: Norton.

Delaney, C. 1995. Untangling the Meaning of Hair in Turkish Society. In *Off with her head: The denial of women's identity in myth, religion, and culture,* eds. H. Eilberg-Schwartz and W. Doniger, 53–75. Berkeley, Los Angeles, London: University of California Press.

Delphy, C. 1996. Rethinking sex and gender. In *Sex in question: French materialist feminism,* eds. D. Leonard and L. Adkins, 30–41. London: Taylor & Francis.

del Rio, M. 2000. *Martín del Rio: Investigations into magic.* ed. and trans. P. Maxwell-Stuart. Manchester and New York: Manchester University Press.

Derrida, J. 1978. *Writing and difference.* trans. A. Bass. Chicago: University of Chicago Press.

Dijkstra, B. 1996. *Evil sisters: The threat of female sexuality and the cult of manhood.* New York: Alfred A. Knopf.

Dio, C. C. 1961. *Dio's Roman History.* Vol. 9. Trans. E. Cary. Cambridge, Mass.; London: Harvard University Press; William Heinmann Ltd.

Doniger, W. and Patton, L. (eds.) 1996. *Myth and method.* Charlottesville; London: University Press of Virginia.

Doty, W. G. 1986. *Mythography: The study of myths and rituals.* Tuscaloosa: University of Alabama Press.

Douglas, A. 1988. *The Feminization of American Culture.* New York: Anchor Press/ Doubleday.

Douglas, M. 1966. *Purity and danger: An analysis of concepts of pollution and taboo.* London: Penguin.

———. 1970. *Natural symbols: Explorations in cosmology.* New York: Pantheon.

Dubisch, J. 1995. *In a different place: Pilgrimage, gender and politics at a Greek island shrine.* Princeton, NJ: Princeton University Press.

DuBois, P. 1988. *Sowing the Body: Psychoanalysis and ancient representations of women.* Chicago: University of Chicago Press.

Dubuisson, D. 2006. *Twentieth Century Mythologies.* trans.M. Cunningham. London; Oakville: Equinox.

Dumézil, G. 1996. *Archaic Roman religion: With an appendix on the religion of the Etruscans.* Vol. 1. Forward by M. Eliade. trans. P. Krapp. Baltimore and London: The John Hopkins University Press.

Dworkin, A. 1974. *Woman hating: A radical look at sexuality.* New York: Dutton.

Eck, D. L. 1998. *Darśan: Seeing the divine image in India.* 3rd edition. New York: Columbia University Press.

Eco, U. 1984. *Semiotics and the philosophy of language.* Bloomington: Indiana University Press.

Edwards, K. 1997. Unspeakable professions: Public performance and prostitution in ancient Rome. In *Roman Sexualities*, eds. J. Hallett and M. Skinner, 66–98. Princeton NJ: Princeton University Press.

Ehrenreich, B. 1997. *Blood Rites: Origins and history of the passions of war.* New York: Henry Holt and Co.

Eliade, M. 1961. *Images and symbols: Studies in religious symbolism.* trans. P. Mairet. New York: Sheed and Ward.

———. 1964. *Shamanism: Archaic techniques of ecstasy.* Princeton NJ: Princeton University Press.

———. 1967. *The Sacred and the Profane: The nature of religion.* trans. W. R. Trask. New York: Harcourt Brace Jovanovich Publishers.

———. 1985. *Symbolism, the sacred, and the arts.* New York: Crossroad Publishing Co.

Elkind, D. 2007. *The power of play: How spontaneous, imaginative activities lead to happier, healthier children.* Cambridge, MA: Da Capo Lifelong Books.

Ember, C. 1978. Myths about hunter-gatherers. *Ethnology* **17**:439–48.

Enloe, C. 1989. Beyond Steve Canyon and Rambo: Feminist histories of militarized masculinity. In *The militarization of the Western world*, ed. J.R. Gillis, 119–40. New Brunswick; London: Rutgers University Press.

Erbse, H. (ed.) 1969–77. *Scholia Graeca in Homeri Iliadem (7 vols)*. Berolini: De Gruyter.

Fash, W. 2005. Toward a social history of the Copán Valley. In *Copán: The history of an ancient Maya kingdom*, eds. W. Andrews and W. Fash, 73–102. Sante Fe and Oxford: School of American Research Press and James Currey.

Fausto-Sterling, A. 2000. *Sexing the body: Gender politics and the construction of sexuality*. New York: Basic Books.

Flavell, J. and Conway, S. (eds.) 2007. *Britain and America go to war: The impact of war and warfare in Anglo-America, 1754–1815*. Gainsville: University Press of Florida.

Flower, H. I. 1996. *Ancestor masks and aristocratic power in Roman culture*. Oxford: Clarendon Press.

Foley, R. 1995. Causes and consequences in human evolution. *The Journal of the Royal Anthropological Institute* **1**(1), March:67–86.

Foucault, M. 1980. *The history of sexuality*. Vol. 1, *An introduction*. trans. R. Hurley. New York: Random House, Vintage.

Freud, S. 1991. Resistance and repression. In *Introductory lectures on psychoanalysis*, eds. A. Richards and A. Dickson. The Penguin Freud Library, 327–43. London: Penguin.

Futrell, A. 1997. *Blood in the Arena: the Spectacle of Roman Power*. Austin: University of Texas Press.

———. 2006. *The Roman games: A sourcebook*. Malden, MA; Oxford: Blackwell Publishing.

Gallop, J. 1982. *The daughter's seduction: Feminism and psychoanalysis*. New York: Cornell University Press.

Gamble, S. 1997. *Angela Carter: Writing from the front lines*. Edinburgh: Edinburgh University Pres.

Garland, R. 2001. *The Greek way of death*. 2nd edition. Ithaca, New York: Cornell University Press.

Gass, J. 1998. Written on the body: The materiality of myth in Angela Carter's *Heroes and Villians*. In *Critical essays on Angela Carter*, ed. L. Tucker, 145–58. New York: G. K. Hall & Co.

Gearhart, S. M. 1978. *Wanderground: Stories of the Hill Women*. (illustrations by Elizabeth Ross) Watertown, Mass.: Persephone Press.

Geertz, C. (ed.) 1974. *Myth, symbol, and culture*. New York: Norton.

———. 1971. *Islam observed: Religious development in Morocco and Indonesia*. Chicago: University of Chicago Press.

———. 1973. *The interpretation of cultures: Selected essays*. New York: Basic.

Gilligan, C. 1982. *In a different voice: Psychological theory and women's development*. Cambridge, Mass.: Harvard University Press.

Gilligan, C. and Brown, L.M. 1992. *Meeting at the crossroads: Women's psychology and Girls' development*. Cambridge, Mass.: Harvard University Press.

Gilman, C. P. 1979. *Herland*. introd. Ann J. Lane. New York: Pantheon Books.

Gilmour, D. 2003 *The Long Recessional*. London: John Murray

Goff, S. 2004. *Full spectrum disorder: The Military in the new American century*. New York: Soft Skull Press.

Goheen, M. 1996. *Men own the fields, women own the crops: Gender and power in the Cameroon grassfields*. Wisconsin: University of Wisconsin Press.

Goldsmith, E. C. 2001. *Publishing women's life stories in France, 1647–1720: From voice to print*. Aldershot, UK and Burlington, Vermont: Ashgate.

Gramsci, A. 1971. *Selections from the prison notebooks*. ed. and trans. Q. Hoare and G. N. Smith. London: Lawrence and Wishart.

Green, M., and J. D. Brown. 2007. *M4 Sherman at war*. St. Paul, MN: MBI Pub.

Greenberg, M. 2002. Molière's body politic. In *High anxiety: Masculinity in crisis in early modern France*, ed. K. P. Long, 139–64. Kirksville, Missouri: Truman State University Press.

Greimas, A. J. 1987. *On meaning: Selected writings in semiotic theory*. intro. P. J. Perron, trans. P. J. C. Perron, H. Frank foreword F. Jameson. Theory and History of Literature, vol. 38. Minneapolis: University of Minnesota Press.

Griaule, M. 1958. *Conversations with Ogotemmeli: An introduction to Dogon religious belief*. London and New York: Oxford University Press.

Grimes, R. 1982. *Beginnings in ritual studies*. New York; London: University Press of America.

———. 1990. *Ritual criticism*. Columbia, South Carolina: University of South Carolina.

Gruen, E. S. 1990. *Studies in Greek culture and Roman policy*. Leiden: Brill.

Gunderson, E. 1996. The ideology of the arena (Rome's Arena). *Classical Antiquity* **15**(1):113–51.

Hall, S. (ed.) 1997. *Representation: Cultural representations and signifying practices*. London; Thousand Oaks; New Dehli: Sage.

———. 1996. Formations of modernity: Introduction. In *Modernity: An introduction to Modern Societies*, eds. S. Hall, D. Held, D. Hubert, and K. Thompson, 3–18. Malden, MA; Oxford: Blackwell.

Hallett, J. and Skinner, M. (eds.) 1997. *Roman Sexualities*. Princeton NJ: Princeton University Press.

Hama, L. 2007. *The battle of Iwo Jima: Guerrilla warfare in the Pacific*. New York: Rosen.

Hanson, A. E. 1999. The Roman family. In *Life, death, and entertainment in the Roman Empire*, eds. D. S. Potter and D. J. Mattingly, 19–66. Ann Arbor: University of Michigan Press.

Hawley, J. S. (ed.) 1994. *The blessing and the curse: The burning of wives in India*. New York: Oxford University Press.

Helm, A. M. (ed.) 2007. *The law of war in the 21st century: Weaponry and the use of force*. Newport, RI: Naval War College.

Herdt, G. 1987. *The Sambia: Ritual and gender in New Guinea*. New York: Holt, Rinehart and Winston.

———. 1994. *Guardians of the flutes: Idioms of masculinity*. Chicago: University of Chicago Press.

———. 1996. Introduction: Third sexes and third genders. In *Third sex third gender: Beyond sexual dimorphism in culture and history*, ed. G. Herdt, 21–81. New York: Zone.

Homer. 1974a. *Iliad*. trans. R. Fitzgerald. New York: Doubleday & Company Inc.

————. 1974b. *Odyssey*. trans. R. Fitzgerald. New York: Doubleday & Company Inc.

Hopkins, K. 1983. *Death and renewal: Sociological studies in Roman history*. Cambridge: Cambridge University Press.

————. 2004. Novel evidence for Roman slavery. In *Studies in ancient Greek and Roman society*, ed. R. Osborne, 206–25. Cambridge: Cambridge University Press.

Horsley, R. 1998. The slave systems of classical antiquity and their reluctant recognition by modern scholars. *Semeia: Special Issue, Slavery in Text and Interpretation* **83/84**:19–66.

Hubert, H. and Mauss, M. 1964. *Sacrifice: Its nature and functions*. trans. W. D. Halls. Chicago: University of Chicago Press.

Hunt, L. (ed.) 1993. *The Invention of Pornography: Obscenity and the origins of modernity, 1500–1800*. New York: Zone.

————. 2004. The 18th-Century Body and the Origins of Human Rights. *Diogenes* **203**:41–56.

Innes, S. A. (ed.) 2004. *Action chicks: New images of tough women in popular culture*. New York: Palgrave Macmillan.

Innis, R. E. (ed.) 1985. *Semiotics: An introductory anthology*. Bloomington: Indiana University Press.

Institoris, H. and Sprenger, J. 2006. *Malleus maleficarum: The Latin text and introduction*. Vol. 1. ed. and trans. C. S. Mackay. Cambridge: Cambridge University Press.

————. 2006b. *Malleus maleficarum: The English translation*. Vol. 2. ed. and trans. C. S. Mackay. Cambridge: Cambridge University Press.

Irvin, F. M. 1992. From renaissance city to ancien régime capital: Montpellier, c. 1500–c. 1600. In *Cities and social change in early modern France*, ed. P. Benedict, 105–33. London and New York: Routledge.

Jackson, S. and Scott, S. (eds.) 2001. *Gender: A sociological reader*. New York: Routledge.

Jakobson, R. 1962. *Selected writings*. Gravenhage: Mouton.

————. 2002. Two aspects of language and two types of aphasic disturbances. In *On language: Roman Jakobson*, eds. L. R. Waugh and M. Monville-Burton, 115–33. Cambridge, Mass.: Harvard University Press.

Johnston, S. I. 1999. *The restless dead: Encounters between the living and the dead in ancient Greece*. Berkeley, Los Angeles, London: University of California Press.

Jones, W. (trans.) 1918. *Pausanias: Description of Greece Books I–II*. Cambridge Mass.; London: Harvard University Press.

Joyce, R. 2000. *Gender and power in prehispanic Mesoamerica*. Austin: University of Texas press.

Juschka, D. M. 2003a. Whose turn is it to cook? Victor Turner's communitas and pilgrimage questioned. *Mosaic: A Journal for the Interdisciplinary Study of Literature* **36**(4): 189–204.

————. 2003b. The writing of ethnography: Magical realism and Michael Taussig. *Journal for Cultural and Religious Theory* **4**(4):84–105. Http://www.jcrt.org/archives/

————. 2004. Cladistics, morphologies, taxonomies and the comparative study of religion. *Method and Theory in the Study of Religion* **16**(1), 2004:12–23.

Kaplan, E. A. 1997. *Looking for the other: Feminism, film and the imperial gaze*. New York: Routledge.

———. 2005. *Trauma culture: The politics of terror and loss in media and literature*. New Brunswick, NJ: Rutgers University Press.

Kaplan, H., Hill, K., Lancaster J. and Hurtado, A.M. 2000. A theory of human life history evolution: Diet, intelligence and longevity. *Evolutionary Anthropology* **9**:156–85.

Kieckhefer, R. 1998. *Forbidden rites: A necromancer's manual of the fifteenth century*. Pennsylvania: Pennsylvania State University Press.

Klaić, D. 1991. *The plot of the future: Utopia and dystopia in modern drama*. Ann Arbor: The University of Michigan Press.

Kraemer, R. S. 1992. *Her share of the blessings: Women's religions among Pagans, Jews and Christians in the Greco-Roman world*. New York: Oxford University Press.

Kramer, L. 2005. *The sociology of gender: A brief introduction*. 2nd edition. Preface by Judith Lorber and foreword by Beth B. Hess. Los Angeles, CA: Roxbury.

Kristeva, J. 1997. *The portable Kristeva*. ed. K. Oliver. New York: Columbia University Press.

Kuhn, T. S. 1962. *Foundations of the unity of science*. Vol. 2, number 2, *The structure of scientific revolutions*. 2nd edition. International Encyclopedia of Unified Science. Chicago: University of Chicago Press.

Kurtz, D. C. and Boardman, J. 1971. *Greek burial customs*. Ithaca, New York: Cornell University Press.

Kyle, D. 1998. *Spectacles of death in ancient Rome*. London and New York: Routledge.

LaFountain, M. J. 1997. *Dali and postmodernism: This is not an essence*. New York: SUNY.

Lacan, Jacques. 1988. *The seminar of Jacques Lacan*. ed. Jacques-Alain Miller. New York: W.W. Norton.

Lakoff, G. 1987. *Women, fire, and dangerous things: What categories reveal about the mind*. Chicago: University of Chicago Press.

de Lancre, P. 2006. *On the inconsistency of witches: Pierre de Lancre's Tableau de l'inconstance des mauvais anges et demons (1612)*. trans. H. Stone and G. S. Williams. Tempe, Arizona: Arizona Center for Medieval and Renaissance Studies.

Langer, S. K. 1942. *Philosophy in a new key: A study in the symbolism of reason, rite, and art*. New York: New American Library.

Laqueur, T. 1992. *Making Sex: Body and gender from the Greeks to Freud*. Cambridge; London: Harvard University Press.

Leakey, R. and Lewin, R. 1992. *Origins reconsidered*. New York: Little, Brown & Co.

Lee, A. 1997. *Angela Carter*. New York: Twayne Publishers.

Lefkowitz, M. and Fant, M.B. (eds.) 1982. *Women in the ancient world: The Arethusa papers*. Albany: SUNY.

Lehman, P. (ed.) 2001. *Masculinity: Bodies, movies, culture*. New York: Routledge.

di Leonardo, M. and Lancaster, R.N. (eds.) 1997. *The gender/sexuality reader: Culture, history, political economy*. New York: Routledge.

Levack, B. 2006. *The witch-hunt in early modern Europe*. Harlow, England; New York: Pearson Longman.

Lévi-Strauss, C. 1963. *Structural Anthropology*. trans. Claire Jacobson and Brooke Grundfest Schoepf. London: Allen Lane, The Penguin Press.

———. 1966. *The savage mind*. The Nature of Human Society Series. trans. J. & D. Weightman. Chicago: University of Chicago Press.

————. 1969. *The elementary structures of kinship*, ed. and trans. R. Needham, trans. J. H. Bell and R. von Sturmer. Boston: Beacon Press.

Lewis, N. and Reinhold, M. (eds., intro. and notes) 1966. *Roman Civilization: The Republic and the Augustan Age, Selected Readings* Vol. I. New York: Harper and Row, Harper Torchbooks/Academy Library.

Lincoln, B. 1986. *Myth, cosmos, and society: Indo-European themes of creation and destruction*. Cambridge and London: Harvard University Press.

————. 1989. *Discourse and the construction of society: Comparative studies of myth, ritual and classification*. New York; Oxford: Oxford University Press.

————. 1991. *Death, war and sacrifice: Studies in ideology and practice*. Chicago; London: Chicago University Press.

————. 1994. *Authority: Construction and corrosion*. Chicago: University of Chicago Press.

————. 1999. *Theorizing myth: Narrative, ideology and scholarship*. Chicago: Chicago University Press.

Lindemann, M. 1999. *Medicine and society in early modern Europe*. Cambridge: Cambridge University Press.

Lloyd, G. 1966. *Polarity and analogy: Two types of argumentation in early Greek thought*. Cambridge: Cambridge University Press.

————. 1979. *Magic, reason, and experience: Studies in the origin and development of Greek science*. Cambridge: Cambridge University Press.

Lorber, J. 1994. *Paradoxes of gender*. New Haven: Yale University Press.

————. 2005. *Gender inequality: Feminist theories and politics*. 3rd. Los Angeles, CA: Roxbury Publishers.

Lorber, J. and Farrell, S.A. (eds.) 1991. *The social construction of Gender*. Newbury Park, CA: Sage Publications.

Lorber, J., Ferree, M.M. and Hess, B.B. (eds.) 1999. *Revisioning gender*. Thousand Oaks, CA: Sage.

Luhmann, N. 1995. *Social systems*. trans. J. J. Bednarz and D. Baecker. Stanford, CA: Stanford University Press.

Mani, L. 1998. *Contentious traditions: The debate on sati in colonial India*. Berkeley: University of California Press.

Marin, J. M. 2007. A Jesuit mystic's feminine melancholia: Jean-Joseph Surin SJ (1600–1665). *Journal of Men, Masculinity and Spirituality* **1**(1):65–76.

Martin, B. and Ringham, F. 2000. *Dictionary of Semiotics*. London and New York: Cassell.

Matthews-Grieco, Sara F. 1993. The body, appearance and sexuality. In *A history of women: Renaissance and Enlightenment paradoxes*, eds. N. Z. Davis and A. Farge, 46–84. Cambridge, Mass.; London, England: The Belknap Press of Harvard University Press.

Masuzawa, T. 2005. *The invention of world religions: or, how European universalism was preserved in the language of pluralism*. Chicago: Chicago University Press.

Maxwell-Stuart, P. 2003. *Witch hunters: Professional prickers, unwitchers and witch finders of the Renaissance*. Gloucestershire: Tempus Publishing Ltd.

Mazzio, C. 1997. Sins of the tongue. In *The body in parts: Fantasies of corporeality in early modern Europe*, eds. D. Hillman and C. Mazzio, 50–79. New York and London: Routledge.

Márquez García, G. 1972. *One Hundred Years of Solitude*. trans. Gregory Rabassa. London: Penguin.

McClintock, A. 1995. *Imperial Leather: Race, gender, and sexuality in the colonial contest*. New York: Routledge.

McCrae, J. 1919. *In Flanders fields and other poems*. B. S. A. M. with an essay in character. New York, London: G. P. Putnam's Sons.

McCutcheon, R. T. 1997. *Manufacturing religion: The discourse on sui generis religion and the politics of nostalgia*. New York: Oxford University Press.

McGinn, T. A. J. 1998. *Prostitution, sexuality, and the law in ancient Rome*. New York and Oxford: Oxford University Press.

Michael, M. C. 1996. *Feminism and the postmodern impulse: Post-world War II fiction*. New York: SUNY.

Miller, J.-A., (ed.) 1988. *The seminar of Jacques Lacan*. New York: W.W. Norton.

Mitchell, W. J. T. 1986. *Iconology: Image, text, ideology*. Chicago: University of Chicago Press.

Monter, W. 2002. Witch trials in continental Europe. In *Witchcraft and magic in Europe*, eds. B. Ankarloo and S. Clark, 1–52. Philadelphia: University of Pennsylvania Press.

Morris, I. 1992. *Death-ritual and social structure in classical antiquity*. Cambridge: Cambridge University Press.

Moss, M. 2001. *Manliness and Militarism: Educating Young Boys in Ontario for War*. Toronto: Oxford University Press.

Mosse, G. L. 1985. *Nationalism and sexuality: Respectability and abnormal sexuality in modern Europe*. New York: H. Fertig.

Most, G. W. 1999. From logos to mythos. In *From myth to reason? Studies in the development of Greek thought*, ed. R. Buxton, 25–47. New York: Oxford University Press.

Mozley J. H. (ed. and trans.) 1928. *Statius: Thebaid V–XII, Achilleid*. Cambridge: Cambridge University Press.

Müller, A. 1997. *Angela Carter: Identity constructed/deconstructed*. Heidelberg: Universitätsverlag C. Winter.

Neimeyer, C. P. 2007. *The Revolutionary War*. Westport, Conn: Greenwood Press.

O'Connell, J. F., Hawkes, K., Lupo, K. and Blurton Jones, N. 2002. Male strategies and Plio-Pleistocene archaeology. *Journal of Human Evolution* **43**:831–72.

Ong, A. 1998. *Appropriating gender: Women's activism and politicized religion in South Asia*. New York: Routledge.

Ortner, S. B. 1974. Is Female to Male as Nature is to Culture? In *Woman, culture, society*, eds. M. Rosaldo and L. Lamphere, 67–88. Stanford, CA: Stanford University Press.

Ortner, S. B. 1996. *Making gender: The politics and erotics of culture*. Boston: Beacon Press.

Orwell, G. 1949. *1984: A Novel*. New York: New American Library.

Osborne, R. 1994. The politics of sacred space in Attica. In *Placing the gods: Sanctuaries and sacred space in ancient Greece*, eds. S. E. Alcock and R. Osborne, 143–60. Oxford: Clarendon Press.

Paden, W. 2000. World. In *Guide to the study of religion*, eds. W. Braun and R.T. McCutcheon, 334–37. London and New York: Continuum.

Parmentier, R. 1994. *Signs in society: Studies in semiotic anthropology*. Bloomington and Indianapolis: Indiana University Press.

Penner, T., and Vander Stichele, C. (eds.) 2006. *Mapping gender in ancient religious discourses*. Biblical Interpretation Series 84. Leiden: Brill Academic Publishers.

Plath, S. 1965. *Ariel*. London: Faber and Faber.

Pomeroy, S. B. 1975. *Goddesses, whores, wives, and slaves*. New York: Schocken Books.

Poole, D. A. 1991. Ritual movement, rites of transformation: Pilgrimage and dance in the highlands of Cuzco, Peru. In *Pilgrimage in Latin America*, eds. N. R. Crumine and A. Morinis, 307–38. New York, Connecticut and London: Greenwood Press.

Potter, D. S. 1999. Entertainers in the Roman Empire. In *Life, death, and entertainment in the Roman Empire*, eds. D. S. Potter and D. J. Mattingly, 256–325. Ann Arbor: The University of Michigan Press.

Powers, S. T. 1992. The battle of Normandy: The lingering controversy. *The Journal of Military History* **56**(3), July:455–71.

Purcell, N. 2004. Literate games: Roman urban society and the game of alea. In *Studies in ancient Greek and Roman society*, ed. R. Osborne, 177–205. Cambridge: Cambridge University Press.

Quinn, M. 1994. *The Swastika: Constructing the symbol*. London and New York: Routledge.

Rabinowitz, N. S., and Richlin, A. (eds.) 1993. *Feminist theory and the classics*. New York: Routledge.

Raphael, R. 1988. *The men from the boys: Rites of passage in male America*. Lincoln; London.

Remarque, E. M. 1929. *All Quiet on the Western Front*. trans. A. Wheen. London: G. P. Putnam's Sons.

Remy, N. 1970. *Demonolatry*. ed. and notes M. Summers. trans. E. A. Ashwin. New York: Barnes and Noble. Facsimile reprint.

Richlin, A., ed. 1992. *Pornography and representation in Greece and Rome*. New York: Oxford University Press.

Ricoeur, P. 1969. *The symbolism of evil*. trans. E. Buchanan. Boston: Beacon Press.

Robb, J. 2007. *Brave new war: The next stage of terrorism and the end of globalization*. Hoboken, NJ: Wiley.

Robinson, S. 1998. The anti-hero as Oedipus: Gender and the postmodern narrative [in *The Infernal Desire Machines of Dr. Hoffman*]. In *Critical essays on Angela Carter*, ed. Lindsey Tucker, 158–75. New York: G. K. Hall & Co.

Roper, L. 1994. *Oedipus and the devil: Witchcraft, sexuality, and religion in early modern Europe*. London and New York: Routledge.

Rubin, G. 1975. The traffic in women: Notes on the "political economy" of sex. In *Toward an anthropology of women*, ed. R. R. Reiter, 157–210. New York; London: Monthly Review Press.

Said, E. 1994. *Orientalism*. New York: Vintage.

Sanday, P. R. and Goodenough, R.G. (eds.) 1990. *Beyond the Second Sex: New directions in the anthropology of gender*. Philadelphia: University of Pennsylvania Press.

de Saussure, F. d. 1966. *Course in general linguistics*. eds C. Bally and A. Sechehaye. (In collaboration with A. Reidlinger, trans. W. Baskin.) New York: McGraw-Hill.

Scott, J. W. 1992. Experience. In *Feminists theorize the political*, ed. J. Butler and J. W. Scott, 22–40. New York; London: Routledge.

Seaford, R. 1994. *Reciprocity and ritual: Homer and tragedy in the developing city-state*. Oxford: Clarendon Press.

Sebeok, T. A. 1994. *Signs: An introduction to semiotics*. Toronto and Buffalo: University of Toronto Press.

Sedgwick, E. K. 1990. *Epistemology of the closet*. Berkeley; Los Angeles: University of California Press.

Segal, R. A. (ed.) 1996. *Ritual and myth: Robertson Smith, Frazer, Hooke, and Harrison. Theories of Myth*. New York: Garland.

———. 1998. *The myth and ritual theory: An anthology*. Oxford: Blackwell.

———. 1999. *Theorizing about myth*. Massachusetts: University of Massachusetts.

———. 2004. *Myth: A very short introduction*. Oxford: Oxford University Press.

Seidl, D. and Becker, K.H. 2006. Organizations as distinction generating and processing systems: Niklas Luhmann's contribution to organization studies. *Organization* **13**(1), January: 9–35.

Sered, S. S. 1994. *Priestess, mother, sacred sister: Religions dominated by women*. New York: Oxford University Press.

Shapiro, W. 1998. Ideology, 'history of religions' and hunter-gatherer studies. *Journal of the Royal Anthropological Institute* **4**(3):489–510.

Showalter, D. and Astore, W.J. 2007. *Soldiers' lives through history: The early modern world*. Westport, Conn: Greenwood Press.

Silverman, K. 1992. *Male subjectivity at the margins*. New York and London: Routledge.

Silverman, L. 2001. *Tortured Subjects: Pain, truth, and the body in early modern France*. Chicago and London: Chicago University Press.

Smith, B. 1998. *The truth that never hurts: Writings on race, gender, and freedom*. New Brunswick, NJ: Rutgers University Press.

Smith, D. E. 1987. *The everyday world as problematic: A feminist sociology*. Boston: Northeastern University Press.

Smith, J. Z. 1978. *Map is not territory: Studies in the history of religions*. Chicago and London: University of Chicago Press.

———. 1998. Religion, religions, religious. In *Critical terms for religious studies*, ed. M. C. Taylor, 269–84. Chicago and London: University of Chicago Press.

———. 2004. *Relating religion: Essays in the study of religion*. Chicago and London: University of Chicago Press.

Srivastava, K. S. 1998. *Hindu symbolism and iconography: A study*. Varanasi: Sangeeta Prakashan.

Stanford, C. B. 1999. *The hunting apes: Meat eating and the origins of human behavior*. Princeton, NJ: Princeton University Press.

Stanford, C. B. and Bunn, H.T. (eds.) 2001. *Meat eating and human evolution*. Oxford: Oxford University Press.

Stanley, S. 1996. *Children of the ice age*. New York: Random House.

Stein, P. 1999. *Roman law in European history*. Cambridge: Cambridge University Press.

Stevenson, J. 2000. Shaman images in San rock art: A question of gender. In *Representations of gender from prehistory to the present*, M. Donald and L. Hurcombe, 45–66. London; New York: MacMillan Press Ltd.; St. Martin's Press Inc.

Strathern, M. 1988. *The gender of the gift: Problems with women and problems with society in Melanesia*. Berkeley: University of California Press.

Strathern, M. and MacCormack, C.P. (eds.) 1980. *Nature, culture, and gender*. Cambridge: Cambridge University Press.

Sturrock, J. (ed.) 1979. *Structuralism and since: From Lévi-Strauss to Derrida*. Oxford: Oxford University Press.

Tambiah, S. J. 1985. Radcliffe-Brown Lecture in Social Anthropology in *Culture, thought, and social action: An anthropological perspective*. Cambridge, MA; London: Harvard University Press.

Tedlock, D. (ed. and trans.) 1996. *Popol Vuh: The definitive edition of the Mayan book of the dawn of life and the glories of gods and kings*. rev. ed. New York: Touchstone.

Tooby, J. and DeVore, I. 1987. The reconstruction of human behavioral evolution through strategic modeling. In *Primate models of human behavior*, ed. W. Kinzey, 183–237. New York: SUNY.

Treichler, P. A., Cartwright, L. and Penley, C. (eds.) 1998. *The visible woman: Imaging technologies, gender, and science*. New York: New York University Press.

Trzaskoma, S. M., Smith, R.S. and Brunet, S. (eds. and trans.) 2004. *Anthology of classical myth: Primary sources in translation*. Indianapolis; Cambridge: Hackett Publishing Co.

Tucker, L. (ed.) 1998. *Critical essays on Angela Carter*. New York: G. K. Hall & Co.

Turnbull, C. 1961. *The forest people: A study of the Pygmies of the Congo*. New York: Simon and Schuster.

Turner, V. 1967. *The forest of symbols: Aspects of Ndembu ritual*. Ithaca: Cornell University Press.

———. 1969. *The ritual process: Structure and anti-structure*. Symbol, Myth, and Ritual Series. Ithaca: Cornell University Press.

Turner, V. 1982. Liminality and the performative genre. In *Studies in symbolism and cultural communication*, ed. F. A. Hanson, 25–41. Lawrence: University of Kansas.

———. 1988. *The anthropology of performance*. (preface by Richard Schechner) New York: PAJ Publications.

van Gennep, A. 1960. *The rites of passage*. trans. M. B. Vizedom and G. L. Caffee, intro. S. T. Kimball. Chicago: University of Chicago Press.

Vermeule, E. 1979. *Aspects of death in early Greek art and poetry*. Berkeley: University of California Press.

Vickers, N. J. 1997. Members only: Marot's anatomical blazons. In *The body in parts: Fantasies of corporeality in early modern Europe*, D. Hillman and C. Mazzio, 3–22. New York and London: Routledge.

Ville, G. 1981. *La gladiature en occident des origins à la mort de Domitien*. Rome: Bibliothèque des Écoles françaises d'Athènes et de Rome.

Waardenburg, J. 1980. Symbolic aspects of myth. In *Myth, symbol, and reality*, ed. A. Olson, 41–48. Notre Dame: University of Notre Dame Press.

Walker, D. 1981. *Unclean spirits: Possession and exorcism in France and England in the late sixteenth and early seventeenth centuries*. Philadelphia: University of Pennsylvania Press.

Walters, J. 1997. Invading the Roman body: Manliness and impenetrability in Roman thought. In *Roman Sexualities*, J. P. Hallett and M. Skinner, 29–46. Princeton: Princeton University Press.

Watson, B. A. 2007. *Desert battles: From Napoleon to the Gulf War*. Mechanicsburg, PA: Stackpole Books.

Weedon, C. 2001. *Feminist practice and poststructuralist theory*. 2nd edition. Oxford: Blackwell.

Weeks, J. 1991. *Against nature: Essays on history, sexuality, and identity*. London; Concord, MA: Rivers Oram Press; Paul and Co.

Westerfelhaus, R., and A. Singhal. 2001. Difficulties in co-opting a complex sign: Our lady of Guadalupe as a site of semiotic struggle and entanglement. *Communication Quarterly* **49**(2), Spring:95–114.

Weyer, J. 1991. *Witches, devils, and doctors in the Renaissance: Johann Weyer, De praestigiis daemonum*. 1583. eds. G. Mora and Benjamin Kohl. trans. J. Shea. Binghamton, New York: Medieval & Renaissance Texts & Studies.

White, H. 1973. *Metahistory: The historical imagination in nineteenth-century Europe*. Baltimore: Hopkins University Press.

———. 1987. *The content of form: Narrative discourse and historical representation*. Baltimore and London: John Hopkins University Press.

Wiedemann, T. 1992. *Emperors and gladiators*. London and New York: Routledge. Ebook.

Williams, C. A. 1999. *Roman homosexuality: Ideologies of masculinity in classical antiquity*. New York and Oxford: Oxford University Press.

Williams, R. 1977. *Marxism and literature*. Oxford: Oxford University Press.

Wilson, A. 1986. *The swastika, the earliest known symbol, and its migrations; with observations on the migration of certain industries in prehistoric times*. Report of the National Museum (1894). Washington: Smithsonian.

Wyke, M. 1997. *Projecting the past: Ancient Rome, cinema and history*. London and New York: Routledge.

Žižek, S. 1994. Introduction: The spectre of ideology. In *Mapping ideology*, ed. S. Žižek, 1–33. London; New York: Verso.

Subject Index

Author Index